Living Among Us

Lucy Palmer

ISBN:
ISBN-978-0-9930600-0-7
©2015 Lucy Palmer

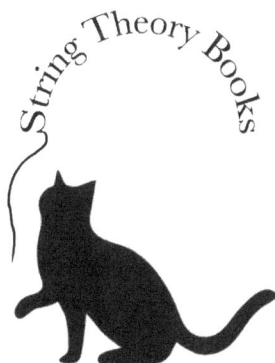

String Theory Books

DEDICATION

FREDERICK WILLIAM DAVIES

16-9-1948 - 31-7-2014

This work is dedicated to the memory of my partner, Fred, who passed with oesophageal cancer during the books final revision. I had eight wonderful years with him when I moved to Manchester in 2007. Fred was a great encouragement to me, not only during the writing of this book, but in everything that I put my mind to. He was so proud of this project that he would always find a way to mention it to anybody and everybody, regardless of what else the conversation may have been about. Following an eight-day road-trip in which we visited various places of interest around Southern England, including my home town of Reading, in order to gather photos for this book, he was taken ill and within three weeks was diagnosed with terminal cancer, and with just weeks to live. The cancer progressed with terrifying speed and Fred passed peacefully on July 31st 2014.

Table of Contents

ACKNOWLEDGMENTS

Thanks to Clive Potter for his meticulous hoarding of letters and files that enabled this book to follow a chronological order.

Thanks goes to Diane Tessman for allowing me to quote at length from her book: *UFO Agenda.* Copyright 2013 and published by Eye Scry Publications

Website: www.earthchangepredictions.com

Acknowledgement also goes to Raven Kaldera for allowing me to quote at length from his website at:

http://www.northernshamanism.org/general/shamanism/classic-core-shamanism.html

and my thanks goes to Jacinta O'Connor for taking the time to read the final version through for me.

Also to the following for their support during the darkest year of my life: Anne Collins. Anne McGarrie. Kerry Sullivan. Laurie Tintinger. Sally Hay. Jan 'Tazzer' Silver. Jan 'Blair Witch' Wilkins. Kelly Jane. Kat Rippa. Brenda Butler. Beth Holtum. Deborah Jane Pearson. Rebecca Lomas. Adrian Riverwolf. Susanne & Beth Swanston. Jill Willmot. Rossann Corrigan. Andy Taylor. Linda Gibson. Paul Muir.

I know there are many more I ought to thank, so thank you for the support.

"Some day the Earth will weep, She will beg for Her life, She will cry with tears of blood. You will make a choice, if you will help her or let her die, and when She dies, you too, will die."

–John Hollow Horn, Oglala Lakota, 1932

FOREWORD

I faced a dilemma when I began my four-year acquaintance with Lucy Palmer and Shelagh Yeoman, because what I thought was going to be just another UFO contact case soon became a free-fall into a greater awareness that challenged my beliefs about the UFO phenomenon.

Living Among Us describes an individual who is human, but also connected to an alien consciousness which has shown itself to a number of unprepared individuals, and demonstrating that Lucy might well be what she claims. Although I have not seen this remarkable transformation for myself, I was present for the occasion when an individual did witness the phenomenon, and I was able to record his reactions first hand.

This has been a voyage of personal discovery and the realisation that humanity is just one of many cosmic intelligences inhabiting a multiverse, with each insight being acquired one step at a time, even having to wait years for another piece to fall into place. In this case, I had the opportunity of gaining access to hidden realms that we are not generally aware of, shown to me by one who is immersed within that reality. I began my association with Lucy and Shelagh in July 1990 after I had co-written an article about UFOs and prophecy, in which I was trying to seek answers as to why many experiencers were describing a catastrophic future, a global Armageddon, often with the nightmare of a thermonuclear war. In this, I was pursuing a similar line of research as Jenny Randles, one of Britain's leading ufologists and a prolific author, in that she too had focused on the source of these contacts as perhaps our inner selves, projecting our fears and portents as UFO contacts, divine visions, spiritual messages, as well as through the medium of songs and novels. Far from being alien, these experiences seemed to be conveying meaningful messages from the future, akin to waves rippling across time from a central core event.

As with many who have embarked on serious involvement in ufology, I came to the subject wedded to the hypothesis that UFOs were extra-terrestrial in origin. I was initially brought up in the beliefs of Erich von Daniken, who wrote popular titles on the 'ancient astronaut' theme. However, such ideas were rudely discarded in the white heat of frontline UFO investigation, where a healthy sceptical attitude was forged on the anvil of experience. Thus, I soon learned to bear the mantle of a sceptic and investigated each case that I encountered with a belief that with enough detective work, any UFO report could be resolved at a mundane level. To be honest, most of the cases I investigated did turn out to be either natural and man-made phenomena that had been poorly observed. A handful of cases, however, were not open to such interpretation, and in the interests of objectivity were consigned to the realm of 'unidentified' or 'unknown'. I eventually decided that the only way to make any sense of the UFO phenomenon was in the study of UFO contactees and abductees - experiencers, as they are now called - and perhaps attempt to communicate directly with the intelligence behind them, be it an external intelligence, the collective unconsciousness or the hidden subconscious of the experiencer. Was there, in fact, a relationship between anomalous objects observed by witnesses, and the entities and even contact that has been recorded? Or were they a totally different phenomenon? Maybe if we could connect with the boundaries that surrounded such phenomena, then perhaps it would react accordingly and we could begin to explore how it all actually worked.

One of the most important features that emerged from observing and listening to Lucy is how the events that I once considered as normal human conflicts within history were often something more; the transcendence of conventional politics into battles of Light and Dark. Humanity has become a pawn in what I term a 'cosmic chess game', but a a special kind of pawn, having the power to transform both, itself and its future through its own choosing. The dark spiritual powers that coexist with us are only able to manipulate and control us through our unconsciousness. And for that darkness to be defeated, mankind has to transform that darkness within its own unconsciousness by bringing the shadow into the light of consciousness.

However, Lucy's understanding, derived as it was from an alien disincarnate source and from her own inner awareness, spoke of there being several intelligences in a spiritual conflict being waged over humanity. Lucy was, in essence, a representative of one group who, as a human in an incarnated form, was an 'agent' performing a mission. It could be compared with the role of the Special Operations Executive, or S.O.E., during the Second World War, agents selected by Allied Command to be sent to Nazi Occupied Europe, destroying enemy targets and training the Resistance in those countries. In a sense, using that simile, this planet is occupied territory and its citizens need to be reached and influenced.

During my research on this case, I found myself an unwitting participant in this 'war' as I encountered representations and manifestations of all the protagonists in one way or another. The representatives were those humans that possessed a non-human spirit, the realisation of who they were and, in some cases, their mission, occurring during their lives as some form of 'awakening'.

One question that stems from this is whether all people on earth possess the same human consciousness, the spiritual identity that marks us out as humans. There is the very real possibility that an alien form of consciousness can exist within human bodies, and that such an alien form of consciousness can also exist alongside other humans without them even realising it. In order for any consciousness to penetrate and operate in this world where the dominant sentient species are human beings, it is evident that such an alien consciousness must be contained in the most appropriate biological vessel, namely a human being with a human consciousness, through which the alien consciousness can function within the human world, in our physical universe.

How would a human know if we all possess the same human spiritual essence, or whether some have a different consciousness, an alien consciousness? The answer is that we would not know. My experience with Lucy and others similar to her, tell me that we can only determine some understanding to that question from both their behaviour and the information that they provide. The ultimate evidence lies within the paranormal phenomenon that they can deliver to us, perhaps a display of their real inner selves, such as Lucy's transformation that occurred before a number of witnesses in the 1980s and 1990s.

This is a quest for a transcendent understanding of where we came from and how we have arrived at the point we are today; it's a quest for the ultimate nature of reality and our place within the cosmos. It is of our timeless questioning about the meaning of our lives, of suffering, of loss, of death and a spiritual purpose to who we are; our collective longing for the essence of ultimate power, love and wisdom within the cosmos, and indeed the very source of divinity itself.

I used to be a sceptic when it came to the existence of alien intelligences, other realities, and the paranormal, refusing to believe anything that could not be seen, felt, understood or proven satisfactorily. I was a product of a ruthlessly cynical society whose culture denied anything that contradicted the established world view of the non-spiritual, materialist universe by generations of scientists.

Then I met Lucy Palmer, and my world view changed - forever.

Clive Potter 2014

SETTING THE SCENE

When I disclosed my experiences to the UFO community in 1990, it didn't take long for me to realise that most ufologists were hunting for metallic craft in the belief UFOs are spaceships from a distant star-system.

An alternative route for some was that the subject could be best understood from a psychological or psychiatric approach, others considered the phenomena to be an effect of electromagnetic fields. In my case, I was told the experiences were most probably caused by mobile phone masts; that we might actually be experiencing what we reported was never given much credibility at that time.

However, opinions and attitudes have changed, and I think the Internet has had much to do with it. It's enabled people to cross-reference their experiences with others through forums and social networking. Indeed, you will read a number of instances where networking has featured heavily in my account. Above all else, the Internet has assured witnesses they're not alone in having these crazy things intruding into their lives. So, now I think it's time for me to tell my story, and I hope this will encourage others to step forward and make themselves known.

Although I now know I'm not alone in having these kind of experiences, back then, I did feel isolated and locked into a crazy world of my own. Even worse, I found it difficult to be taken seriously, mainly because what I was reporting led into regions that, at that time, was rarely acknowledged within ufology, but are now gaining credibility, even among mainstream physicists; the contentious subjects being parallel dimensions, alternative universes and time-travel.

On the professional circuit, there were pioneers whose works have become classics. Dr Jacques Vallée, for example. Two of his books: *Dimensions* and *Passport to Magonia*, made a study of ancient and medieval texts, describing what appear to be encounters with otherworldly beings. Vallée is of the opinion that these beings are not extraterrestrial, but are inhabitants of our own planet.

His theory is that the beings behind these experiences are connected intimately with the planet and act as a kind of control mechanism with an ability to influence the course of human development, and as part of his argument against UFOs coming from distant planets, he points to the overwhelming number of sightings, which stack against the idea.

The parallel dimension theory is steadily gaining popularity now that physics hint at alternative universes brushing against our own, and this is leading scientists and ufologists alike, to probe the outer edges of a multiverse, a concept that has been recognised in occultism for centuries. My story is steeped in this parallel world, from shamanic initiation across dimensions, to Men in Black and human/alien hybrids all forming my narrative backbone. The human hybrid is becoming an increasingly recognised element in the phenomena, also with its parallels in fairy-lore, as explored in the works of Vallée. But the first modern abduction suggesting hybrid creation is the experiences reported by Antônio Vilas-Boas

On October 16, 1957, 23-year-old Brazilian Farmer, Antônio Vilas-Boas (1934–1991), was ploughing fields late one night – he did it at night simply because it was cooler than during the day - near São Francisco de Sales when he spotted a 'red star' in the sky. This 'star' grew in size until he could identify it as a circular craft, with a red light on its front and a rotating cupola on top. The strange craft extended three legs, and Boas realised it was about to land in his field.

At this point, with common sense getting the better of him, he decided to leave the area. Initially, he tried to make his escape on his tractor, but its lights and engine died after travelling just a short distance, (the sudden failure of electrical equipment is a common effect and includes not only tractors and cars, but even aircraft and weapons systems). So, abandoning his now dead vehicle, Boas continued on foot, but again, he didn't get far, and was seized by a 1.5m tall humanoid that wore grey coveralls and a helmet through which Boas could see small, blue eyes. Instead of speech, the creature apparently made something resembling barking noises.

Three more beings joined the first and between them, they dragged Boas into their craft. He was stripped naked and covered in some kind of gel, before being taken to a second room where the aliens extracted blood samples. In yet another room, he was left alone for around half an hour, and then a gas was pumped in, this made Boas feel sick. The farmer was then joined by a naked female creature: she had a pointed chin and large, blue eyes that Boas described as 'cat-like'. The hair of her head was long, straight and blonde, in contrast to her pubic hair, which, was bright red. Boas became aroused enough for them to engage in sexual intercourse, the alien showing her affection by nipping him on the chin, presumably their alternative to kissing.

When this act was completed, she rubbed her belly and gestured upwards, which Boas assumed to mean that she was now pregnant and was going to give birth away from planet Earth. Boas was handed back his clothes and allowed to take a tour around the ship, sometime during which, he attempted to steal a clock-like device, because he wanted to bring back something as proof of what had occurred, but the aliens wouldn't allow it, and took it back off him. Only then was he permitted to leave the ship, and when he arrived home he discovered that four hours had passed.

Although he hadn't been able to bring back the clock-like device as evidence of his encounter, he did return with something; suffering with nausea, headaches, loss of appetite, blurred vision, and skin lesions. Boas was examined by Dr. Olavo Fontes from the National School of Medicine of Brazil, and it was discovered that the farmer was suffering with a mild dose of radiation poisoning! No rational explanation could be given as to how he might have acquired this condition, and although he was questioned over the years, Boas never contradicted his story, sticking to the details right up to his death.

One man who propelled the human/alien hybrid phenomenon to the high profile stature it enjoys today was Budd Hopkins. Hopkins was born in 1931 and raised in Wheeling, West Pam. Graduating from Oberlin College in 1953, he moved to New York City, where he remained throughout the rest of his life. An accomplished painter and sculptor, Hopkins became interested in the abduction phenomenon during the 1970s and choosing hypnosis as his main tool, he studied the reported abductions and slowly began to recover details that built into dossiers of previously hidden memories.

Hopkins was soon to become one of the leading exponents in this line of research, and by the late 1980s, he was very prominent in Ufology, even gaining serious mainstream attention - no easy feat. He authored several articles and books, including *Missing time, Intruders*, and *Witnessed*, and all considered to be among the most influential books published on the abduction phenomenon. Hopkins died in 2011.

Alongside Jacques Vallée stand other academically qualified names, including:

Dr John E. Mack, born in New York City in 1929 and graduating from Horace Mann-Lincoln School in 1947, he received his degree from Harvard Medical School after undergraduate study at Oberlin in 1951. He was a graduate of the Boston Psychoanalytic Society and Institute, and certified in child and adult psychoanalysis.

Mack's views were inspired by spiritual and philosophical traditions in which people are connected to one another; and this led him, in the 1990s, to make a study of 200 men and women who reported alien encounters. He later considered the notion of an expanded reality, which allowed for experiences that don't fit into the Western materialist paradigm. His second and final book on the encounter experience, *Passport to the Cosmos: Human Transformation and Alien Encounters*, connected spirituality and the findings from his research with what he termed 'experiencers' - a word which soon replaced 'abductees' and 'contactees' because It encompasses much more than simply UFO and alien contact, so from here I will, more often than not, use the term 'experiencers,' to identify the witnesses to any paranormal phenomena.

However, in May 1994, Mack faced a problem when the Dean of Harvard Medical School appointed a committee to review Mack's clinical care for the people who had discussed their alien experiences with him. It was the first time in Harvard's history that a tenured professor was subjected to such an investigation. 'Kafkaesque,' was how Mack described the proceedings; he never quite knew the status of the investigation, and the specific complaints were not even revealed to him until the committee had their draft report prepared some eight months later.

As this wasn't a disciplinary committee, it didn't follow the established procedure, which made Mack's defence both difficult and costly. Nevertheless, concluding what amounted to a fourteen-month investigation, Harvard issued a statement acknowledging Dr. Mack's academic freedom to study what he wished and to state his opinions. But less than a decade later, on Monday September 27 2004, while in London to lecture at a T. E. Lawrence Society conference, Dr Mack was killed by a drunken driver while walking home alone after having had dinner with friends. He lost consciousness at the scene and was pronounced dead shortly thereafter. Mack remains one of the most esteemed academic names to have studied the subject.

The next two researchers believe there's an underlying hostility behind the alien agenda. Dr David Jacobs obtained his Ph.D. from the University of Wisconsin-Madison in 1973. He wrote his dissertation on the controversy over unidentified flying objects, and a revised edition was published as *The UFO Controversy in America*. As a faculty member of the Department of History at Temple University, Jacobs specialised in the history of 20th-century American popular culture, and for more than 25 years, taught a course on 'UFOs in American Society'. He has written four books on the subject, arguing that alien/human hybrids are engaged in a covert program to infiltrate human society with the goal of taking over the planet. He also suggests there are humans teaching hybrids to blend into society so that they cannot be differentiated from humans.

Dr Karla Turner earned her Ph.D. in Old English studies and taught in a university in Texas for more than ten years. In 1988, she, her husband and son underwent a number of experiences that forced them to face the fact that they were all abductees. This seems to have been a powerful enough motivation that led Karla to drop her academic career to focus full-time on abduction research. *Into the Fringe*, told of her family abduction experiences, while her second: *Taken - Inside the Alien-Human Abduction Agenda*, profiled the abductions of eight women. *Masquerade of Angels*, was co-written with psychic, Ted Rice, and details his encounters with beings that exist within a region between angelic and demonic. Dr Turner was working on a further book when she became ill in early 1995, and tragically died of cancer on January 9, 1996. Like Dr Jacobs, Dr Turner's hypothesis was that the Grey aliens were operating on earth with nefarious objectives.

Any debate will invariably focus on the motives of these aliens, as made clear in the research data of Hopkins, Mack, Jacobs, Turner, and many others. This debate usually spotlights the 'Greys', which are a central feature throughout this book. You will notice that I spell them with an upper case 'G', this is to distinguish the species from the colour. So, let's take a look at this being, these Grey aliens of dubious repute. For one thing, the Greys rarely seem to display emotion, and on the few occasions they do, it's at a very superficial level. They also react with apparent indifference toward the suffering and confusion of the humans they abduct.

It has been reported that they experiment with human emotion, and are intrigued - perhaps mystified - at the range of responses they elicit from their captives, and there does seem little doubt that humans are treated as exploratory subjects. From there it is easy to jump to the conclusion their motives are therefore 'evil'; but is this necessarily the case? It could be comparable to humans sitting a chimp in a laboratory environment, giving it a stack of building blocks and rewarding the animal if it manages to construct a pre-determined configuration. Indeed, some experiencers have reported being in exactly that situation! The Greys also perform communication experiments, something else we do with primates.

Game wardens tag animals to observe their movements and habits. Couldn't these beings be doing much the same with 'endangered' humans? Especially if, as some suggest, the Grey are, in fact, humans from the far-distant future. This is the hypothesis supported by Diane Tessman, a researcher and author from Iowa, USA, who in her book: *UFO Agenda*, champions the theory of a future humanity harnessing time-travel, perhaps sending their consciousness back through the ages to their distant and primitive ancestors - us - with a contact and research agenda.

If that's the case, maybe these time travellers are as far removed from us as we are from our original biped ancestors on the African Savannah. Would our scientists act any differently if they encountered a prehistoric humanoid species? They'd observe habits, social conditioning and the range of emotional expression - and probably be thoroughly puzzled by some of it - which is why they'd most likely engage in lengthy research programs.

Maybe we'd lift one or two specimens from their wilderness habitat and place them in a laboratory environment, and create what we think would pass as a few comforts to lessen the impact of their temporary abduction. We would also make attempts to communicate, as one alien culture to another, before returning them to their community. Couldn't this be precisely what the Greys are doing? However, even if it is, there's a very important difference, humans are not chimpanzees, we feel violated by these experiences. Trauma runs deep after these encounters, and the quality of life can never be the same again.

Because of their notoriety, the Grey is now hardwired into the human psyche and pop-culture images can be found everywhere. You will find them on website banners and Pin badges, from toys, to computer games and TV series. Take 'Babylon 5', as an example: In that series, The 'Vree' are a race that has been observing and abducting humans since the 1940s, in ships characteristic of flying saucers. This race is modelled on the infamous Grey to such a degree that in one scene, a human is demanding compensation from a Vree for the emotional damage caused by the Vree's grandfather abducting his grandfather!

The 'Strieb' is another race in the series that's reminiscent of the Greys. The Strieb regularly abduct individuals from other species for experimentation; this fictitious alien was named for Whitley Streiber, a horror fiction author who went on to detail his own abduction experiences. However, this fact-based book, *Communion*, stirred such controversy that its knock-on effect was for his sales as a fiction author to suffer.

But if there's a single event responsible for catapulting the Grey to worldwide prominence, it's that of Betty and Barney Hill and extensively recounted in many articles, books and a film; it's one of the most famous abduction cases on record.

At 10. 30pm, on September 19th, 1961, the couple was driving home to Portsmouth, New Hampshire, after a vacation to Montreal and Niagara Falls, in Canada. Betty spotted a bright light in the sky which at first she took to be a shooting star, but then it moved upwards and began behaving erratically. She urged her husband, Barney, to stop the car, so she could observe the light through binoculars, and what she saw was a strange-looking craft with multiple coloured lights. At first, Barney suggested it might be an aircraft, but when it then started moving towards their vehicle, he had a change of heart.

They travelled slowly until they reached Franconia Notch in White Mountains. Stopping again the couple watched as the craft disappeared behind Cannon Mountain only to reappear as they started off again, but this time the object began to close in on them.

Roughly two miles north of North Woodstock, the glowing, blue-white, disc like craft descended to about one hundred feet. Barney stopped yet again, only this time he got out of the car and approached the craft with his pistol, and used his binoculars to get a better view of the vessel. He could clearly see several figures standing behind the craft's windows. They watching him for several minutes before they began to use the controls of the ship. The apparent leader of the group became Barney's focal point as he began to have a creeping fear that he was about to be taken hostage. The strange craft was, by now, only seventy-five feet away.

Barney ran back to the car screaming, 'They're going to capture us!' jumping in beside Betty, he started the vehicle and sped along the highway while Betty rolled down her window and searched the sky for their pursuer; but all she could see was a suddenly starless sky. Barney was certain this was because the object was so large it had blocked their view of the sky. The couple soon heard a strange beeping sound that originated from the rear of their car and both felt tingling and drowsy as they experienced some kind of altered state of consciousness that numbed their minds.

When eventually they regained an awareness of their surroundings they discovered that they were 35 miles south of where they should be, and their most recent memories were little more than a vague recollection of the road being blocked by a strange craft.

After a series of inexplicable dreams, and a general feeling of unease, they submitted to hypnosis, and this took place from January 4th to June 6th 1964, under the guidance of Dr Benjamin Simon. These sessions, which Dr Simon conducted on them separately, revealed that the couple had been taken into the craft, parted from each other and subject to intense medical examinations.

Communication between the couple and the aliens seemed to differ, depending upon who you asked. Betty heard the beings speak English, whereas Barney said they spoke in some mumbling language that he wasn't able to understand. But on the occasions they wanted to communicate directly with Barney, it was via thought transference; he believed this because he couldn't recall seeing their mouths move.

Betty was shown a holographic three-dimensional star-map which, following her hypnosis sessions, she was able to draw. This map depicted a number of stars connected by both solid and dotted lines; she explained how she'd been told that the stars joined by solid lines were trade routes, while those connected by dashed lines were stars not so often visited. This map was included in *The Interrupted Journey*, by John. J. Fuller, the first in-depth account of the Hills' abduction, gaining the couple, and the star-map, worldwide fame.

In 1968, the map so intrigued amateur astronomer Marjorie Fish, that she wondered if it might be used to discover where the UFO had come from. Assuming that one of the fifteen stars on the map must represent our sun, she constructed a three-dimensional model of nearby Sun-like stars using thread and beads. Then, using stellar distances from those published in a star catalogue, she studied thousands of vantage points over the course of several years. Eventually she found that the only one that seemed to match the map configuration was from the viewpoint of binary star system, Zeta Reticuli, which lies in the southern constellation of Reticulum. This announcement inevitably led to the Greys being referred to as 'Zetans', or 'Reticulans'.

The Hill case has come to represent the classic textbook abduction, because it includes missing time, medical experimentation, and the taking of biological samples, and in return, information being given, (in this case it's the star-map suggesting where the Greys might originate from.) There were also physical effects left behind, Betty's dress was torn and had a strange pink powder on it, there were shiny, concentric circles on their car's trunk that hadn't been there before the experience. Experiments were made on these using a compass, and it was discovered that when the compass was moved towards the circular marks, the needle spun wildly, but as the compass was moved away, it settled down again.

Betty Hill was also memorable in another respect; this was the first of what would be numerous reports of females being subjected to terrifying and invasive medical procedures.

I will leave the final word on Betty and Barney Hill to Philip Klass, who until his death in August 2005, was the arch sceptic of all things UFO:

On one tape, I heard Barney Hill relive his close-quarters encounter with the UFO. At the start of the interview, his voice was quite calm, but as he "approached" the UFO, hovering over a field near the highway, Barney screamed hysterically. Dr. Simon told me that he had never had a patient become so excited under hypnosis. At one point, the doctor said, he feared that Barney might try to jump out of the office window. ... As I listened to Barney reliving his UFO encounter, I could agree completely with the doctor that Barney had indeed seen "something," and it had been a terrifying experience.

Philip Klass, UFOs—Identified (1968)

Today, following many cases of abduction, women miss their period and report unexplained pregnancies that seem to terminate after around three months of gestation. Physical examination often shows that they were pregnant at one point, but the pregnancy seemed to terminate without the expected foetal tissue. The women might then, at a later date, report being taken aboard a UFO to see a child, which they are told is theirs. The explanations given by the aliens for these hybrids can vary, but usually it's described as an ongoing program to nudge human evolution.

As the decades rolled on and abduction reports increased, they began to incorporate an increasing number of paranormal qualities. However, I'm using the term 'paranormal' with some caution, because what we are probably looking at is an extraordinarily advanced manipulation of light and matter to create what our current understanding can only perceive as a paranormal effect. With the advance of quantum physics and species field theory, we might well be in pursuit of some of the 'physics' they employ, such as vehicles levitated into hovering ships via beams of light, and people taken from beds and passing through solid walls or windows.

As for myself, I can't remember any time during my life when I didn't feel different from the people around me. There were even occasions when I asked my mother where my real parents were; which was the only way I could articulate the difference I felt. My mother's response would always be the same. 'What sort of daft question is that?' So, I would walk away from her and continue to puzzle over why I felt no emotional link to this family, it was a kind of dead-zone. My father also seemed to have a strange relationship with me, he never - and I do mean *never* - made physical contact with me. For example, if he had to cross a road with me in tow, he wouldn't hold my hand, as any other parent would, he'd hold my sleeve between thumb and forefinger, so as to make as little contact as possible. More than that, whenever he referred to me, I was always an 'it'.

'I will take *it* to the park for a few hours.'

'I will take *it* to buy some new shoes.'

Things got worse when *it* was five, and had to go to school. The exposure to other children in greater numbers than *it* had experienced before being nothing short of traumatic. This exposure to the childhood community with its forced attempt to have me socialise, did absolutely nothing to help my profound sense of alienation. What it did, however, was teach me how to pretend to have fun and join in. I made no friends and even into adolescence, I found it virtually impossible to form a close relationship with anyone. During the most introspective moments I would ask God, or the universe - any higher power that might happen to be paying me attention - 'why am I here? What am I?' The estrangement, this remoteness, went deeper than simply external relationships, I didn't even have one with myself!

Sometimes I found these thoughts, frightening.

Until the truth came storming into my life - and that's when things started to get really frightening.

BUILDING THE BRIDGE

Fairies, Unicorns and Spaceships

I was born in Saint Mary's Hospital, in Croydon, England, on January 5th, 1958. The night was a full moon, one that the Native Americans call the Wolf Moon; when wolf packs are howling outside the villages.

But there's one thing that I must now make clear before we go any further; I was born into a male body. It wouldn't be until 2009 before that situation would change with gender reassignment surgery. I need to make this very clear at the outset because it's a powerful contribution to the later stages of this story. However, from the beginning and throughout, I have referred to myself as my legal status of Lucy Palmer; that's to avoid sudden confusion and to retain a consistency throughout.

I sometimes wonder if my father suspected, or knew something about me, even if it was just intuitively, because, according to my mother, he had an aversion to me within weeks of her taking me home from the maternity hospital. In fact, it wouldn't be an exaggeration to say that his reaction was almost pathological in nature, and his refusal to pick me up or even touch me, bordered on repellent.

Many years later, my mother told me that he'd attempted to bribe her, just to get this baby of less than a month old out of his house. Apparently, if she agreed to have me adopted, he'd buy her a full-length fur coat, and in 1958, a mink coat was a luxury that many women coveted. However, as it turned out, my mother decided to keep me and would remain furless for the remainder of winter, but this does demonstrate how far he was prepared to go to have me removed from his family circle. So I stayed and eventually became the eldest of five children, and none of them generated the same inexplicable attitude from him as I continued to do.

There was, however, one family member I did have an enduring relationship with. Two years younger than me, Penny was the eldest of my brothers and sisters. Because we were both dark-haired, the same height, build, it was often assumed we were twins, especially as we went everywhere together; we might as well have been joined by an invisible umbilical.

Perhaps she saw my father's aversion to me and tried to compensate for it, but even if that was the case, there was a genuine bond between us. Our life as 'twins' hinged principally on the use of our imagination, especially in Penny's case. She was a very talented child and loved to sing at every given opportunity. She was also a natural artist, and often drew fantastical imaginary fish, unicorns, and fairies - the fairies, in particular, had the most intricately produced wing and clothing detail, and she'd tell us: 'that's how they look,' as though she was an authority over the subject - and who knows, maybe she was.

We would often sit in the garden if the weather was good, and sing along to pop records on our blue plastic turntable. Our two favourites at the time were *Chirpy Chirpy Cheep Cheep* by Middle of the Road, and *In The Summertime*, by Mungo Jerry. At one point, Penny thought we could form a duo, maybe we could have been like The Carpenters; but I didn't fancy the idea, so our singing career died its death there and then.

Unlike me, Penny was able to make friends with ease and had plenty of them around the village and at school. Even so, she sacrificed much of her time with others to be with me, and that's why we were each other's companion, whether it was out riding our bicycles, building secret camps, or exploring the dense woodland and open fields around our village near Reading in Berkshire. Ryeish Green consists of a single road, with houses along one side, the school, a dairy farm and a big orchard on the other.

The orchard was owned by an old lady, well into her seventies and surrounded by a population of Dachshunds. Many of the children believed she was a witch simply on the evidence that we never saw her unless she was going to or from the local store with her shopping. She never spoke to anyone, nor did they to her so far as I know. Inevitably some of the local kids dared each other to steal apples from the her orchard; undoubted, it was believed that if any were caught by her, they would disappear into her house and never be seen again!

Towards the end of summer most of the village kids would help as the harvesting was done, we usually raked the grasses together and watch as they were baled to dry as hay for cattle winter feed - these were the halcyon days of childhood, there must have been bad as well as good, there always are. But my memories are of an ideal childhood. When not hanging about the village, Penny and I loved being in the woods, deep among the trees and hidden from the rest of humanity; the village had a small enough population as it was, but deep in the woods it was absent of any sound of human life at all. This was where we could explore imagined worlds, lands we populated with her beloved unicorns and fairies. It would be where we lay upon the grass in the summer warmth, and with our eyes closed, build imaginary environments, each of us in turn describing a section of an adventure while we both visualised ourselves in that environment.

For instance, one might describe a path through a forest, then the other might describe a cottage up ahead, and so it would go. When I think back on it now, I'm rather impressed with the visualisation training this game actually entailed. As it is with all children, our imaginations had no bounds, and even when simply walking through the woods, Penny would point to birds and 'squittles' - she couldn't say 'squirrels' - and tell me what they were thinking. I now see Penny as having been something of a teacher' to me, because embedded in these games were lessons in reaching out with our sixth sense and creating empathic bonds.

I think we were very intuitive and psychically aware, because what we sometimes engaged in went beyond simple games and fantasy. We seemed to be practising specific occult disciplines without even realising it. Of course, at our ages, neither of us could have grasped the concept, but undoubtedly, that is what we were doing. Penny was so much more than you would expect a regular five or six-year-old to be.

When I was eight, we had some kind of spontaneous 'moment' in which it was decided we'd actually go and visit the imaginary worlds created in our minds. I don't know how it came about, but we totally convinced ourselves that these places existed and that we could get there if we had the right kind of transport. With impracticalities and common sense swept aside, we sat in our tree camp and planned the construction, which simply involved finding as much scrap and unwanted bits as we could, then being led by our imagination as to what we needed to do with it. So, over the summer months we built our 'flying saucer', and with it, my first conscious attempt to leave Planet Earth. We decided to construct this thing at the far end of the garden because it would be far away from the house, therefore, we wouldn't be moaned at by our mother. But, the part of the garden we chose also had a particular significance that we didn't even realise at the time.

We pursued our construction project with a lot of enthusiasm and a lot of wood and rusting, corrugated metal that we found dumped in the undergrowth at the sides of the lanes around the village. In the middle of this - and let's be perfectly honest, and call it what it really was - 'rubbish heap', we placed two chairs borrowed from the kitchen, after all, we'd need somewhere to sit for the duration of our flight, which we knew wouldn't take long, if any time at all. In fact, we'd probably be back in time for tea. But this was no game of make-believe; this was serious stuff, and we genuinely believed that somehow, miraculously, we could fly the thing.

'It doesn't have an engine!' Penny stated.

I told her it didn't need one; we could 'think' it to fly, a clear reference to levitation and mind control.

Now, back to what I was saying about the place where we built the thing. My sister claimed she could actually see the fairies that she drew with such precise detail – in other words, what looked like fantasy images, were, she claimed, drawn from life; she told us that she'd regularly sit in conversation with them in the seclusion of our garden.

Our property was on a large piece of land, it was the length of a football field and almost half as wide, but only the quarter closest to the house was tamed into submission; the remainder was nature in growth frenzy. It was a jungle of trees, gorse, and blackberry and gooseberry bushes, all within a knee-deep ocean of ankle-snagging weeds, thorns and nettles. Nevertheless, we did have a single path hacked all the way to the far end, where an orchard extended across the back for the length of six or seven houses. The path had been made in the first weeks of us moving in, and what a tremendous adventure that had been! Slashing our way to find the furthest end of the garden, and no doubt pretending to be jungle explorers seeking one of our lost kingdoms - well, that's how our minds worked. It was at the end of this path, by the orchard boundary, where she went to hold those conversations with the fairy-folk.

Even today, as a mother of three, she maintains she was telling the truth. I believe her, and I have assumed these 'fairies' to be a manifestation of the force that was guiding our project. Perhaps they were what Dr. Jacques Vallée described in his hypothesis: a non-human intelligence masquerading in a form conducive to the people and culture they're interacting with. That's what makes it particularly intriguing, because this was the location where we built our spaceship. However, and as with many projects we undertook, within a few weeks of it being built, the 'flying saucer' was abandoned and the components returned to the garbage where they rightly belonged.

Even so, I do think that some underlying objective, the real purpose behind the construction had been achieved. I believe that through prolonged and focused concentration on that location, and with a clearly defined intent, we opened what might be best described as a 'dimensional wormhole' - a portal of some kind that bridged worlds. Although there was nothing tangible to show for it, I believe this was my point of First Contact, and that 'something' reached out to me from - from where? A parallel universe? Or, perhaps, from the future. Regardless of wherever it was, I know they packaged this other world as a fantasy realm and as a consequence, the bridge was formed. This intelligence had a plan behind the project, and it had driven us on, using Penny as the medium. Of course, none of this was thought of at the time, it is only when you consider the events that followed.

Why do I seem so sure that Penny was being used as a medium? Because several days after we had abandoned our flying saucer, Penny started telling us that she was being woken during the night, her sleep being disturbed by the sound of soft footsteps walking across her bedroom floor; they would stop and she'd feel a weight at the end of her bed as though the spirit was sitting down. This spirit turned up at random over the next two years, always walking across her room and unfailingly sitting at the end of her bed, but never once was she able to see what it was. Penny believed in ghosts and was sure this was a friendly one, so she didn't fear it. Within a couple of months of the ghost taking residence, things started vanishing while other items were found in random and unexpected places all over the house.

On one occasion a heavy flower vase tipped from the mantle shelf and smashed into fragments, and because it had been there for such a long time, we could think of no reasonable cause for it to suddenly happen. I don't recollect them all, but there was an almost continuous period of unaccountable phenomena in the two years we had our ghost around the place.

We had two Siamese seal-point cats that used to spend the night on Penny's bed, but as soon as the ghost arrived they stopped going into her room altogether, even during the day.

Penny thought this spirit was her new friend and was quite happy at the thought of having her own personal ghost, but that pleasure was to be short lived as the visits to her bedroom ceased. I remember we were sitting at the kitchen table as the discussion turned to the ghost, and that's when she told me it had gone.

'I thought it was here to be my friend,' she said. 'But I think it changed its mind. It's here to be with you.' She never did explain just what she meant by that statement or how she arrived at such a conclusion. She didn't need to, it wasn't too long before I found out for myself.

Mirror Image

I was eleven years old when I had a preview of what my life held in store for me, and this terrifying experience happened when I was in the bathroom making wearisome preparation for another day at school. I remember my total lack of interest in facing a morning of something boring, perhaps it was maths and double geography, my two least favourite subjects. The cabinet with toothbrushes, paste and an assortment of other bits and pieces was on the wall to the left of the mirror, so having finished splashing water in the general direction of my face, I turned my attention to the cabinet and trawled around for my toothbrush. I squirted paste onto it and returned my attention to the mirror, and that's when I saw the mutation to the left side of my face.

I fell into a complete paralysis as my senses struggled in a futile endeavour to rationalise the image being relayed to my brain. My left eye had turned into what I believed, in horror, was a big black hole.

In that sanity-shattering moment I thought my eye and a part of my head had vanished, terrifying me in a way that's utterly impossible to describe. Even now, writing this and being forced to recall that moment, I still shudder at the cold terror of what I saw.

I now know that my eye and upper cheek had turned into a large and perfectly black alien eye, shaped like an almond and wrapping around the side of my head; but as a child gripped by terror, a vivid imagination convinced me it was a gaping hole. Then there was the flesh around the eye. It was a mottled grey, which, further away from the eye, blended with my own pale skin. As I looked at it I began to realise my face had changed, not disappeared.

I had this vision for maybe a second - perhaps it was only a fraction of a second; I have no real idea of how long it stared back at me - but while in my transfixed state of incomprehensible terror, it was there long enough to sear the image indelibly, clearly, into my memory for the rest of my life.

Then it vanished. No fading away; one moment it was there, the next it was gone. I stared at my recomposed face a moment longer before snapping out of that fearful paralysis.

That's when the screaming began.

Today, we would call it the eye and cheek of a 'Grey', but this was 1969, just eight years after Betty and Barney Hill had been abducted by the Grey aliens, and only five years after their regressions yielding all. So we didn't know anything about these beings, they certainly hadn't yet become iconic, and I hadn't been exposed to their imagery.

With the onset of my ear-piercing screams, my father came rushing into the bathroom, probably expecting to find blood on the floor and me bearing a severe cut. I imagine he was puzzled to see me standing with my eyes transfixed on the mirror and screaming in apparent fear of my own reflection. It took some moments for my stare to be broken from it, and for my mother to get me out of the bathroom and through to the sitting room – my father wouldn't touch me, even in a situation such as this!

It was the best part of an hour before I was calm enough to tell them what I had seen. But at eleven, I just couldn't find any words to adequately describe it, but they obviously believed my trauma was genuine because they kept me off school for the day.

It haunted me for a very long time, and it was when I was in bed, alone and in the dark, I would remember it clearest of all. Even then when I did eventually sleep, I was gripped by nightmares which persisted for months after the event.

I asked Penny, some years later, if she remembered this event. I wanted to know what she thought of it, both then and now. She told me that at the time, she and my other sister and brothers were quite shaken and scared at my reaction to whatever I had seen, but what it was, they couldn't imagine; but my experience was enough to make them wary of the bathroom for several days. Penny acknowledges that we both had an unusual childhood, living as we did, mostly inside rather than outside of our fertile imaginations, so she doesn't doubt or question what I saw - but remember, she grew up socialising with fairies, so how could she possibly criticise?

This terrifying reflection left me with a fear of mirrors so great that even now I'm still so wary of them. I'm apprehensive of looking at pictures of myself, such was the impact that scarred my young mind. Stranger still, since that time, I haven't been able to sleep if my face is exposed. For some reason I had developed a fear that it might creep up on me in the night and 'do something' to my face.

This irrational fear developed very soon after the bathroom experience, and so makes me wonder if a sense of purpose had been planted in my subconscious, perhaps a game-plan of the future. However, it would be many years before the reason for this sleep problem would be made clear to me. At this point, nothing more happened, even though I was terrified to go into the bathroom by myself for several weeks after the event. If I needed to use the toilet I'd always leave the door slightly ajar so I could make a quick run for it if 'That Thing' came back.

My parents tried to rationalise it all, insisting that I'd imagined it. I might only have been a child but I wasn't stupid; I knew I'd seen it. I quickly realized that arguing with them wasn't going to change a thing, so, with my parents being total disbelievers in the paranormal, and insisting that what I'd seen was nothing more than an over-active imagination; this was my first brush with debunkers.

However, as terrifying as that experience was, I managed to put it behind me when some months later, excitement gripped the family. What could help me bury the memory of such a shocking vision? My father saw work opportunities in New Zealand and he wanted us there within the next couple of years. We had so much planning and preparation ahead of us, but more importantly, what I didn't know it at the time, was that I had a date with destiny on the far side of the world.

The Maori Mystic

Australia had devised a scheme to increase its population and supply its industries with a boosted workforce, and this opportunity was available to Europeans who were lured by subsidised travel costs which amounted to adults paying just £10 for their fare. This was an attractive proposition because the Australian government offered good employment prospects, housing and an all-round more optimistic lifestyle than could be found in the UK at the time.

1945 through to the 1980s, was the period of a migration known as the 'Ten-Pound Poms', and more than a million Britons were involved in the exodus to Australia and New Zealand. The catch - and when is there never one? - Was that migrants who went into the scheme were obliged to remain for two years or refund the full cost of their assisted passage. My father was optimistic because he'd been planning this for around three years, a full year before he even told the family anything about the opportunities that now lay before us. I think he was just being cautious because such a move with a family was a feat of logistical planning.

As a further incentive, children didn't need to fit into the financial equation because, they were able to travel free - and because there were five of us kids that was quite a saving! Thrown into this mix was the fact that my father was an amateur radio operator, so he was in a position to contact radio enthusiasts in New Zealand and get information and request home movies about the far-off land; aside from the armfuls of brochures we harvested from travel agents – all necessary without the now so convenient internet. My father soon struck up conversations with fellow radio enthusiasts in Christchurch and Auckland, the two options as our eventual destination.

To compensate for the time-zone difference, he was awake by 4:30am, and trudging with his coffee to the shed that served as his radio shack. This didn't really bother him because he virtually lived there; it was carpeted, had a heater for the winter months and was even furnished with an armchair and a television. This garden shed even had a silent claim to fame, In July 1969, my father had a brief conversation with a radio operator on the USS Hornet, as it was sailing into the Pacific to pick up the astronauts of Apollo 11 when they splashed down.

So, it was in the shed that he'd spend a couple of hours of the early morning before work, chatting to his mates and arranging for those pictures and home-movies to be sent to us, and discussing accommodation arrangements for when we arrived. Eventually, he set his sights on Christchurch, and by April, 1971, we set off, having abandoned virtually all our existing possessions. My father insisted the entire family buy complete new wardrobes of clothes, our English clothes consisted of a lot of winter wear that wouldn't have been suitable. So we went shopping.

My new wardrobe of choice was a mix of tops, jeans, soft shoes and sturdy boots as I imagined a life of horse riding and hiking.. The money we spent must have been breathtaking, but he'd saved over a number of years for an adventure such as this so the budget must have been able to sustain it without too much difficulty. However, as if a bad omen for the rest of the adventure, it soon started going wrong.

We flew out to New Zealand while our packing cases went by sea, I don't remember how many weeks they took to catch up with us, but it must have been at least eight, maybe twelve or thirteen. This resulted in not one item of clothes fitting. We had all outgrown hundreds of pounds worth of brand new gear! There were a few things that could be passed on to a brother or sister, but not much.

Things didn't go as planned from that point on, and I'm guessing that we wouldn't even have contemplated the move if the incentives hadn't existed. But it wasn't just us that faced unforeseen obstacles, it caused untold problems for many 'Poms' during these years, ranging through missing the British weather, feeling isolated from family and friends left in Britain, not able to settle into a new work environment, or into the culture in general.

But least our father had the foresight to establish a secure beach-head before we left, so he had a job and a temporary house all arranged. Unlike so many who packed their bags, paid their Tenner and went with no arrangements whatsoever. A lot of people really did just step off the plane after having travelled half way round the world, and only started considering what they might do as they walked through the terminal.

As we slowly settled into new schools, him into his job, and my mother made friends around the neighbourhood, we waited for the deep-seated homesickness to evaporate. I felt very few effects of this move, I did miss one or two school chums, but little more than that. I was still a solitary soul, and even with a new start in this country, I remained inward-looking; spending my first months alone at the beach and watching the surf crashing in. The only discomfort I felt was the heat. I don't like heat at all, and felt uncomfortable even in the British summer, so New Zealand Summers with many weeks of heat wasn't my favourite season by any means.

However, try as we might, things became decidedly precarious because my father did not like the company he worked for, which meant he became increasingly restless. Then, true to his nature, he made a sudden decision to uproot us and move. The reason being that a friend on the North Island had discussed a business partnership with him, they were in the same line of business and so planned a domestic refrigeration engineering company.

After talking it over with our mother, and her agreeing to give it a try, we sold the house we'd owned for a little over a year, packed everything, and went to Gisborne, on the North Island's east coast. My mother never settled at all, hating both Christchurch and Gisborne, and generally disliking the country from the very start. The homesickness and not being able to integrate into the culture affected everyone deeply, but as I have already mentioned, it didn't affect me so greatly because I simply didn't feel settled wherever I was.

In 1972, I was fourteen, and having discussed it with my parents, decided to leave school. Two things prompted this decision; the first was that the school-leaving age was lower than in the UK, making it possible. The second was that the education was different to what we were used to in the U.K., and to qualify for anything I would have needed to gain what was known as a 'School Certificate.' I was of an age where even attempting it was outside of my ability because I had missed the necessary education leading towards it.

On top of that, I suffer Dyscalculia, an inability to cope with even the most basic mathematical calculations, in the '70s, the condition didn't exist in any recognisable form apart from being 'thick'. So I abandoned school and started my first job, a shelf-filling position in a town centre department store, called Gisborne Sheep Farmers. This wasn't as rural an institution as the name suggests, but a store comparable with the likes of Debenhams or Marks & Spencer.

Because we lived on the outskirts of town, I usually walked the forty-five minutes to work rather than catch a bus. I've always liked walking, and would wander to work, taking a detour from the high street into side roads to avoid the traffic. It's along one of these side-roads that I first noticed him. I'm not sure precisely when I first saw him, but some months after I started work I began noticing what I took to be a homeless loner sitting in the doorway of a shuttered shop that displayed a 'To Let' sign. At first, I ignored him, I was like that with most people. I was never one for coming forward at all.

Eventually we began passing random pleasantries, a 'good morning' or 'hi, how are you?' I don't recall who began, but I imagine it was him because I didn't start chatting to someone I didn't know. I'm still awkward when I meet people for the first time, and if I am at one of the few social gatherings I ever attend, you'll find me in the corner, cradling a soft-drink and people-watching. Invariably I'm asked why I am not joining in, and am I not enjoying it. But I would be enjoying myself, by just watching people - observing them. Therefore, with the homeless man getting things underway, it wasn't long before we were having brief but regular exchanges of conversation.

The man – who never told me his name, and for some reason I didn't ask - was a Maori, an indigenous New Zealander. I hadn't even heard of a Maori before, so was curious about him and his culture . In contrast to being stand-offish and self-isolating in new and unfamiliar social situations, if I'm inquisitive about someone, I open up and relentlessly throw questions at them. That's precisely what happened as soon as I got talking to this man.

I questioned him about why he existed the way he did and what he got out of life. My bonding, if it could be called that, was established when he said much the same as I felt, being an outsider looking in on society without being a part of it.

'I might as well be from another world; do you ever feel like that?' He asked me one time.

I told him I often felt that way, but it was good to know I wasn't the only one.

Warming to this man, I was soon opening up and talking about myself: discussing the things I did, the places I liked to go, and not feeling at all comfortable around people. All this, yet in the months of talking to him, I never asked his name; it just didn't seem important. Even so, it was puzzling that he knew my name, even though I am as sure as I can be that I never told him. I can remember when he first used it, and I recall thinking I must ask him how he knows me. By the time he did stop chatting in his usual animated way, I'd completely forgotten to ask him because the conversation had, by then, moved on.

He was a shaman, although he didn't actually use that term. Among others things, he was a healer and mystic traveller, having learned the craft of his ancestors from his father, who in turn had learned from his father. He also told me some of the mythology of his people, and his own beliefs regarding the afterlife. Of how the spirits of the land and the waters were important to him. He told me that a Polynesian demigod called Maui was his mythological hero. He told me how Maui was a protector of the weak and underprivileged. About how Maui flaunted convention to side with humans rather than the gods. One instance to demonstrate this was when he slowed the passage of the sun so that humans might have more time for cooking!

He told me that Maui created New Zealand's North Island while out on a fishing trip. Apparently, he fell asleep while his bait was in the sea, and when he awoke, he'd hooked a fish that was a real monster the size of an island. He and his brother grappled with it, and it took them three attempts to haul the fish to the surface, where it became the North Island.

Maui's crescent-shaped fishing hook, which obviously was very large, became Hawkes Bay, which was just around from Poverty Bay, Gisborne's location. The canoe that Maui and his brother were in became the top of Hikurangi, the tallest of the North Island mountains. Then, as the fish dried in the sun, it became the hilly folds which characterise the Island.

'Maui of 1000 Tricks' would, I think, be a Polynesian equivalent of the Norse god, Loki.

All the time he talked to me, this man would be working on wood with his knife, carving staffs and walking sticks. Never selling them, but giving them away to people he thought could use the 'magic' in their lives.

I found him and his stories utterly fascinating, and even if for no other reason, it was worth me going just for the opportunity to sit and listen to him. He left me with a feeling that I too would have liked to walk away from society and live a free life, me and the land.

However, the family situation continued to deteriorate as my father's business partnership began failing inside a year, and the thin dream of emigration was quickly evaporating. As kids, the five of us did enjoy the place, especially me, as I sometimes visited a friend whose parents managed a sheep station in the hills,

I loved going there to ride her horses across the wide-open hill-country, and is the the most exhilarating thing I have ever done, even more so when I she taught me to ride bareback. Outside of a few leisure pursuits that we would otherwise never have experienced; it all sank to such a low that we were quickly becoming a 'Ten-Pound Pom' statistic of failure. If nothing else, my father was tenacious to the last and simply couldn't cope with the thought of having failed, and he was never short of job opportunities because he was good at what he did.

Abandoning his company, he sought regular employment. His problem was he had a bad habit of setting his ambitions to a quixotic level - a trait I inherited from him - and I think his ambitions for being in New Zealand were just a little impractical in some ways. He went with the aim of running his own business and becoming wealthy. That is how it worked out for some, but not for countless others. Maybe if he'd been single, without the commitment to a family, his ambitions might have worked out for the better.

Eventually, having to face failure, my father gave the family an ultimatum: do we go home or do we try again, in Australia?

We knew this would be our last journey, as available finances were nearing the point of exhaustion. Aware of how much mother hated being out of the U.K., we decided to come back, and so planned our return much faster than we had gone. In January 1974, the day before we were to fly out of Gisborne to join our connecting long-haul out of Auckland, I took a final walk on my old route to work. I wanted to find The Mystic and say goodbye. I went to where he always sat, but couldn't find him. I looked around the nearby streets, in the local convenience store, in the newsagent and off-license. But I didn't see him again.

Not until I was back in England.

REVEALING TIMES

The Visitor

A few weeks after our return to England, and living within five miles from the village we'd started out from, my father found employment as a refrigeration engineer with a local company. It so happened they were also recruiting sales staff for their town centre store, so I applied, and succeeded in gaining employment with them. With it, life returned to a semblance of normality not known since before we embarked on that ill-fated New Zealand adventure.

On a July afternoon in 1975, eighteen months after our return, I was making myself useful in the shop. It was hot; perhaps a foretaste of the 15-day heat wave that was to bake Britain the following year. The shop wasn't busy, and I was the only staff member working; the other two were on their lunch breaks, which puts the time somewhere between 12 and 2pm. I had been occupying my time by replenishing the smaller items of stock and dusting the glass shelves, I was still engrossed in some mindless dust-flicking when I heard someone open the door and walk in.

I put on my best customer-service smile and turned to greet a man who was around six feet tall with scalp-cropped black hair. He was wearing a dark suit, white shirt and a dark blue tie. His eyes were hidden behind reflective sunglasses, probably Foster Grants, which were extremely popular at the time. In fact, I can't think of anybody who didn't own a pair. I would have said this was a businessman - perhaps a travelling salesman - who cared about his appearance; he had a broad face and swarthy complexion and might have been of Mediterranean origin.

As soon as I looked at that face, I was hit by a sensation of deja-vu, that he and I had some connection; that I knew him from somewhere and should be able to remember. It was so strong that my greeting smile almost became one of recognition and relief at seeing him and I wouldn't have been at all surprised if he'd reminded me where we'd met. But then those out-of-place feelings evaporated, and I snapped out of it.

Regaining my composure, I went behind the counter to attend him. He began asking about freezers, cookers and washing machines, because he was refurbishing one of his houses and wanted to turn it into small apartments. He travelled a lot and was back in England to see a friend, and so was taking the opportunity to change the layout of the house - or so I was told. Then the conversation shifted almost imperceptibly. He continued to peruse the brochures I had put on the counter for him, but with no obvious reason , he asked if I was interested in UFOs.

I had recently developed an interest in the subject, and been reading books by authors such as Dr Allan. J. Hynek, Brad Steiger and Erich von Daniken. Of particular note, I had read *The Sky People*, by the 8th Earl of Clancarty, Brinsley Le Poer Trench.

Le Poer Trench succeeded his half-brother as 8th Earl of Clancarty in 1976, and immediately set about using this position to put pressure on the British Government regarding the UFO enigma. He became quite a thorn in the side of the Ministry of Defence, because Clancarty knew his subject well and the MoD had nobody they could field against him, which left them floundering with embarrassment. On 18 January 1979, one of the best ever attended debates took place in the House of Lords; the public gallery was full to bursting. Why? Clancarty had used his position to initiate a debate about UFOs.

This was an amazing episode in the history of not only UFOs, but of politics, and the Hansard transcript is well worth reading. The debate lasted three hours and Clancarty began the session by calling for an intra-governmental investigation into the subject, he also appealed for the MoD to release what they had, pertaining to the subject. Unfortunately, most of what Clancarty asked for failed to materialise, but one thing that did come of it was the House of Lords UFO Study Group, which held meetings over several years. Le Poer Trench died on 18 May 1995. At the back of Clancarty's book, *The Sky People*, I found the Oxfordshire address of Contact International, a UFO research organisation Clancarty had founded in 1967. I decided to join and in mid-1974 I paid my subscription fee and eagerly looked forward to receiving their quarterly journals. I told The Man of my interest, and even about how me and my sister had believed we could build a flying saucer when we were children.

I also told him what I had experienced with the mirror, which was unusual in itself, because I never told anybody about that. But The Man took it in his stride, simply nodding a response as he continued leafing through a glossy brochure. When I finished talking, he told me in a rather matter-of-fact way that he'd seen flying saucers; he also stated - as though an authority on the subject - that they were real, just not as most people thought. Then he asked me if I'd ever been abroad, but without waiting for an answer, he went on to tell me that he had been. In fact, he'd had some of his best UFO sightings while trekking around New Zealand.

I was astonished. 'You were in New Zealand?'

'Yes, until quite recently.'

I told him how that was such an amazing coincidence, because we'd been back from there just over a year. I told him of our initial optimism, followed by the failures and the rapid return home. There was, however, one thing about the New Zealand trip I didn't mention; I didn't have to, The Man mentioned it for me.

I no longer thought much about the Maori until The Man reminded me, and it was extremely unnerving that this stranger could replay a lot of my conversations with the Mystic, and all I could do was look on in bewilderment. Then he hit me with a statement that shook me to the core; he told me he knew me very well indeed, and that there was a purpose for me being here. He said he understood me, but my being here was important. The Man then picked up a brochure and left the shop.

I spent the four years between 1976 and 1980 mainly reading history, and writing science fiction. The latter being the only hobby I got any real pleasure from. I never wrote my fiction with an aim to publish, although the writing bug did start to bite deeper and one or two short stories found their way into competitions. I even wrote two novels, but the ever-mounting rejection slips soon put me off the idea completely. Still, I wrote for myself, and perhaps it was a way to revisit the worlds that we had created all those years ago.

It was around this time I developed an urge to find somebody I could spend some quality social time with and talk history, especially Roman history. I began to toy with the idea of forming a small group to recreate Roman gladiatorial combat at local Fayres and carnivals, the fact that such a group would cost an absolute fortune to furnish with replica equipment didn't really enter my mind. I had no finances whatsoever, so how I imagined I would accomplish such a feat defies me even now; that is an example of inheriting my father's habit of setting sights beyond what was realistically achievable.

But having decided it was I wanted to do nothing could shift the idea, and as with our 'spaceship', all impracticalities were swept to one side as I put my plan into action. In 1978, I placed a postcard on a newsagent's personal ad's board, appealing for people to contact me if they were interested in forming a Roman re-enactment group. It was in the window for a month before I forgot all about it, until a year later in mid-1979 when I got a reply.

Meeting Shelagh

A beautiful spring morning in Mid-March of 1979 brought a knock on my front door, I opened it to be faced by the person who was to usher profound changes into my life. This smiling woman started the conversation by telling me she was responding to a postcard that had been in a newsagent's window, and when I pointed out that it had been and gone more than twelve months, she admitted that it had been 'quite some time ago.' I invited her in and while I made us a pot of tea, she explained that she'd copied out the details from the newsagent window, but the slip of paper had gotten lost somewhere in the bottom of a handbag which she no longer used.

Apparently, just some weeks before arriving on my doorstep, she'd decided to send some of her old belongings to a charity shop, and this included the obsolete handbag. Checking to make sure it was empty, she found the piece of paper, and - well - here she was. As we drank tea and ate biscuits it was soon discovered that we had a lot in common, and so spent the next few hours moving from subject to subject. At one point she asked how the re-enactment group was going, and I had to admit it wasn't going anywhere, and confessing that she was the only response I'd had.

From that day on, we spent many afternoons chatting about both Roman and Tudor history. The subject of the re-enactment group did surface now and again, as we continued to wonder if it could be done, but we usually ended up agreeing that it was a non-starter.

Fifty-one-year-old Shelagh Yeoman was a large lady with a bubbly personality to match. She lived with her teenage son and a husband she didn't get along with at all, it was a marriage under strain, but kept hidden behind her bright and infectious smile. I learned that life at home was difficult, and she didn't know what she'd do if she didn't have her son, Julian, for support, and comfort from her German shepherd dog, Kali.

Our afternoon tea- and biscuit-supported chats soon broadened out until I was accompanying her when she took the dog for its afternoon walk across an area of East Reading called White Knights. This picturesque 321 acres of lush meadow and woodland paths is part of the Reading University campus,and regularly used by the public, and especially favoured by dog-walkers and joggers. During these afternoon strolls through the woodland and circumventing its artificial lake, we told each other our life stories. Shelagh was particularly fascinating because her younger years had been spent in Southern Rhodesia - now Zambia - where she had been a police inspector with the CID in Broken Hill, now Kabwe.

She had been there during the uncertain years of the Mau Mau uprising that took place between 1952 and 1960, and although the dispute took place in Kenya, more than a thousand kilometres away, it inspired Zambian nationalists, and was fanned by the fact that Northern Rhodesian troops were deployed in active combat to Kenya.

However, things got even more interesting when she started talking about Mambwe. This man had not only been the Transport Sergeant, responsible for the upkeep of the vehicles at the police station, but was also a witch doctor and a Headmen in the Bemba tribe. The stories she told me about him was my first exposure to practical tribal magic.

Mambwe

She told me of occasion when he arranged to perform a spectacular display of his abilities at a police social function. Dressed in tribal regalia, consisting of animal skins and furs with bone decorations and totems sewn into it, and a headdress of more dried animal skins and feathers, he began dancing, chanting and shaking.

He had requested that four of the Rhodesian Ridgeback's be allowed in the room, and these lay obediently under their handlers' tables, but at Mambwe's request, had not been leashed. As he continued his dancing and chanting, the dogs became increasingly agitated, and the handlers were finding it difficult to keep them calm.

Mambwe increased the momentum of his ceremonial dance and moved into an empty area of the room, creating a safe distance between himself and the occupied tables. Then, as if at a signal, the four dogs launched themselves in a frenzied attack from under the tables. The animals clamped their jaws on his arms and legs and held firm. Shelagh said that Mambwe remained with them in this position for just a few moments, before uttering a single command at the dogs which sent them slinking back beneath the tables with their tails between their legs. Shelagh said this was the most spectacular exhibition of control she has ever seen.

Mambwe was very protective towards Shelagh, and seemed to treat her as being special. He put protection on her, and explained that while in Africa, no animal would touch her; no insect would bite her; no native would harm her. He proved right on all counts, because in the years she spent in Northern Rhodesia, she said she saw virtually no wildlife at all. Nothing apart from a giant tortoise, a water buffalo and a troop of baboons - and even those were on a game reserve.

On another occasion, a colleague offered to take her to a beauty spot where she could watch the annual mass migration of the elephant herds from one part of the country to the other. Of course, she was eager for that experience, so off they went. They waited, and they continued to wait. Nothing happened and her colleague was left perplexed that on this occasion the elephants didn't pass by on their regular migratory route. He told her that he'd never known it to happen.

Shelagh habitually walked through the long grass with her feet and legs bare, but never once did she receive a bite from an insect. Finally, and rather embarrassingly for her as a CID officer, she hired a native houseboy that turned out to be a convicted murderer on the run. How did she discover this fact? Some months after hiring him, she noticed some new 'Wanted' posters on the board at the station, and identified him in one of the mugshots!

'That's my Solomon!' she uttered in disbelief. The houseboy was immediately arrested, and while in custody, it transpired that he was sympathetic to the Mau Mau cause, and had even arranged with a neighbouring houseboy that they would murder their white homeowners! It may be down to Mambwe's influence that she was still alive to recount any of these experiences.

Introduction To The Paranormal

It was these stories about Mambwe that guided us to the subject of the occult in general, and Shelagh revealed to me that she was a practitioner, Wicca. I had taken some interest in Wicca and witchcraft, but in those pre-Internet days, it was all very hush-hush and I lacked anybody to discuss it with. Therefore, Shelagh seemed to be the answer to a silent prayer that I'd been putting out to the universe, as she began to open out as much as her coven oaths would allow.

During the 1950s, she had been a High Priestess in a Brighton coven, which had hived off from it's parent situated in The New Forest. from what Shelagh was saying, this sounded like it might even have been the coven taken over by Gerald. B. Gardiner in 1939. This was the man who in the 1950s, was in London establishing the modern Wiccan framework after the repeal of the 1736 Witchcraft Act. If not *the* coven, it most surely hived off from it. Shelagh always remained very secretive about her coven work because, as she should, she took her initiation vows seriously, even though the coven had ceased to exist many years before she met me. On other occult and pagan topics, she was open and forthcoming, always happy to give her views and opinions when I asked for them.

In March 1982, I had to leave my rented flat and needed to find somewhere else to live. Shelagh had a spare room she leased to university students, but it so happened that the room was vacant because its former occupant had suddenly decided to leave, which couldn't have been better timed. Shelagh never believed in coincidences, but that everything came about for a reason. The postcard advertising a group that I had no chance of creating had been a means to draw us into a lasting friendship had been one such 'arranged' coincidence. Likewise, she had no doubt that the student had suddenly departed because he was 'making way' for me to have the room. It's by way of this logic - also known as 'synchronicity' - that she offered it to me.

So I took the room, but not before trying alternatives, after all, isn't that what family is for? By now, my parents were divorced and my father was living in a small house by himself. I had been given his number and wondered if he could assist me for a few nights, just until I could get sorted. My mother couldn't help, she had remarried and was living in Sussex. So, I phoned my father on the morning as I was leaving my flat, but he acted as if he didn't know me, like he had no recollection of who I was. That's how he had always been with me, so nothing new there!

I moved into Shelagh's spare room and it wasn't long before our mutual interests helped deflect her worries from her husband whose regular Saturday night binge in the pub had her locking herself in her bedroom by 10pm. I became acutely aware of how bad things were when she said: 'I told him just months after marrying him, that I didn't plan to grow old with him. I will have left long before then.'

A seriously good advantage for me moving in was that Shelagh opened her library to me, and I marvelled at shelf after shelf loaded with books across the breadth of occultism and witchcraft. She had books by such stalwarts as Doreen Valiante, Hanz Holzer and Alice Bailey. There were more by Madam Blavatsky and Sybil Leek. Sybil was of interest for two reasons. She was one of the first English witches to publicise her craft to the media, and secondly; Shelagh and Sybil were distant cousins. In fact, looking at pictures of Sybil Leek and Shelagh, you could see the close family resemblance.

I took a lot of interest in the Theosophical books, some of which, mapped the invisible worlds of existence. This was my introduction to the concept of alternative states of reality, the various astral, mental, emotional and etheric planes. These books explained how those who have passed on, work their way through these levels before reincarnation.

I also read books by Ruth Montgomery. *Strangers Among Us: Enlightened Beings from a World to Come*, was my introduction to 'Walk-Ins', this process describes how under a pre-birth agreement, the natal-soul departs the body, to be replaced with a new soul, which could be either temporarily or permanently. This isn't to be confused with 'possession': a forced takeover of a person by a malevolent, invading spirit. Possession is a different thing altogether. A 'Walk-In' is said to occur when a human has some work to perform, this might be in assisting the human collective consciousness, or delivering a teaching of some kind, maybe demonstrating a lesson in compassion.

Missing Time

One subject I found lacking in this otherwise extensive library was that of UFOs, I had expected to find at least a few books on the subject, maybe even just the one nestled somewhere between Bigfoot and the Loch Ness monster, but I found nothing.

I asked her why this was, pointing out that she had just about everything else you could think of. Her reply was that lights in the sky were boring and didn't interest her. I tried to generate some enthusiasm by explaining that it wasn't all lights in the sky, and that there were reasonable grounds to believe spaceships had landed and the occupants been seen, even spoken to, humans. I told her there were many stories of interaction between the species. However, there was simply no in-road with Shelagh.

I soon realised that at just the mention of the subject she'd suddenly be busy and refuse to even listen, and any comment she did make was to repeat her utter disinterest. She seemed to switch off at the very mention of the subject. But then, one day, something did change. By chance, I said that many witnesses suffered periods of missing time; an otherwise perfectly normal day would have a mysterious period of missing time.

That's when Shelagh interrupted me in mid-sentence and told me that reminded her of an odd experience she'd had some years previously. She said, to my astonishment, there was a whole chunk of time missing from her life, and try as she might, she'd never been able to remember what happened. I asked her if she were OK to tell me what she could recall, and she agreed.

It was during the summer of 1975, she began by reminding me that she always took Kali a walk at the same time every day, at 2pm. The timing was that precise so she could be home for when her son came out of school at 3.30pm, and on the day in question, seven years previously, it was no different. However, by the time she was halfway through her walk, something she couldn't seem to understand or identify, was totally out of place.

She said she had the memory of emerging from a clump of trees and with it, a sensation of being watched; She also pointed out that these trees weren't on her usual route, they were located way off across open grassland.

I asked what made her divert her course, and she shrugged and chuckled, 'I have absolutely no idea. I was just suddenly aware that I was walking in an unfamiliar area and that the day looked wrong.'

'Wrong? How was it wrong?'

'I had no idea, not until I got home and that's when it hit me.'

I asked her how she felt when she went across to the trees, but she surprised me by saying she had no memory of even approaching them. What she recalls is walking along a track with open land on either side, and Kali running free from her leash. Then her attention was drawn to the line of trees that lay some way off to her left. That's the point when her memory is a blank, and there's nothing more until she's walking out from among the trees.

She got Kali back on the leash as quickly as possible, spooked by a notion that she needed to keep the dog close, but with no idea why; all she could identify was an eerie sensation that her every movement was being watched; being monitored by something unseen.

Even with everything she'd experienced in the African Bush, this was the strangest and most unreal she'd ever undergone. Gathering her wits about her, she hastily made her way home. She told me that as she headed out of White knights, she was puzzled because something about her environment was 'different', there was something 'wrong'. upon arrival home, she took off her coat and filled the dog's water bowl and noticed that Kali lapped the bowl dry; barely lifting her head once until the water was gone. Shelagh was also unusually thirsty, and drank a glass of water without pause.

Then she walked into the sitting room, and that's when her world went completely crazy.

Not only did she find Julian watching television and eating burger and chips, but her husband was home as well - and he wasn't supposed to finish work till 6pm.

'Where have you been?' Peter asked her.

'I've been walking Kali, why?' Even as she answered his question, her own mind was asking *why are you both at home so early?*

Then Peter drew her attention to the wall clock. 'But where have you been?'

Shelagh glanced at the time and couldn't believe what she saw - it was just after 6.30pm - more than three hours later than it had any right to be. That's when realisation smacked her between the eyes, and she understood why the day 'looked wrong', It was because the sun was three hours lower in the sky!

Hypnotic Regression

Her missing time intrigued me because it was the first time I had ever met someone who'd experienced it directly, but there was nothing more she could add to what she'd already said. There was simply no memory of veering off the track and walking towards the trees. One moment she was on the path, then the next she was emerging from the trees with three hours of her life missing and no indication of what had happened in that time.

I wondered whether hypnotic regression would be of some help; it's considered by many to be a controversial tool in aiding recall, but even so, it was implemented by Budd Hopkins in his research, and had been used to recover details from Betty and Barney Hill. Furthermore, there were many less well known cases in which it had been successfully used. I discussed all this with Shelagh and she seemed happy to try it.

I knew someone who I thought might be able to help us. He was retired, but in his time had been in the medical profession and was qualified in hypnotherapy techniques. I had Len's number so phoned and asked if he might be interested in having a subject regress back over a few years. I didn't suggest to either Shelagh or Len that there might conceivably be any link to aliens, and although it did seem to follow the pattern, there wasn't anything to suggest this was actually the case, so I kept all thoughts on that to myself.

I was now seeing myself as something of a UFO investigator and so tried to uphold a degree of what I hoped was professionalism. I didn't want to 'pollute' the scenario by seeding thoughts into Shelagh's mind, which would contaminate her recall, and all I told Len was that Shelagh seemed to have an unaccountable memory loss in the summer of 1975, and that maybe he could help her get through it to discover what had happened. He agreed to try, and so undertook the project; Shelagh was more than happy to be his subject, and arranged her schedule with him. Within the month, we began to explore the lost three and a half hours.

Abduction

Len began his session by verifying what information he could. Having regressed her back to the day in question, he asked for details, such as what clothing she wore at the time, what the newspaper headlines were that she'd read on that particular morning, plus any other small and insignificant detail he could find to support the clarity of her recall. He even asked her the precise date and what day of the week it fell on – and she gave this information without hesitation, which, when checked, helped to confirm the accuracy of her memory.

He conducted the session in Shelagh's home, he felt it was important that she explored this missing time while in an environment where she could feel comfortable, relaxed and safe. I sat some distance away at the table, poised to switch on the cassette tape recorder when Len indicated for me to do so. The therapist sat on an armchair next to the couch upon which Shelagh lay with a blanket covering her. With Peter at work and Julian at school, the house was silent and still.

Len began the session, and Shelagh told him that the dog-walk began at 2.05pm. She didn't recall anything unusual as she made her way along the side of the school that Julian attended. She walked past the playing-fields and the tennis courts, and then into the White Knights campus that lay at the back of the school. Everything progressed uneventfully, and to be honest, I was expecting her to say that she developed a seizure and passed out long enough to explain the time lapse. But then about halfway around her circuit, she mentioned spotting something like a shiny metal disk in the tops of the trees.

Those trees were some distance away across open ground. I knew exactly where she meant, because she had taken me past that point during our dog-walks, and although these trees were off of her route, she felt compelled to walk across to investigate whatever was flashing in the sunlight from the treetops. There was a pause for some moments as in her mind she covered the distance in real-time, but this pause was punctuated with remarks about the 'shiny disk' that seemed to increasingly intrigue and captivate her attention as she closed the distance. It had her helplessly hooked and was now reeling her in; then she reached the edge of the trees, and the unexpected kicked in:

'Oh.'

'What's wrong?' Len asked.

'I don't know. I'm going through something.'

'Can you describe it?'

'I don't know what it is; it's like thick ropes and thin threads, thousands and thousands of them; they look like they are made of mist and hanging down from the sky - my God It's even hanging from the trees.'

'Describe to me what's happening.'

'I can feel that I'm brushing through this stuff. I've stopped and I'm looking around, and... and... I... I'm lost. It's all around me... oh, which way is out?'

There was a lengthy pause. 'Are you still lost?'

'I'm in somewhere.'

    We noticed her voice had now changed, just moments ago she had sounded lost and confused, but now she was calmer; her tone was relaxed, and even carried a dreamlike quality to it.

'Where are you?'

'I don't know.'

'Describe what you see.'

'A room... a white, round room. They are at the end of the room on a raised bit.'

'Who are at the end of the room?'

'I don't know - things - they are… oh my dog. Where is she?'

Unprompted, Shelagh relaxed a moment later.

'Where is the dog?' Len asked

'She's stood near me, but I don't understand it, she's frozen.'

'What do you mean, "frozen"?'

'Like a film that's stopped, she's frozen in mid-stride.'

He then asked her how many people or things were in the room.

'No, not people, just things. Three are on a raised bit, and one off to my left.'

She was asked to describe this strange environment in more detail. We already knew she was in a white, round room with a 'raised bit' at the end. She went on to describe banks of lights behind the three beings at the far end, and midway between them and herself, was what looked like a dark grey steel table. Another creature was off to her left.

The beings were bipedal reptilians with necks 'like a turtle', long, stretched and wrinkled skin. Those necks fascinated her so much that she frequently broke off her commentary to mention them. Shelagh estimated the heights of the beings as between seven and eight feet. Their hands were long, clawed and articulate. She held up her own hand and slowly flexed her fingers in an attempt to aid her description of how they moved. Then she sounded unnerved, describing how one of the creatures lifted a hand, and with a single finger, beckoned her forward.

An instant later, and with no recollection of moving, she found herself standing beside the table, and the three beings that had been on the 'raised bit' were now standing directly in front of her. Then - and without a word being passed between her and the beings - she gazed at the one who had beckoned her forward, staring into the black pits of its eyes. She felt information start to pour into her mind, slipping past her consciousness at blinding speed. She tried to grasp it, to become aware of what was going into her mind, but she failed. Then, as suddenly as it started, the information-flow ended. The creature that had fixated Shelagh with its eyes and conducted the information transfer, inclined its head very slightly to one side. Again, with no awareness of having made a move, Shelagh was face-down on the table with all four beings crowding around.

'Oh God!'

'What is it? What's the matter?'

'My back. They've pushed something into my spine.'

Len prompted her with questions but she couldn't add anything further, just that something cold had been pushed into the base of her spine. She described as like a cartridge being rammed into the breach of a shotgun, a downward then sharp upward movement.

'What's happening now?'

'I'm no longer on the table. I'm standing before them.'

'Have they said anything at all? Have you asked anything?'

'No, they've said nothing, and I don't feel I want to ask.'

The beings guided Shelagh to the wall opposite that from which she'd entered, and this seems to have been the first physical movement she experienced while in their presence; she passed through the solid wall and found herself out among the smoky ropes again. She walked through this and out into clear air. She now seemed to be standing with her dog at her heels as though nothing had occurred, but she said she was confused. This was the point where, during our previous conversations, she seemed to be aware of walking out of the trees.

'Can you see anything?'

'No, it's all gone. I have to go home and forget what happened.'

'They told you this?'

'No, not told me, but I know that's what they want me to do.'

Bringing the session to a close, Len went home to transcribe his tape-recording to paper. Over the next couple of sessions, he regressed Shelagh again in order to check on little details, even asking misleading questions, like asking about some minor point, and maybe distorting a minute fact. However, even when he did that, she would correct his detail. Everything seemed to correspond to the initial regression, and throughout the days between sessions, I was sure not to discuss any of it with her.

So much for Shelagh finding 'lights in the sky' and UFOs a boring subject!

Perhaps the lack of interest was planted in her mind to deter her from questioning the missing time too closely? It would make sense, seeing as how compliant she appeared to be with the creatures, such as having no desire to question them, and that she needed to go home and forget what happened. If I hadn't arrived in her life, with my interest in UFOs, this abduction might never have come to light - or maybe her 'disinterest' had been placed there to keep this abduction secure and untouched until I did come along, and my mentioning of 'missing time' being the key needed.

As an addition to this experience, years later, in 1990, I discovered that on separate occasions, two security guards on the campus witnessed unidentified lights while crossing a bridge over a river on the campus. When they took me over to White Knights, and pointed to where they had seen the dancing lights, they told me they had investigated, assuming it was a torchlight, but found nothing to explain what they saw.

What I noted, however, is that they had seen the dancing lights among the trees where Shelagh had had her experience.

Red Eagle

The consequence of this regression started just a week later, when we were sat watching television; Shelagh suddenly looked towards me, frowned for a moment and then said that she could see a Red Indian standing behind me. 'It's rather odd, because I haven't seen him before. He's just suddenly appeared from nowhere.' She continued to stare at a space behind my right shoulder.

'What does he look like?'

Shelagh closed her eyes and attempted to make psychic contact with the apparition.

'He's at least six-feet tall, very tall indeed. He has a broad face and an amazing head-dress. It's just so full of eagle feathers and extends down his back to below his knees.'

'Can you ask him what he wants?'

'He says he's with you.' Eyes still closed, she pointed towards me to emphasise her comment. 'Yes, he's with you and says you "need to be ready to learn."'

'Need to be ready to learn what?'

She shrugged, 'I don't know, he's just repeating that you need to be ready to learn.'

'Does he have a name?'

Shelagh went quiet for a few moments, and then chuckled to herself, 'Oh, here we go - I hate Red Indians and Red Indian names; everybody seems to have a Red Indian or a Chinaman as a guide. I've tried to wipe his image and name out of my mind, but he keeps repeating it – well, not as words, I can see him squatting in the sand. He has a teepee erected behind him, it's on a cliff-edge. He's writing his name in the sand with a finger. It says: "Red Eagle". They all seem to be Red Eagles, White Eagles and Running Horses.'

I did understand the point she was making, as a long-term member of the Spiritualist community, she'd come across a lot of mediums and their spirit-guides, and she was right in what she said, there was a preponderance of Asian and North American guides. But if Shelagh said this Indian was there, I certainly wouldn't question it. She had demonstrated her psychic ability to me time and time again, so I had no reason to doubt that she was indeed seeing this Indian that had appeared unannounced, nor was I prepared to question the accuracy of whatever information she got from him. An example of her accuracy as a psychic was when she was a child at school, no more than seven years-old. She had a major argument with another girl in the playground and spinning to face her in fury; Shelagh yelled for all to hear, 'At least my dad is my REAL dad – unlike yours!'

That really hit the fan because no one aside from the girl's parents knew they had adopted her as a baby!

So, Shelagh's clairvoyance and mediumship had an amazing track-record which I unashamedly exploited over the coming weeks as her link to Red Eagle strengthened, which suggested that he planned to be around for some while. I plied him with questions, mostly about his life as a Native American. Obviously, nothing she gave me was verifiable, but I wasn't looking for evidence; it was of entertainment and curiosity value alone. But then, about a month later, she told me something that knocked me sideways:

'Red Eagle is telling me about your time in New Zealand.'

'Really?' I muttered; my attention not focused on her at all.

'Yes, he is showing me a man squatting at the side of a road.'

My attention was suddenly fully switched on, because I had only briefly mentioned the Maori Mystic to her, and even that wasn't in any great detail. In fact, it was simply mentioned in a response to her telling me about Mambwe.

She continued: 'I'm not sure what he means, but he says that he was that man, and he wanted to see if you would bother to stop and talk to him. He needed to test you.'

'He had a life as that man?'

Shelagh shook her head, now looking slightly puzzled. 'No, he says he became physical.' Her eyes still squeezed tightly shut; she tapped her forearm to emphasis her point. 'He took on a solid existence, just for that encounter.'

There was a lengthy pause, her brow furrowing as though she might be concentrating, or focusing her attention on something. 'He's talking about marks you wake up with. He says you have been finding them for years, and you don't know how you get them.'

While we were in New Zealand, I started finding marks on my body that had not been there the previous day, and I would have no recollection of how I got them. It had an alarming side to it, because during my sleep, I would have had a nightmare involving the alien in the mirror, and in the morning I'd find perfectly round bruises, about the size of a two penny piece on either side of each knee. I also found them on each side of my elbows, all circular and identical in size. I got so used to seeing them that I eventually paid them no attention, and they continued to appear at regular intervals right up to 1980, at which time they - and the nightmares - stopped.

I asked her what he knew about me having those marks, but I was careful not to tell her what the marks were; I wanted to see if she could get it from him.

'He's showing me round bruises, on your arms and legs?'

'I used to have them, but not now, I haven't seen them for quite a while. Ask him what they were and why I had them.'

Shelagh shook her head slowly. 'He's not telling me, he just says it's "to make you ready."'

If I was astonished that she had picked up where the bruises had been, I was in for another surprise just a moment later.

She opened her eyes and stared at me. 'He says you met him twice. You met him here, in England as well.'

I remembered The Man who had come into the electrical shop back in 1975, and how he seemed to know all about me, then a second realisation hit me; The Man, who Red Eagle was claiming had been him, had occurred in the same month and year as Shelagh's abduction by the reptilian aliens.

This Red Indian had suddenly appeared in my life with a series of astonishing revelations, and it seemed he'd started as he intended to continue.

BIRTH OF A GREY

Communication

In September 1982, five months after uncovering Shelagh's abduction memories, the night-paralysis began. Coming out of nowhere, it struck me suddenly at some point in the early hours of the morning. I woke up but found I couldn't open my eyes or move my limbs, no matter how much I tried; I was paralysed. I was aware of what had woken me, a mild vibrating sensation rippling through my body from head to feet.

Initially, there was something strangely relaxing about it, maybe that was because it was barely noticeable. However, over the next several seconds the intensity increased until I was hit by the convulsive waves of a tsunami that felt as though it were ripping every molecule of my body apart. I tried to open my mouth, wanting to call out for help – or scream - for all I knew it could have been an epileptic seizure. As I tried to cry out for help I felt something open, it felt like it should have been my mouth, but it couldn't have been as I could still feel my mouth paralysed shut.

Then something like eyes behind my physical eyes opened and I could see the ceiling above me, It was as if my sealed eyelids had suddenly become transparent, and shutters behind them had abruptly opened. As confusing as these sensations were: a mouth that wasn't my anatomical mouth opening to scream, eyes that weren't my anatomical eyes opening and registered on my senses as vision, I came to understand this, much later, as some form of 'split consciousness'. In other words: I was aware of my physical body being rendered powerless as something else - either within me, or merging with me - became the only part with any self-control at all.

But at the time it happened, and because I had been reading Shelagh's Theosophical books, I naturally assumed it had to be the mouth and eyes of my astral body opening, and that was why I could see the bedroom so clearly. This sight wasn't anything like my normal vision, everything was bathed in a vivid electric blue glow. This was nothing like previous Out Of Body Experiences I'd had. My usual OBE would consist of flying sensations within dreams, sometimes waking with memories of seeing people and visiting places I didn't recognise. These recalls would most often be little more than vague feelings, indistinct and woven into dreams. They certainly bore no resemblance to what was happening this night.

But as suddenly as it had started, and as my panic was reaching a peak, this 'Juddering' subsided from being akin to a choppy sea and back down to the gentle rippling sensation I had experienced on waking. Then it ceased altogether, my blue-tinted vision also switched off and I was plunged into gloom as I found my physical eyes were now able to open. That's when I saw an optical phenomenon along the coving of the wall opposite my bed, a strong white strip of light a few inches thick, and about six feet long. As soon as I looked at it, the light snapped down to a pinprick, like a point of laser light that hurt my eyes to look at. This thing remained visible for a moment or two before winking out of existence.

When it did vanish, and I could finally move my arms and legs, how did I respond? I got out of bed, went for a glass of water, then returned to bed and went straight to sleep without giving the experience a single thought. I know how anti-climactic that sounds, but it's exactly what I did. I can only guess that as soon as the light vanished, my brain went into some kind of 'normality' mode and forced me to engage in a mundane activity, which just happened to be getting a glass of water. Perhaps it was the reaction of a brain that had, for a few moments, lost all contact with its understanding of reality, and so going for a glass of water was its way to ground itself back in the physical world.

This sleep-paralysis - or call this well-documented phenomenon what you will - continued at frequent intervals across the next two years. Each time It was exactly the same, and included the light strip which I came to think of as an energy source connected with, or was itself, generating the experience rather than being the random optical illusion which at first I thought it might be. I came to this conclusion because on one occasion, I was floating very slightly out of my body. Conscious awareness of my OBE's had become normal for me since the sleep-paralysis began, No longer was I experiencing the vague sensations of flying, but I could clearly recall stepping out of my sleeping physical form - and I could see this strip of light along the coving, bathing my body in pale light.

This light didn't seem to touch anything else in the room, not even the bed beneath me, but only illuminated my sleeping form, as though I was under a soft spotlight. I also understood what was happening. Even though the thought was crazy, it was there in my head – a second 'me' was in the process of being twinned with my human form.

Around two months after these particular experiences began, I not only saw, but actually became the being I had 'conjoined' with. I also decided that this entity was quite probably connected with the creature whose eye and partial face I had seen in the mirror so many years before.

This particular night in November 1982, I awoke to the now-familiar Juddering, and, as usual, was unable to open my eyes or move my body, but I no longer panicked. I would lay still, be as relaxed as I possibly could, and ride it out, so to speak. However, this time, moments after the intensity of the Juddering increased, I was ejected from my physical body; or rather, a part of my consciousness, housed in a non-human form was ejected from my body.

The ejection was violent enough to catapult me clear across the room, and I tried to brace myself, knowing I was going to slam against the wall. But instead of the expected collision, I landed squarely and lightly on my feet. Even more surprisingly, I'd been thrown barely halfway across the room by a force that should have splashed me across the wall. I looked back at the bed and saw myself asleep. I don't know if my physical body was still experiencing the Juddering, but if it was, I could see no external sign indication. I could also see that my sleeping form was bathed in the pale glow from the intense white bar of light that, as usual, was nestled along the coving. Up to this point, I assumed I was having a regular OBE, even though it was a particularly forceful one.

This sudden ejection was very different from any that had gone before, not least was that I couldn't sense Red Eagle's presence anywhere. Until now, I had always been aware of him accompanying me on nocturnal journeying. He had started being my companion since September of that year, but, so far as I could determine, he was never a part of the experience; he was simply a companion, an overseer. I assumed that for reasons best known to himself, he needed to be somewhat obscure, shadowing me without participating, as he trained me to travel across dimensions. During these nocturnal travels, I became aware of a multitude of very different forms of life, all linked in various ways, not only to humanity and each other, but to the planet itself.

It was astonishing for me to discover that there are parallel worlds, and that what happens in one can affect the balance of another. He educated me on what I simplistically thought of as 'lower astral and higher spiritual planes'. He introduced me to the subtle and not so subtle energies that thread their way through them, and all of which can interact with the human mind, even having the ability to manifest visually. So much was shown, yet a great deal was simply not understood.

On this occasion, however, he wasn't with me. I was alone.

I looked back to my sleeping form, but felt little association with it. I saw the body in that bed as human, therefore, not me. That was a very strange thing to have gone through my mind. Then I looked down at my hand: My arm was thin, lacking anything much in the way of muscle; it could have been no more than flesh covered bones, and very delicate bones at that. My hand was elongated and I remember a thumb and three fingers, each digit longer than a human equivalent, and they each had an extra joint. I was dark grey in colour.

This change of appearance didn't generate the same terror I'd experienced as a child, this was full of intrigue and curiosity. I wasn't human. I was thinking as this entity; as that creature. I also knew that the Grey body I occupied wasn't biological, at least, not in any way that humans understand the word. I somehow felt it was something manufactured, and my consciousness was inhabiting it. I didn't move from the spot where I had landed as I stared at the bedroom wall. I knew I was in a room that belonged to the person in the bed, and as with the body in the bed, I felt an almost complete disassociation from it. I remember my last thought before this experience ended, being:

I'm undergoing a process of splitting into two.

Then I woke in bed, restored to human form and with a clear memory of what had happened. However, in the moment before I woke, I had two images in my head that I would need to remember to tell Shelagh in the morning. I laid there in the dark and no longer able to sleep. As I waited for daylight to catch up with me, I replayed the entire sequence events in my head, getting up as soon as I heard Shelagh downstairs.

Over tea and toast, I asked Shelagh if she had seen or felt anything unusual during the night. She barely hesitated as she went on to say that she'd woken during the night and felt a 'presence' which she thought, at first, was in her room because it was such a strong feeling. But when she woke fully, she realised it was coming through the wall from my room. As she was telling me this, I remembered that as the Grey I had stared fixedly at the bedroom wall, and it hadn't registered with me before this moment that it was the adjoining wall between her room and mine. Had the Grey been motionless and staring at the wall because it was communicating something to her? Or had it been making her aware of its presence?

I had no answer even though, rather confusingly; it had been me standing and doing the staring – and yet it wasn't me! Shelagh told me that she'd reached out with her mind to try to make contact, asking it to identify itself. She told me that it hadn't responded to her, not in the way she had requested, but what it did was to transfer information to her mind. She saw images flashing through her mind: In the first, she saw a hole in the ground, deep and glowing.

'I don't know what it was I saw, but it was somewhere cold and fairly barren. I think there's going to be a big nuclear disaster; I can see empty streets and abandoned homes and vehicles. I am wondering if I am seeing a nuclear Armageddon. It's frightening. They will be doing something - experimenting; I think - and it will go wrong and pollute everything. I saw empty streets; it's going to be dreadful. Then I saw images of a war between Europe and the Middle East, Crusaders and Saracens' fighting, and it's going to spill all across the world. There is going to be a Holy War.' Shelagh shook her head in frustration. 'I know there can't be crusades today, but it is the kind of thing I'm see.'

Because of the images the Grey transmitted to Shelagh, we quickly fell into the group of experiencers who believed that a global Armageddon was about to strike the planet. With the Millennium fast approaching, there were increasing numbers of people expecting such an event to erupt. But in years to come we were to identify the 'hole in the ground nuclear disaster' as Chernobyl, and as the horror of 9/11 came to pass, bringing with it the consequences, I recognised the 'Holy War', and the crusading armies as the terrorist-linked bombings and George Bush's War on Terror. But until that all became obvious we were convinced we were going to see a nuclear war within our lifetime, maybe no more than a decade away.

When Shelagh finished speaking, I told her what had happened to me. That in some way I knew this entity was meshed with me, each of us with a separate awareness, but both being processed by my human brain. I described how it had ejected from my body and immediately stared at her wall, perhaps, that was the moment it had transmitted to her, not that I had felt anything. I thought it was staring at the wall for no reason. We decided not to tell anybody about all this, because even by our standards, it was way off the weirdometer. An etheric metamorphosis complete with an alien mental process, was too crazy.

I then told her about two future events I'd seen in the alien mind just moments before I returned to my human body. I think they were transmitted to me at the same time other info was being sent to Shelagh. Both my own pieces of information would have a significant impact upon our lives in the future, if they were true. In the first, I saw a man I didn't recognise, standing on our doorstep, and being welcomed in. With this vision came the overwhelming feeling that whatever we were doing; we wouldn't be doing it alone. It would be misleading to refer to this knowledge as 'predictions', because in the Grey mind, it was a plan in place and scheduled to happen at the right time, in contrast to something abandoned to fate or chance.

I told Shelagh that plans were being made for a UFO investigator to be brought to us who would help our work. But what precisely that work was I did not know, and how was I able to know this was a UFO investigator? I didn't know that either, but it was in the mind of the Grey and it was now in mine. I then went on to tell her we would be working with a music band from the South of England, possibly from the coast. Again, this was something the Grey knew about, but I didn't have even the slightest clue as to what it could mean.

I couldn't understand where this sudden psychic connection was coming from. What was that Grey? How could I know what was in its mind? Was I the Grey? But that was ridiculous, how could I possibly be the Grey?

I had those and so many more questions racing through my head, but not a single answer came to either of us.

Spiritualist Church

Although we discussed this Grey on a number of occasions, neither of us could come up with anything that could explain it. Red Eagle wasn't helpful either, he was absolutely silent on the subject. About this time, I began catching fleeting glimpses of shadowy figures, usually from the corner of my eyes. I was also seeing small orbs of light, flitting around the house, or through the trees in White Knights. I had not experienced anything like it before, and Shelagh suggested that latent psychic abilities might be coming to the fore. She told me that the orbs were psychic energy.

She suggested I visit the Spiritualist Church with her. Shelagh was no stranger, attending most Sundays and Thursdays. I wasn't that keen on going, but with the Church only a couple of streets away, there seemed to be no excuse not to go at least once. So, the next available Thursday I went along with her to see what it was all about.

Shelagh had been a member for some years and had a small group of regular friends she'd meet up with, and so she introduced me to some of them as a way to help me settle in. This included a lady called, Vera, or 'Vee', as Shelagh knew her. Vee and Shelagh had been best friends for many years and often spent time at each other's house drinking tea and musing over everything from spiritual topics to the state of the weather.

I sat among the audience for several weeks , all hoping to get some kind of message from spirit. I was particularly optimistic in expecting an explanation of what I was experiencing. Maybe Red Eagle would give me something useful. However, when I did start getting messages from the medium, it was mostly my grandfather making himself known.

'I have someone here for you.' the medium stated, pointing emphatically at me and filling me with a mix of excitement and anticipation. I'd never had a message through anyone but Shelagh before. I sat slightly more to attention, hoping some revelation would be handed down. I would even be happy if it was couched in cryptic language, giving me something to go away and think about, so long as it offered some kind of answer.

'I have an old man wearing what looks like a chef's hat and smock. I think he might have been a cook…'

I smiled at the description, since this had to be my grandfather, but he wasn't a cook or a chef. His name surname was Baker.

Frustratingly the messages from Grandpa Baker were mundane and rather generalised, as were many Spiritualist messages any of us received. He had passed when I was six years old, so there wasn't an awful lot I could remember or confirm about him. The medium did see a Red Indian guide which I assumed to be Red Eagle, but he played the part of a regular spirit guide and offered none of the sensationalism I had hoped for.

Then one Thursday evening, some months after I had been in regular attendance, and still hoping for a revelation, I walked into the Church and made my way to where we usually sat up at the front near the platform. On this occasion, I had to sidestep past two men who were standing at the front and admiring the table that was at the base of the mediums' platform, long and draped with a beautiful, white lace cloth with heavy vases displaying splendid bouquets of flowers, brought in by the Church Wardens.

One of the men looked to be in his twenties, wearing a dark-brown roll-neck top and jeans, and seemed quite ordinary. The other man, however, was really quite odd. He was perhaps in his thirties or forties, but with such dreadful skin, it was near impossible to guess his age much more accurately than that.

The anachronism was his clothing, which was so old fashioned that it looked medieval. I even wondered if he was dressed like that to represent something. He was wearing a short wool tunic with a hood that was down, the tunic being brown in colour and belted around the waist. He also wore dark woollen trousers and badly deteriorated shoes. I heard this very strange man say:

'It looks set for a banquet.'

'It is,' replied the younger man, 'It's set for a banquet of knowledge and understanding.'

That seemed such an odd thing to say so I turned to Shelagh and asked what she made of the two men standing just a few feet from us. She looked puzzled and shrugged; I turned back towards the men, but they were gone. They had vanished in the space of time it had taken me to speak to Shelagh and turn back to them. This was my first encounter with human souls who had passed from this life.

The afterlife had suddenly been opened to me, but these weren't spectral figures floating over the ground. They weren't transparent, ghostly images; they were as real and solid as everyone else in the room. I also went on to learn some time later, that one of the Spiritualist rescue circles - a meeting in which a number of sitters help distressed and lost souls find their way - had been working with a number of medieval souls. It seems that what I had seen was one of them emerging from his confusion, and the younger man was, in fact, a spirit guide helping him towards the light.

Nothing was the same after that evening as my psychic development went forward in leaps and bounds, and within a month I was seeing and hearing spirits so clearly that it was sometimes as though our worlds were superimposed over one another. I am not sure if that was the intention or if it was my brain trying to cope with the diversity of signals and senses, it was suddenly receiving. Whatever the case, things continued to develop until after around three months I was even passing messages to others in the audience at the Church.

On one occasion, a regular attendee, a young woman seated next to her mother told me that she had received wonderful news just a month earlier, she was pregnant with her first child and had been told at the hospital that the baby was a girl. What I had noticed was that a third person had walked into the Church with them. This older person was a lady and appeared as solid as anyone else, but I guessed that the mother and daughter couldn't see her because at no point did they speak to, or even acknowledge her presence. Furthermore, when they sat down in their chairs, she stood directly behind them even though there were empty seats either side of the couple.

I asked her mentally who she was, and the reply came back that she was the pregnant girl's grandmother, and this grandmother reacted to the statement of the baby being a girl by shaking her head. Grandmother told me they were mistaken and that she was going to have a boy. By now, the girl's mother had gone on to tell me that she'd knitted a number of pink baby girl clothes, and was starting on a small bedspread for the crib.

That's when I suggested she stopped knitting pink and get some blue wool, and that they should start expecting a little boy. Both mother and daughter sat in silence for a moment, then asked me how I knew that, after all, the hospital was sure it would be a girl. So, I told them that grandmother was standing with them and seemed to know more than the scan had revealed. Perhaps the baby had been lying in a position that obscured its genitals? I had no idea, but I told them to hold up on the pink stuff. I didn't even know why I was telling them all this, I just knew it as surely as if all this had played out somewhere or sometime before, and I felt as though I was repeating something I already knew. It was a most strange experience.

However, the result of all this was that they did indeed abandon Project Baby-Girl in favour of Project Baby-Boy, and all based on nothing more than my words from grandmother - and thank goodness, she was correct - a boy was born.

Things continued like this over the following year, as I pursued my new-found spiritualist interest.

Eventually, I decided that I would like to train as a medium, and Shelagh supported this idea wholeheartedly, especially as I was still developing breathtakingly fast. I enrolled for the Church development circle, and almost as soon as I sat down with the group, I was picking up messages for some of the sitters. Things progressed from this circle as I was encouraged to train to be a medium and represent the church during their meetings.

Although I made an effort, I didn't feel comfortable getting messages for the general public. I pursued it, and seemed to do quite well, but I just didn't feel this was my future - it didn't fulfil my sense of something missing. The training and discipline I learned through the church served me well, teaching me that regardless of what wanted to work through me, I was in control, and I was the one to control any spirit wanting to use me as their medium. So, although I didn't work long-term with the Spiritualist Church, it taught me what I needed to know.

Then the first of the reality-bending paranormal experiences began.

SIEGE OF MADNESS

Jurassic Junction

It was a Friday night in October, 1983, and we were off to a showing of *The Twilight Zone - The Movie.* There were three performances; midday, evening and a late showing. We decided to go for the late, which started at 11.15pm. It wasn't a cold night, so we decided to walk home after the show, which put the time at around 1.15am.

We had enjoyed the film and were talking about it enthusiastically, discussing sections we each liked, as well as the not so favourable. Our film review didn't last too long and had pretty much fallen into the background as we left the town centre and started off along Wokingham Road, which stretches for some miles. At this time, we lived just off Cemetery Junction in East Reading. It's not an old cemetery; the first burial there took place in 1843.

Wokingham Road is generally a busy dual carriageway, but was deserted and almost completely traffic-free at this early hour of the morning. We only saw an occasional taxi passing us during our entire walk.

We were half of the way through our unhurried, one hour stroll home when I first became aware of footsteps some distance behind us. I glanced round, casually inquisitive, but as I did so the footsteps fell silent. The road and pavement behind us were deserted and so I assumed I had misheard the echo of our own footfalls. I didn't bother mentioning it to

Shelagh. However, what I had failed to realise was that when I had turned, we were still walking, which means the sound could not have been our echo otherwise they would have still been heard. We continued on for perhaps five minutes before I distinctly heard the footsteps start again, this time they sounded closer. We both glanced back this time, and again, the footsteps fell silent as we turned our attention to them.

'What was that?' She asked.

'Perhaps our feet echoing off the buildings.' I thought it was an idea worth pitching to her.

'I guess it could be.' But she sounded as unconvinced as I felt.

I shrugged and followed her as she resumed walking. In the next instant, we heard the footsteps resume. Sounding closer still. I heard them; but I still saw nothing stalking us – and stalking is exactly how I was now starting to think of this.

I wasn't prepared to jump immediately to some paranormal explanation, although on a lonely road in the early hours it would have been easy to do so. I told Shelagh to stay where she was while I walked back along the pavement to find out who was following us. So I made my cautious way back, retracing our steps and looking into the dark shadowed driveways and gardens, while being sure to stay as close to the road as possible. If there was a mugger, I didn't want them rushing out at me.

I went back some five or six houses - as far as we would reasonably expect to find someone – I then made my way back to where Shelagh still stood, watching me anxiously. I shrugged and gave an empty-handed gesture as I reached her. 'I can't find anyone there.'

We walked on, the phantom footfalls picking up moments after we started. But now sounding as though they were directly behind us, so close that we would have seen someone almost looking over our shoulders had they been there.

But, of course, there was nothing.

We were being stalked by something, there was no doubt about it now. Not only that, it had to be something paranormal.

'Try to "see" what it is.' I asked her under my breath.

So Shelagh concentrated, her brow furrowed and her eyes narrowed to slits as she directed her thoughts at whatever was following us. After a few moments, she looked at me, 'I can't sense anything - there's nothing there.'

'But we can hear it.' I tried to reason with her by stating the blatantly obvious.

'I know what we can hear, but there's nothing behind us - nothing at all.'

I couldn't believe this. She should have sensed something, just a presence, even if she couldn't identify it. But here she was stating there was nothing, when we could clearly hear it virtually on top of us.

About fifty feet ahead of us and barely two hundred feet from the cemetery junction, we saw the pedestrian crossing, which are insanely familiar to use. You press the button, the traffic lights switch from green to red; Traffic stops; Green man flashes; and you cross the road accompanied by an electronic beeping. The beeping then stops, the lights switch back to green, which allow the traffic-flow to resume.

However, we were about thirty feet from the crossing when, for no reason whatsoever; the lights went from green to red. Seeing that happen took us by surprise because there wasn't anybody waiting to cross. The road was as empty as it had been all along, no pedestrians or traffic - just the pair of us and the footsteps. In fact, with the absence of traffic, a pedestrian would have no need to change the lights; they could have easily strolled across.

As soon as the traffic lights had inexplicably changed to red, the footsteps ceased and the beeping started. Then a weird sensation struck our senses, the electronic beeping suddenly sounded muffled, as though someone had blocked our ears with cotton wool. By now, we were standing still again, our eyes fixed on the crossing. At that moment, there was something about the environment that had an unreal quality to it; the mid-October air had, all of a sudden; become humid and sticky.

I don't know why we stopped walking and stood to stare at the crossing, there was nothing to see apart from the lights inexplicably changing. With hindsight, it's as though we were expecting to see something without even realising it. Then the spectacle began.

'Look!' Even Shelagh's voice sounded muffled.

I don't remember answering her; I do recall being paralysed with shock.

I saw a dinosaur suddenly appear on the pavement ahead of us. This was long before The Stephen Spielberg film, *Jurassic Park*, but if the incident happened now, I would be saying it looked very much like the Raptors from that movie. The creature was a little over nine feet tall with mottled green and brown skin. The thing became visible and bounded across the empty dual-carriageway with movements that reminded us of an ostrich. In fact, its gait was the single thing we remarked on for days after. In four strides, it was across the road, and as it touched the opposite pavement, it vanished.

The beast wasn't accompanied by any sound, but did appear to be perfectly solid, and gave every indication of being so. We could even see the street lighting on its skin, and we could see the shadows on it where the lighting didn't reach. There is a small island in the middle of the road with railings, to control pedestrian movement. The dinosaur even weaved around the island railings, suggesting that it was aware of physical obstacles. This added to our conviction that the creature had substance and was not a hallucination or an apparition.

At the same moment that the creature vanished, the beeping stopped and the traffic lights returned to green. That's when we felt the chill seep back into the air around us, and the 'cotton wool' plucked from our ears.

'Did you see that?' I was numb and shaking as the shock took hold of me.

'I saw a dinosaur.'

'I did too.' I took her hand, a gesture more for myself than for her, as a way to ground myself with something securely anchored in our world. Cautiously, we walked onward, and when we passed the point where the dinosaur had materialised, it was done with a certain amount of trepidation. That the prehistoric creature had used a designated pedestrian crossing simply added to the urban absurdness.

Surely a random apparition would have appeared anywhere along the road, but lights changing and this thing on the crossing suggested intelligent design, and hopefully one displaying irony rather than a threat. We also quickly attributed those phantom footsteps to what we had just seen, assuming they must have played some part in all this.

As we recovered our composure we realised the footsteps weren't following us, and we hoped - we prayed - it was a signal that tonight's events were at an end. So, still buzzing from the dinosaur experience we began comparing notes on what each had seen. It was incredible, because each point one of us mentioned, the other could confirm it; we had seen exactly the same thing. We believed this thing might have come through a hole in time, maybe a portal of some kind had opened and caused the past and the present to splice together for that moment. We had no evidence to suspect any of this, but was the idea any more crazy than what we'd just seen?

For the remainder of our walk home, we continued to discuss and speculate on what had happened, and as with many conversations of this nature, it eventually spiralled deeply into the highly improbable and most unlikely. Then we turned into our road and stopped talking as we realised the footsteps were in pursuit of us again; they weren't so close this time, but nonetheless, still following. We had no idea how long they had been back with us because we'd been too busy talking about the dinosaur.

While Shelagh was getting the door open, I glanced behind us, the footsteps had fallen silent again and the road was empty; all we had was the illumination from street-lighting, beyond which anything could have lurked.

There was an immediate feeling of safety as we closed and locked the door. The irony of just having returned from *The Twilight Zone* movie was not lost to us, but suddenly any film seemed superficial compared to what we had just undergone. We brewed a pot of tea and sat with our coats on, discussing what had happened, but with no idea why it had happened. With our tea finished, Shelagh decided to cast a protection around the house. I asked her what she was expecting and she replied that she expected nothing and hoped it would stay that way, however, the witch wanted to play on the side of caution.

When she finished, she had created a psychic defensive ring around the house and doubled it on the inside at every window, at the back and front doors, and at every open chimney. Her expertise in occult protection was well tested and I couldn't have felt safer. But would it be any use? After all, we had no idea what had followed us for more than half the distance home. Then, with nothing more to be done I went to bed and lay awake for some time, staring at the ceiling and pondering what we had been through. I had never seen anything like it in my life. I switched off the bedside lamp and dozed, only to be woken by the bedroom light being switched back on.

I sat up thinking that for some reason Shelagh had come in, but the door was closed and I was alone - alone with a bedroom light that had switched itself on. There was no lamp shade it was just a bare bulb hanging from a light fitting cord. I climbed from bed and went to turn the light off. Then I glanced back up at the bulb, attracted by a flicker of movement. I dropped my hand from the switch and stared. There were three fish, each about two inches long and silvery gold, their mouths were opening and closing and their gills fluctuating, just as they would in the water - except these fish were 'swimming' equidistant from each other in orbit around the bulb. This vision felt as though it went on forever, whereas, in reality, it must have accounted for seconds - or maybe a minute at the most - I have no idea. Time becomes redundant when these things happen.

I walked to the centre of the room and stood beneath the bulb, the goldfish now above my head. Now the light was starting to hurt my eyes, then I realised why; the bulb was beginning to burn brighter. I squinted against the light, feeling it burning into my eyes, but I was unable to look away. The goldfish continued to orbit the bulb, seemingly oblivious to the heat now being generated.

Maybe the paranormal absurdities of the night were getting to me, because I started laughing at this ridiculous image. Even so, the sight itself wasn't humorous; it was rather chilling to witness something so harmless operating with such normality outside of its environment. I just knew I had to have Shelagh come and see this, regardless of what time of night it might be.

I went to the door and pulled at the handle, but it wouldn't open. I turned back to the goldfish and told them – yes, I told them - I needed to get out of the room, and that their antics must cease. I don't know if I really expected a response, but there certainly wasn't one forthcoming.

At this point, I didn't know what to do, but realising my options had diminished to zero; I did something that now sounds a far too casual reaction to what was manifesting around me. I sat on my bed and watched the fish. I wasn't too bothered because although I had no control over this thing, it wasn't displaying malice towards me. Furthermore, I was fairly convinced that what we experienced on the way home had been a demonstration of some kind. Maybe something had decided to show us what it could do. Maybe it was a way of explaining something that I didn't, as yet, understand.

I also convinced myself that what was happening here in the bedroom was the same thing as at the lights, just different props being used. That's why I decided to sit on the bed and watch. Then, after what may have been several minutes, the bulb dimmed back to what it should be and the goldfish vanished suddenly, as if they had never been there to begin with. I now expected everything to be over and so rose from the bed. I wanted to try the door again, fully expecting to be able to open it. As it turned out, I could, and everything seemed to have returned to normal. I glanced at the time. It was 3am. I decided not to wake Shelagh, that could wait until later in the morning. I would also be asking her why her defences had been powerless.

I left the bedroom and went into the kitchen to get myself a glass of water and a biscuit, a grounding procedure I often used. Then I went back upstairs and straight to bed, glancing at the ceiling, just to be sure there were no other aerobatic teams. I went to sleep - and that's when I plunged into a real nasty nightmare.

Invasion Of The Mind

There was a story segment In *The Twilight Zone - The Movie*, called *Out Of Time,* in which Vic Morrow - who, along with two child actors, tragically died during the filming when a helicopter crashed onto them - played a bigoted man thrown through time. He goes from being a Jew in Nazi-occupied Europe, to a Vietnamese being pursued by American soldiers, to being lynched by the Ku Klux Klan, and in each scenario he's a victim of his own prejudices. So I can only think that the cyclic nightmare that now engulfed me was plucked from that movie. In effect, my own memory of the film was turned as a weapon against me.

I felt myself suddenly surrounded by rushing air sucking me into a black void, and I emerged to find myself in a railway wagon. With the omnipotent perceptions only available in dream-states, I knew I was in a cattle wagon that was part of a Nazi train and bound for a concentration camp. I was sitting hunched in the corner, but the wagon wasn't crowded with other victims, as would have been the case in truth, I was on my own but could smell the urine and faeces from terrified victims in other wagons.

Outside I could hear shouts in German, as the guards herded people aboard the train. Then a whistle sounded and the wagon jerked, as the train heaved its way from the platform. I remained motionless, wondering what was happening, and why imagery had been taken from a movie, if indeed it had been. At the time, I didn't know about lucid dreaming: a state in which you know you are asleep and dreaming, and can actually control your dreams. I knew I was dreaming, however, I was powerless to do anything. I was trapped inside it.

Then to my astonishment, the train was standing at the platform, as though the scene had looped back - which, in fact, is exactly what happened. I heard the very same sounds of soldiers shouting and heard the whistle; the train pulled away. The engine built up speed for several seconds, before I was back in a stationary train. Those same seconds repeated in my head on an eternal loop.

I did manage to tear my eyes open at some point and even believed, for a moment, that I'd escaped that shocking nightmare. But then as if a blind were drawn back, and proving that something else, not me, was in control of this night, I could see the wagon in my mind and hear the sounds I now associated with it. I was not lucid dreaming, not now. I was fully awake and sitting up in bed, gripped by panic as I closed my eyes, scrunching them tightly shut in an attempt to remove this hideous repetition that just went on and on:

Wagon doors, sliding and slamming shut.

Guards' shouting and dogs barking. Then that whistle.

A jolt as the train moves forward, with me sitting on my bed, but my mind projected into a crouch in that corner of the cattle truck.

Something in my head telling me over and over again that I was being sent to die – sent to die alone.

I don't know how long this horror repeated itself, but after what seemed like many hours I was physically off the bed and crouching in the corner of my bedroom, arms wrapped around my knees, my body rocking back and forth as I wrestled with this horror. Sobbing to myself and unable to shake off the terrible, haunting sight and sounds that nudged me gently towards the edge of madness. I could feel the foundations of my sanity crumble beneath the weight of this onslaught that was coming from God knows where.

There came some point when it did stop and I was released, But having been locked into a kind of sensory deprivation I had no way of knowing how long it had lasted. To my shattered ruin of a mind, it could have been moments, days, or even weeks; I barely even knew where I was. The vision had been so violent and sustained that my mind had been blitzed to shreds, leaving me incapable of forming a single rational thought.

However, my instinct for self-preservation was still intact; nature's inbuilt life-support was functioning, keeping mental activity and responses alive, and even when I realised the horror had finally ceased I continued to cower in the corner of the bedroom; I was fearful that I was being teased, and remained fearful of its return at any moment.

However, given enough time, and feeling a little confident that it really had finished. I slowly looked up, and through the parting in the curtains, I could see the sky was streaked with pre-dawn light. This means I'd experienced the concentration camp train for perhaps three or four hours without pause - not just experienced it; I had actually been there at some level of perception. No wonder I was a mental wreck. I climbed shakily to my feet and managed to reach the bed before collapsing into an uneasy and trauma-filled sleep.

I woke with an awful headache, so lay for a minute or two before peering at my electric clock. It was 8am, which it meant I hadn't slept for more than an hour or two, and after last night's horror I'd expected to be knocked dead for most of the day. I went downstairs to find Shelagh in the kitchen, then I saw the clock on the cooker: 11am. I didn't think anything about this until I carried my first coffee of the day into the sitting room, and saw that the clock in there also displayed just after 11 am.

'Shelagh, what's the time?'

'About eleven; I thought you were getting up early so we could go to the rummage sale?'

I went back into the kitchen and sat with her, delaying our trip while I related the terrifying experience; and as I did so, she got some pills to deal with my headache. I also pointed out that my clock had lost two hours during the night, which was a strange effect after something that had presumably been all in my mind. If not for the dinosaur we both saw before getting home, I might have been convinced it was all subjective. When I asked her about the failure of her magical protection, she couldn't respond to that, apart from the obvious conclusion, that whatever had caused the experiences was much more powerful than she was.

She said that she hadn't heard anything during the night and had slept soundly. In fact, she didn't even get up for the bathroom, which was quite unusual as more often than not she did. We were in agreement over one thing, however: what had followed us home from the cinema was either the culprit, or had been a beacon tracking us to our home. Further theorising had us consider that possibly the dinosaur was some kind of test, perhaps to ensure one or both could see what would be presented during the early hours of Saturday morning - that must have been the tenth theory of ours on what the dinosaur might have been.

We tried consulting Red Eagle to find out what he could tell us about it all, but, no matter how much Shelagh tried, he refused to communicate. He did this sometimes. If there was something he wanted us to handle ourselves, he'd show he was observing but would remain silent. It's as though he deliberately stepped back, wanting to see how I resolved whatever was at hand. I found this infuriating, especially when my own well-being could be at stake. However, if I thought that was the end to the torment, I was wrong. An even more mystifying experience was to follow that very next night.

Although she continued trying to coax something from him, Red Eagle was having none of it, and without his help neither of us could come to a satisfactory explanation to what the death train and goldfish could possibly have meant - it was plain crazy stuff. All we could do was write it into our journal and leave it at that, hoping an answer would present itself at some later date.

Saturday afternoons usually meant rummage and car boot sales, but as neither of us could drive, it would just be a visit to the nearest church halls and schools. Invariably, we would amass a good number of bargains. Today proved no different as we trawled around a local church hall. I still nursed a headache and was so tired I dragged my body around, spending most of my time looking through piles of books while Shelagh dug through paste tables loaded with clothes and bric-a-brac

Within an hour, she had five bags crammed with the stuff; and she was still finding more. I'm not exaggerating, when that woman hit a room filled with jumble, she became an elemental force to be reckoned with! Even so, she didn't buy junk; she always found good-quality clothing, ornaments and jewellery that were worth more than she ever paid for it. You wanted something at a good price? Shelagh had an inbuilt Rummage-Sale radar that would find it sooner rather than later. Being pre-Internet days, this talent made her very useful to know.

Needing free hands to continue her relentless assault on those paste tables, she suddenly had a bright idea - she'd leave her bags in safe hands and come back for them later. So she approached a stall-holder and asked if she would be able to look after them for about a half hour.

The girl agreed and said she'd put labels on the bags to indicate them as purchased property. Then about forty-five minutes later, we returned to find a different woman at the table. The girl we had handed the bags to was nowhere to be seen. Then, horror of horrors, Shelagh recognised one of her precious purchases on the paste table! Then she saw another, and then another. The truth quickly dawned on her that the girl hadn't put a label on the bags and someone else had put it all out, thinking it was a donation to their cause.

The woman stepped back dumbfounded as Shelagh snatched items up from the table in a frenzy and clawed other things she recognised, from the hands of unsuspecting punters who were preparing to make a purchase.

'That's mine. That's mine - and that's mine too!'

I can't recall a single person who dared oppose her onslaught!

To her credit, she got virtually everything back. Maybe one or two items escaped, but all in all, it did turn out to be a successful day. After Shelagh had calmed down enough to explain what had happened, the stall-holder said that her daughter had needed to get away rather urgently and must have forgotten to mention the bags.

After Shelagh had calmed down, I wandered off to look around more tables and that's when I found one in the corner. A woman had a stall of bric-a-brac, and next to her, seated at a small card table was a young girl, probably around ten or eleven years old. She had a silk scarf wrapped round her head, and held a pack of tarot cards in her hands. While Shelagh's keen vision scanned across the table in Terminator-like rummage-mode, I asked the woman about the girl. She said this was her daughter, and she had brought her mum's cards with her because she wanted to do some readings. I asked the child how much she charged and when she said fifty-pence, I sat opposite and crossed her palm with silver.

The child shuffled the cards, which in those hands, were over-sized and clumsy, then asked me to pick five from the deck which she had now fanned face down. With my selection made, she closed her eyes for a few moments before turning the cards face up. I don't know what I was expecting, but I was quite astonished when she said 'you and that lady over there work together. I don't think its work, like in a shop or anything. It's different, important stuff and you have an Indian man looking after you both.'

I encouraged her, telling her how accurate she was, and that I would like to know more. I knew the cards, so could see she had a good grasp of the basic meanings, but with how she frequently closed her eyes while not referring to the cards, I could see she had mediumistic skills. She then told me there were 'bad things' trying to hurt me, but I wasn't to worry because the 'Indian man' was looking after me, and, so the 'bad things' could only scare.

'Will the bad things try to scare me again?'

'Yes. But I don't know what they are.' She sounded almost apologetic.

I smiled to reassure her, and asked: 'Do you know why they are trying to scare me?'

She shrugged. 'I don't know.'

I assured her it was OK, and I paid her an extra three pounds for her effort. That little girl was quite remarkable, giving me one of the best psychic readings I have ever had, and I really hope she went on to develop her abilities further as she got older.

That night, 'the bad things' came back.

After a bath, I went to bed around 10pm, and lay awake for a while reading. My throbbing headache lasted until about four o'clock that afternoon before eventually fading, but I was still fatigued and very tired from the exhaustion I'd suffered the previous night. I must have switched the light off and slept because I then remember suddenly waking with a start.

Having flown as a youngster, I'm aware of the effect air pressure has on the ears, they feel blocked; I woke with precisely that sensation now. What I didn't consider is that it was also the same effect as when Shelagh and I had encountered the dinosaur. I sat up, wondering what had woken me. Then something attracted my attention. At first, I thought what I saw was on the wall, but as I looked at it for longer, I became aware that it was *within* the wall's surface.

A slowly rotating circle of blackness, its edges smudged into the pale blue paint which was distorted and streaked to the right, as though the hole was spinning clockwise and dragging the paint on the wall with it. The hole was about two feet across, but that's just a guess; I certainly had no intention of going near the thing to measure it accurately. There was no sound, and at first I detected no sensations. It was a black hole, or some kind of void; somehow I knew I was peering into the darkest possible black that had no end to it. It plunged so deep into nowhere that I was stricken with vertigo when I gazed into its centre. I climbed from bed and stood facing this thing. I seemed to recognise it; something deep within me reacted at confronting this unknown. It was the face of evil - pure, untainted and absolute evil.

An identity for it suddenly came to mind: 'Event Void Singularity'. I didn't know what that meant then, and I still have no idea now. Maybe it's another way of describing a place where reality collapsed in on itself and created a singularity where matter, even in a quantum state, was impossible. Perhaps it indicated a pocket without space and time, a pre-Big-Bang nothingness existing like an airless bubble between two universes. Whatever the case, I shall continue to call it an Event Void singularity (EVS); regardless of it holding no meaning for me whatsoever.

From the moment I climbed from bed, I'd been gripped by a curiosity about this thing - this EVS; I even took a few hesitant steps towards it. I glanced at the bed and saw my human form still asleep. Then looked down at myself and saw what I somehow expected; I was Grey. As I write this, I'm still puzzled, and not knowing at which point I Shifted from human to Grey. During these early days, I was a kind of hybrid when I shifted. By that I mean that although I was in a Grey form, and had a partial Grey awareness, I was still overwhelmingly human, which is why I might have not have been aware of what point I crossed from one to the other. I, (the Grey?) returned my gaze to the languidly spinning blackness - a bottomless bore-hole drilling into something outside of time and space.

I was becoming aware of something deep within its depths, something with consciousness looking out at me, studying me. The Grey consciousness that was entangled with mine, seemed familiar with this phenomenon, had possibly even encountered it before, but I didn't know where or when. I was experiencing a very strange kind of cross-species consciousness.

I took another step forward as something touched that alien component in my mind; inviting the Grey to go through, to step into its unreality. I know it was only a couple of feet across, but I was aware that if I got close enough, it would have opened like an iris, and by the time it had done that, I could not have stepped away. I can only speculate that I would have been trapped there as a Grey, and as a consequence my human body wouldn't have been able to wake. I would have been found sometime the following day, at worse dead, at best lapsed into a coma from which it would never return.

Although I expected something more to happen, the night of this swirling portal was to prove anti-climactic. Maybe I would see something as spectacular as the dinosaur, as baffling as the goldfish, or as terrifying as the concentration camp train. But it wasn't to be. I do not know how long I stood watching this thing screwing slowly clockwise while feeling a curious need to step through, but gradually this urge faded away and within a couple of minutes, I was staring at a smooth blue wall.

Perhaps it realised it had been beaten, and that the Grey consciousness wasn't going to step through. I walked over and gingerly touched the wall with those three fingers spread wide apart. I remember the Grey putting its face close to the wall and analysing the point where the disturbance had been

I don't know how the eyes of a Grey work, but they are multi-sensory organs. The entity wasn't simply looking at where the EVS had been, it was taking readings of some kind in case it had left any residue. I'm not aware of anything detectable, in fact; through the Grey's vision, I could see through to Shelagh's room.

The next morning I detailed the strange experience to Shelagh, but she hadn't sensed anything, in fact, as on the previous occasion slept undisturbed. I couldn't understand why that would be, There was so much going on, surely she had to have sensed something - anything. She closed her eyes and focused Red Eagle in her mind's eye, asking him why she hadn't been alerted to anything on either night.

She opened her eyes, and she appeared puzzled. 'He's keeping me safe from what he's teaching you.'

'Teaching me?'

Shelagh nodded,

'What does he mean? Keeping you safe from what?'

She shrugged helplessly. 'I don't know, he's not saying. He's repeating that I need to remain isolated from some of it.'

As unsatisfactory as this reply was, I didn't bother labouring the point. I knew when he was being uncooperative, and this was one of those times.

Shelagh fell silent for a few moments longer. Maybe he wasn't being so uncooperative after all, because I saw her brow furrow in concentration, and I knew Red Eagle was showing her something that she was trying to understand. Then she shared what she was being shown.

'He's braiding a single eagle feather into your hair.' further silence. Then: 'No, that's not quite right. It's your name. He is telling me that you are "Eagle Feather."'

'He's giving me an Indian name?'

'It's the first of your three initiation names. He says he will give you two, and the third will be chosen by yourself. He's telling me that your path has begun.'

Departure

This is how it continued, with us having no clear idea of what we were dealing with - or to be more accurate - what was dealing with us. Even Red

Eagle seemed less a conventional spirit guide than an impersonal mentor, who with a single-minded determination was focused on elevating me to some, as yet, ill-defined state.

All we did know is that he chose the guise of an American Indian so that when detected by a psychic - the young girl at the rummage sale, for instance - they would see a typical spirit guide who blended with regular spiritualist phenomena. I even started to wonder if this would be an excellent disguise for a truly alien intelligence, it would be stealth in plain view.

That would make Shelagh's initial reaction at seeing 'yet another Indian guide', exactly the response he expected to generate. So in truth, we didn't even know what he was.

I couldn't see how all this came together; it was a chain with links that began with a period of missing time, and seemed to be leading to the revelation that I was either a Grey non-human in a human form, or I was meshed with the consciousness of a non-human, possibly from another dimension or from our own future.

Whatever the case, it was an identity that I felt comfortable co-existing with, Presumably because it seemed to be in a more advanced state than my human mind. By that I mean it was uncluttered by the superfluous and irrelevant, nor did stress or anxiety seem to be present. Furthermore, with the passing of information to Shelagh through the wall, whilst simultaneously allowing me to be aware of future plans, it had shown it could conduct at least two separate thought processes at the same time.

Alongside this, we had the mind-blowing visual experiences and out-of-body journeys to a myriad of worlds that co-exist with ours. Parallel realities and astral existences, most of which are familiar to occultists and shaman, but, until now, were entirely unknown and forbidden landscapes to me. Nevertheless, not only were they being shown. I was waking of a morning with the knowledge of how to interact with them; and how they affected this planet and the life upon it; I was being handed keys and shown how to unlock doors.

I would often discuss these out-of-body journeys with Shelagh when we were walking Kali across White Knights, a few hours respite from a house Shelagh was beginning to loath living in. We had a favoured spot where we would sit on fallen tree trunks and watch the dog run off to investigate doggy-interesting things, these were the quiet moments when I would explain to her about the astral environments I was experiencing, and that I was establishing an active connection with the human collective consciousness.

I was beginning to realise that I housed a human mind that the Grey was modifying into something it could use to connect to the species field; I was becoming a conduit of some kind. The only way I could visualise the connections being made was as strands: I was at the centre, with a connection through these strands to every living thing on this planet and across the many universes.

The beauty of the complex metaphysical architecture I witnessed is that everybody is that individual centre, with threads linking them to everything else in creation. So no matter what shoes, paws or claws you possess, you are the centre of everything. Words do nothing to convey the impact of the experience, and I feel cheated in that I cannot show you by direct experience. However, it would be some while yet, before I understood what this would mean, but the realisation that I was learning something new each time I left my body was enough to know that progress was being made.

There were, of course, darker days, when we sat on our logs in the glade and Shelagh would talk about her desire to leave that house. At first, these were just moments of wishful thinking, and it did her good to talk the frustrations from her system. Besides, if she really left home, where would she go? She had no family in the area and only one truly good friend, Vee, but she didn't have accommodation space to help Shelagh out. So for now, the talking remained just that. However, her situation gradually deteriorated to the point where she decided she had to leave the house, whatever the cost and outcome. She couldn't take any more of it.

She didn't want to engage in any lengthy legal battle to try to keep the house; she simply wanted out. My option was to find a room or flat to rent. I certainly didn't want to stay there any longer either; I had been thinking about leaving for the last few weeks, but my friendship with Shelagh kept me in place. I told her that so far as I was concerned we were now a team and that when she left I would go with her, we'd stick together no matter what. I felt I had a loyalty and care for her after everything she had done for me in the past, there was too much history between us for me to pack and walk away.

It was while we were sitting discussing this, that I felt there was a need to cast off any cautions I felt, and take an ultimate responsibility for what we would have to do. I knew we had a specific value to whatever Red

Eagle was, and that he'd seen us through everything so far. My trust in him had developed to such confidence that I said to her: 'Red Eagle will see we're OK. All we need to do is leap and just know that he'll catch us. He won't let us fall, nor will he fail us. He knows you're unhappy and is aware of the suffering. It's time we break from our past and go for it.'

This was quite a speech for me, but I knew we'd be fine. I then had Shelagh's trust in me proved the very next day when we packed a couple bags and walked out of the front door.

We went for it.

THE WILDERNESS YEARS

Politics

Julian, Shelagh's son, decided to stay with his father for practical reasons such as his school being across the road from the house, and because he had a comfortable relationship with his father. Shelagh didn't expect him to come with us since he wasn't a part of what we were engaged in at the time. It's as well that she thought this way because the next five years were to be an existence of destitution, vulnerability and constant uncertainty, with 1987 to 1989 being the most insecure of all.

With no other options available, we descended to temporary housing, euphemistically referred to as 'bed & breakfast accommodation'. This was a time of loosely regulated accommodation agencies; they would pay a flat rate to a house-owner, and then sub-divide rooms into smaller rooms with plasterboard walls, and charging £150 per person a week for nothing but an ill-maintained room with the minimum of legally required essentials. To ensure legality, and qualify for the government money, the 'breakfast' would consist of a small cardboard box, delivered once a week and containing the cheapest and often out of date milk, sugar, eggs and bread. As a treat, a pack of digestives or bourbons might be included. Convicted criminals had a better existence than an entire silent sub-class in Margaret Thatcher's Britain in the 1980s.

Throughout those five years, we never even once thought we'd made the wrong decision, in fact, we came to believe we had to see the depth to which people in a so-called 'civilised' nation could sink and still retain dignity and self-respect. Shelagh soon made a lot of friends, and through them we became acquainted with the appalling levels of drug and alcohol abuse, the general lack of qualifications and few work prospects for many of the people in our situation. Then there were the shocking number of people with mental health issues. Many whom we met had recently been released from institutional care and landed straight into the arms of these B&B landlords who were quick to capitalise on the misfortune of the victims who were soon in poor physical health, due to the mismanaged housing conditions.

All this inevitably leads to shoplifting and exacerbated drug addictions. Others were prostitutes because they felt this was the only way to make enough money to escape the cycle of destitution, and there were the single mothers, desperate to get their babies and toddlers out of such an inhumane and dangerous environment, some even falling pregnant as a desperate hope to get onto the emergency housing list. I spent most of my free time helping at a local homeless drop-in centre in order to talk with, and try to help some of the people as best as I could. Often this amounted to little more than cooking meals, or Shelagh buying them fresh clothes from charity shops.

The trouble was that the economic and housing policies pursued by the Conservative Government from around 1979 provoked the homeless situation. The 1985 Housing Act consolidated legislation that distinguished 'intentionally' and 'unintentionally' homeless; 'Priority Need' categories were also introduced; none of this helped the community within which we existed, in fact, it worked against them because none of us were no longer considered 'priority' or even 'homeless.'

Further legislation was proposed that would force those in our situation to move from a town or city after having been there for a few months, and not allowed to claim benefits in that same town for a period of six months from their last Social Security signing date. This was, apparently, to encourage them to move around the country in search for work in different areas. Perhaps this was engineered as a result of party Chairman, Norman Tebbit's suggestion at the 1981 Conservative Party conference, calling for the jobless to 'get on your bike' and look for work.

This situation is what encouraged me to make my incredibly brief foray into politics. I did this by organising meetings in the unemployment drop-in centre, planning protests in the street; two of our girls even handcuffed themselves to a desk at the local Benefit office! We were aided by an eager Labour councillor who helped us petition parliament and lobby our MP. This seemed to generate enough media publicity to motivate significant numbers of people across the country to do the same and to even coordinate with us.

The project went well, and it was not long before the government shelved the plans. It gave me such a good feeling in knowing that I'd motivated a community of people who had fallen under the radar and felt they were being carried on a political tide, and incapable of defining their destiny. I had empowered them.

We soon realised this was one of the reasons we had been forced into homelessness. I had been given a test which I had passed. I had amazed myself in that I'd helped reshape a little of the political landscape. Everything we experienced during these wilderness years were lessons of one kind or another, things that had to be observed and learned; things that had to be touched and changed. Our descent to the lowest strata of living in urban Britain was tough, it was really tough, but unlike the truly unfortunate souls, we managed to rise above it and survive. Shelagh maintained her link to Red Eagle who regularly prompted us not to lose hope. He told her at moments throughout those years that we'd be offered a way out, and all we would need to do is recognise it when we saw it.

This is what Shelagh had to say about it:

The years between 1984 and 1986 seemed like an utter eternity. I lost my home, but Lucy said, "Don't worry, walk away from it." That may have been so, but where could we go? Lucy said: "Trust Red Eagle, he will see we're safe." I thought she was mad, but I loved her so much that I followed her blindly into destitution; living on benefits and at the hands of unscrupulous landlords.

'I eventually began to go through severe depression and at times like this would go downhill emotionally, retire to bed and shut the world out. It was in these moments when Lucy would sit on the edge of the bed, and I would see a look in her eyes that seemed a "different" her, and she would begin to say the most beautiful things I have ever heard. I would begin to cry, not through depression, but through the mixture of emotions which her words seemed to invoke. I cannot remember now what she said specifically, but I do

know that what she said seemed to make a terrible way of life somehow sensible and meaningful. It gave an indefinable hope and promise.

Shelagh had an issue which became the catalyst for the next shape-shift; the first to be witnessed by anyone other than myself. Shelagh's problem was the age difference. She was twice my age and knew we wouldn't be together forever, this problem was always a temporary phase that she soon passed through, but it struck so deep it could sometimes border on manic depression. On one of these occasions, when I heard her crying to herself, I went into her room and asked what was wrong - like I didn't already know - she said: 'I'm happy. I've found someone I get on with so perfectly, why did I have to live all those years with such unhappiness? Why has it all been so unfair to me?'

'But your marriage gave you a son, that must be worth it to you?'

'Yes, but I need to know why it's all so necessary.'

I had no answer for her - but someone did.

Up Close And Personal

This is from Shelagh's journal:

One of the most momentous events occurred in 1985. This was when Lucy showed me exactly what is with her. One night, she came and sat on the edge of the bed. Then, with her face a few inches from mine, and almost immediately, I saw a mistiness emanate from her left eye. This began to flow over and coat her face. It was like very bright wriggling tadpoles. Her face seemed brilliant and alive – a true transformation if ever I have seen it. The whole shape of her face began to change; her nose became almost a beak, and her eyes turned into what I call "Dame Edna Everage glasses." I was not worried about this at all; I was fascinated. I was just inches away looking at what Lucy had told me was a dual consciousness that existed alongside her. I then said, "You're changing, do you know that?" 'Lucy didn't reply verbally, but her alien head gave a slight nod. Having worked in Spiritualist circles for a number of years, I have seen ectoplasm, the dead and smelling "clay" which mediums and spirits use. Lucy was not like that at all. What built over her face was alive and vibrant. Lucy later claimed that what I saw was, indeed, not ectoplasm, but whether what I saw was her or something else, I'm not too sure. Lucy says: "I know when it is happening; However, Red Eagle controls it, not me."

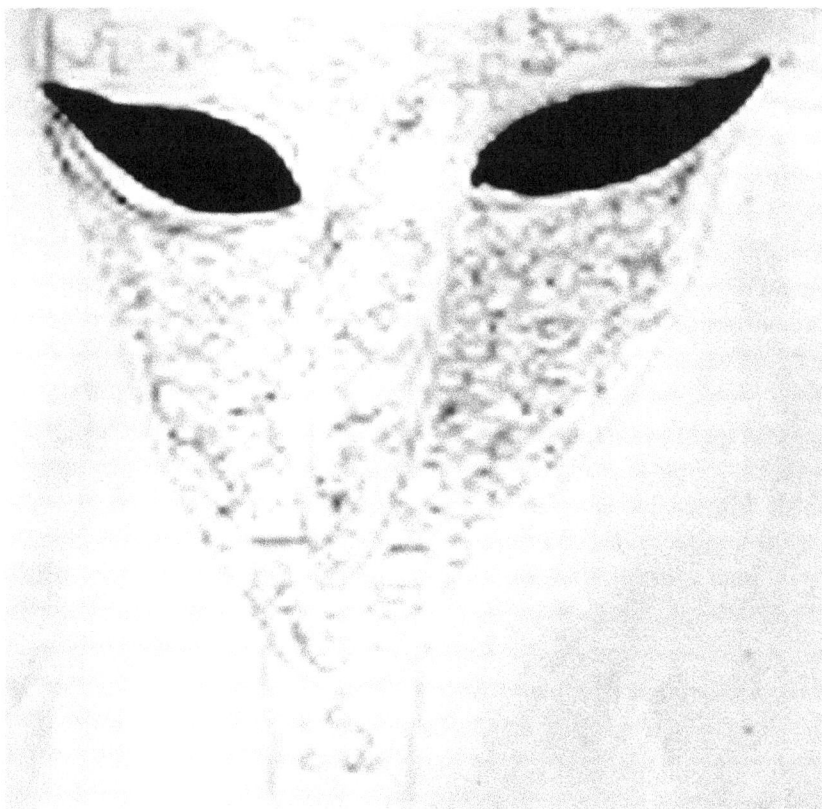

Indeed, I was aware of what Shelagh was experiencing, because as I sat beside her, I heard a voice inside my head say: *we need to show her; she has reached a point where she needs to know more.* With that I leaned close to Shelagh's face and felt a strange sensation, as though my vision was moving to the back of my head; as though I'd taken a rear seat. Then a tingling began at my left cheek that spread across my face until it stretched from forehead to chin. At that point, a most curious emotion filled me. I looked at Shelagh and felt a deep and passionate love, not just for her, but for everybody on this planet. I felt a sense of responsibility for the path their lives, their spirituality, their politics, and their military were taking them. In the immediate aftermath of this shape-shift, I thought this experience had been to touch what is often termed as the 'Christ-consciousness'.

But in hindsight, I came to the conclusion that this isn't what actually happened. I believe this was, in fact, the first and only occasion when my human mind and the Grey consciousness became united as a single and complete awareness. In that entangled state of perfect balance I could know the human condition through the Grey consciousness, and the Grey had experienced an emotional state for humanity through my own; we shared alien emotions with each other.

Had this been a brief glimpse of what humanity is evolving towards? Whatever the truth, this was a moment when both our minds became forever entwined; a dual consciousness, sharing a single awareness. Then, with the shape-shift complete, this alien head, still radiating its white luminescence, looked into her eyes, and Shelagh later told me that she received this directly into her mind:

Two beings of a single spirit that can never part; when one leaves the flesh, they will return to being one flesh, reunited as a single soul.

I was aware of words sliding through my conscious mind, a 'thread of words' uncoiling and passing through to her. These words were meaningless at the time, but would have a striking significance some years later. Unlike many familiar images of a Grey, this one, aside from being luminescent white, had a beak-like appendage, extending to just below the slit of a mouth. This 'beaked' alien appeared on more than this one occasion when I Shifted.

Invisibility

Through the months of October and November 1986, we had a number of things occur in rapid succession, and all seemed to be indicating an attempt to manifest the Grey in its entirety. The first had been witnessed by Shelagh, and the second was to be seen by both Shelagh and her son. These were experiences that featured my body moving out of the visible range. This is what Shelagh had to say:

> *We were in the town centre, and I went into a shop, while Lucy*
> *waited on a bench outside. When I came out, I looked at the*
> *bench only to find she had gone. I even walked to the bench and*
> *remember thinking, 'oh no, where has she wandered off to?' I*
> *looked along the road, then turned back to the seat and saw her*
> *sitting there! I don't know how, but she seemed to be invisible*
> *for a few moments. It had to be invisibility, because the bench*
> *was in the middle of a pedestrianised area and there was no*
> *way she could have left the bench and returned without me*
> *seeing her movements. Furthermore, I was walking towards the*
> *empty bench and would have seen her sitting there. I did not*
> *find it too surprising that she had vanished momentarily, as she*
> *did it before I left my marital home, in 1983. On that occasion I*
> *walked into my room and went past the bookcase to look out of*
> *the window. I was alone, which is strange, because I thought*
> *Lucy had come in a few minutes before, to find some books she*
> *had asked me about. Then, as I turned from the window I nearly*
> *died of shock, Lucy was standing at the bookcase just a few*
> *yards away, holding a book and staring at me. I told her what*

had happened, and she was as surprised as I was. She'd wondered why I had entered the room and walked past without even looking at her. This seems to have happened on several other occasions. Just a couple of months ago I was telling a friend about this, she looked quite startled and said that after a visit to our home, Lucy had escorted her to the railway station. Lucy then stood on the platform until my friend's train departed. This friend sat near the window, and after briefly looking away from Lucy, Lucy had gone. My friend looked as far down the platform as the carriage window would allow, then saw Lucy standing in the same location. She had puzzled over this momentary disappearance until I told her about my own experiences.

I had no knowledge of any of this taking place. In those first two instances, I wondered why Shelagh had ignored me, why she seemed to look through me, and I now know that is exactly what she did! In the case of her friend, I couldn't understand why she suddenly appeared to be puzzled and looking out of the carriage; seemingly mystified by something. I didn't feel any effects when this invisibility occurred, so whether I actually vanished or whether some illusion was being used to bend light around me, I do not know. With the absence of any sensation to indicate something out of the ordinary taking place, I tend to think it was an illusion. When we stop to consider the holographic nature of the universe, and that matter isn't really solid at all, it starts to make some kind of sense. The only constant with the invisibility is that in each case I was motionless, so if it was a light-bending effect, my lack of movement would make it easy for that level of technology to accomplish.

The Second Shape-Shift

Three weeks after Shelagh saw the changes in my face while she had been lying in bed, Julian, who was now 19 years-old, witnessed my shape-shifting for himself. Some Saturday nights he would come round to our dingy little bedsit with a sleeping bag and making a temporary bed between two armchairs pushed together, would stay for the night.

On this particular occasion, we had been watching some television and during the commercial break I decided to go make a pot of tea. This was about 8pm and it was dark outside.

I was passing the window when I glimpsed a brilliant white speck in my left peripheral vision. It appeared to be in the sky, but as it was out the corner of my eye, that is only what I perceived, for all I know it could have originated in my eye. I turned to the other two and was about to ask if either of them had seen a brilliant spark of light in the sky when suddenly I froze and couldn't move my limbs or my head. As I was turning to them, I had started to point out the window, so an arm was upraised in a pointing gesture.

Then I heard Julian utter 'Mum, can you see that?'

I saw her nod, and reply that she could. From their point of view, I had begun to transform into what they described as a 'typical Grey'.

'Typical', aside from Shelagh described it as possessing a beak-like nose that came down to just below the line of its mouth, whereas the usual reported Grey is reported as having none.

This transformation started, as with the previous, in my left eye and then spread across my face. That eye always seemed to be the point where everything started, all the way back from when I saw my eye change in the bathroom mirror as a child. As a point of interest, in later research I stumbled across a very obscure North American shaman practice referred to as Dead Crow Magic.

The brief passage explained exactly what was happening to me from a shamanic perspective, and was the first indication that what I was experiencing might really be shamanic in nature. Dead Crow Magic described the shaman undergoing a physical shape-shifting, becoming one with the creature they wished to turn into; the energy to accomplish it would emanate from their left eye. I only ever found that single reference to it and never saw it again. All subsequent inquiries during the writing of this book, including exhaustive Internet searches, came up with nothing. Curiously, I never even saw the original source book in the library again.

Unlike the childhood bathroom horror, or the almost Christ-like alien image that Shelagh saw, this time the shape-shift went further than just my face. This time it spread down from my head, across my chest and arms, progressing as far as my waist. I could still speak, but at first I didn't because I assumed that for some reason I wouldn't be able to. When I did eventually say something, it was a simple statement, made in a rather pathetic voice.

'I can't move. I feel frozen solid'.

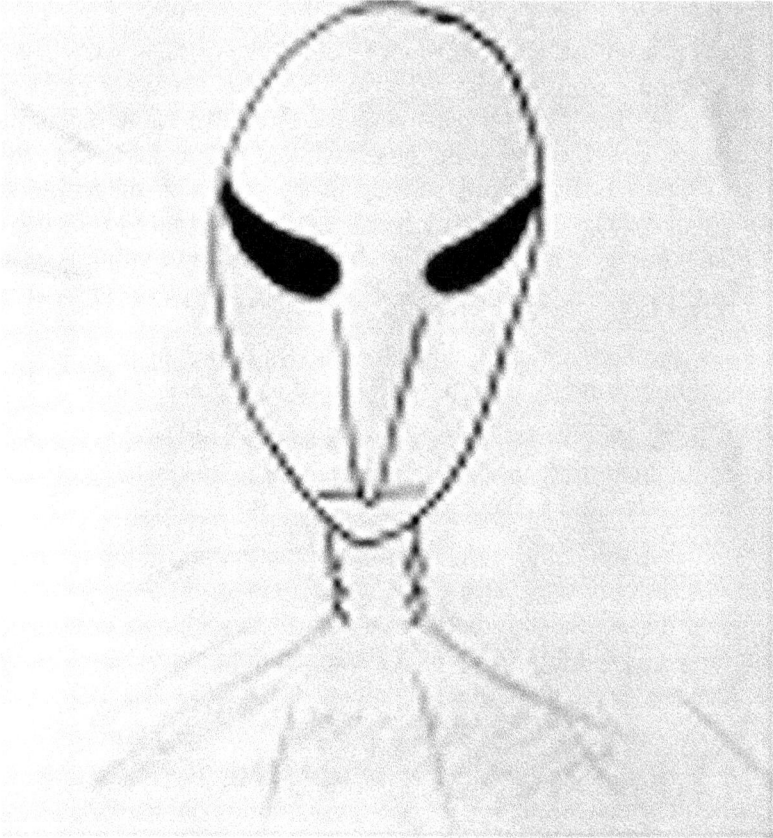

Julian rose from his chair and walked, rather cautiously, towards me. He stopped at around three feet from me when he seemed to collide with something he couldn't see.

My own experience of what happened is that I spotted the flash from the corner of my eye, and then turned to my friends, which is when my body stopped moving completely. I didn't feel any exterior or interior force do this.

My body simply failed to respond further, like a film suddenly paused, which reminded me of Shelagh's remark about Kali being frozen during their abduction. My friends asked me what was wrong, but I didn't reply. I was too busy trying to figure out why my body had stopped moving. Then I felt a thick rope of intense cold encase me in a single coiling movement from feet to head. I didn't feel chilled and my temperature remained consistent, but the surface of my skin sensed the coldness.

Then I realised I wasn't frozen quite as solid as I had first assumed, because I could move fractionally, but it took a tremendous effort to do so. It felt like the air around me had turned into an invisible molasses which left me feeling cut off from the outside world. I gave up my struggle to move. That's the point when Julian said; 'Oh God, mum, can you see that?'

Apparently, I had now begun to shape-shift but felt nothing, not even the familiar tingling across my face. Maybe the cold sheath encasing me was isolating me from it. I told them I couldn't move and tried to explain what I was feeling. I think they heard me, but all they did was stare. Shelagh was slowly shaking her head, a look of total disbelief on her face - and for her, that's a very rare expression.

Julian stood up and came towards me, asking if I could lower the arm that remained pointing out of the window. I told him I couldn't. He almost reached me, but at about three feet away, he said he could feel a cold barrier between us. However, it didn't turn out to be quite as impenetrable as I had at first believed, because he managed to move into it until he was beside me.

What they both saw from their seated positions was my form 'morph' into that of an alien. They said at the time it was like the transporter effect in Star Trek, but in my case, it was a wriggling white-light effect. I immediately thought of the white tadpoles Shelagh had seen across my face during that first close-up facial shape-shift. It was now that I began to realise that the bright pinprick of light in my left peripheral vision wasn't in the sky, but in my eye, and might be an indication of when the left-eye shape-shift would take place.

I wonder if when Julian broke through the cold barrier, he might have interfered with the shift. Which might be why I started 'flickering' between human and Grey form, which is what Shelagh reported to me later. It might have been like a holographic image being disrupted. As had been with the invisibility, I felt no sensations of the shape-shifting, and because of the 'molasses-effect', I couldn't move my head or eyes enough to look at my body.

Julian grasped my arm and said it felt normal. He tried to push it down to my side, and although he felt a little give, he couldn't move it with any noticeable effect. I told him I couldn't even feel him touching me, so he should put more pressure. I was sure he wouldn't be able to injure me. Taking me at my word, he eventually hung onto my arm like it was a bar and his feet swinging off the ground! He was not usually giver-upper, but this was defeating him completely.

Nothing he attempted seemed to have any effect. Moreover, as crazy as all this was for me, I am quite sure that as he applied pressure on my arm, the coldness tightened in response, holding me even firmer. In other words, this invisible barrier was reacting to him and countering his every attempt to move my limb. Julian then realised he was defeated and backed off. He stepped out of the cold barrier and went to sit down, both of my friends utterly powerless to do anything but watch. However, none of us had anything to fear because as soon as he sat down the coil unwound, the shape-shifting faded from view and I was free to resume my life. I had no after-effects, and it was as though nothing had happened.

I spoke with Julian in May 2014, and discussed his memories of the incident. Now aged 46, and living in Salisbury, he understandably remembers the experience with clarity. He told me:

The alien meld started like mist, which covered your head and moulded to your face; then it seemed to become part of you, covering your head, a bit like a mask or Exo-skin. The air went strange, and I remember a smell. It wasn't unpleasant, but was indescribable. This all became a bit of a goosebump moment because the air around you felt frosty; as though there was crystallisation, the air solidified.

None of this was frightening, but there was something else; a lot of emotions, but emotions that were different than all others. You became ridged and motionless, and there was initially a blank look on your face as you went stationary. Then your face slowly morphed into nothing like I've ever seen before, not even in comic books. The face was grey as I recall, and there was an underlying motion, but it wasn't veins throbbing, but it was the face itself that had an underlying motion. The eyes were mainly pupil, but not catlike, so it was different. It was quite dark in the room, but something about you was giving off a dull glow which got brighter as the morphing progressed.

Julian's recollection of the light and the undulation that he saw under the skin might well have been the same wriggling tadpole effect Shelagh had reported during her first experience, as was the dull glow, reported by Julian as this latest experience progressed.

I had just experienced phase two of a plan for the Grey to manifest physically in the real world, and I told my friends that I thought this was the plan. With the dispersion of the cold, I was left with a feeling that this was all intended for future exposure to the public in some form. This thought was confirmed and played out by the third and the most spectacular shape-shift of all; but that was a few years away. Before then, we faced two more years of domestic trials and tribulations that would test our resilience to the limit.

TULPA AND PORTALS

A New Home

In May 1986, we had the opportunity to rent the ground floor of a large house that had been turned into two flats, and this seemed to be our one chance of escape from the degrading bed & breakfast habitations. Since we left Shelagh's home and put our faith in Red Eagle, we had been forced to move from house to house on no less than ten occasions; one of these moves was outrageous, because it was close to midnight when we were told we had to do it.

I don't know what laws he had been breaking, but this landlord had to get us all out of bed, hastily dress and pack our belongings. Then he gave us directions to one of his other near-derelicts, but as we were living on State handouts how could we complain? What rights did we actually have?

But then the opportunity of a privately rented flat turned up because one of the girls who worked in the office of this particular B&B landlord was emigrating, and as we always got on well with her, she offered us the landlord's contact details. Then, when she gave one-month notice on her tenancy, she put our names forward to him, even offering to supply character references in our favour. He in turn phoned us and asked if we would like to see the flat.

Oh would we!

It was the ground floor of a house on Reading's very busy Oxford Road. This was a two storey building with a basement accessed from the street, and from where the landlord ran his plumbing and heating business. Compared to the cramped, single-room occupancy we were used to, this was Heaven! It had a sizeable bedroom situated next to an equally large sitting room, there was a nice bathroom and, for once, a hygienic kitchen without food rotting in a refrigerator that didn't work. There weren't even any mice feeding in the cupboards, or piles of dirty nappies next to the waste bin. The top-floor flat was reached through the communal front door and up the stairs, as you would expect in a regular two storey house, so there was no door dividing the two flats. Nonetheless, the occupants respected each other's privacy, and what to most people would be 'average', was, to us, palatial.

We had not even gone looking for the flat, it had come to us. We knew Red Eagle would be true to his words, in that he would organise an escape from our situation – and he had.

Shelagh's journal:

In early May 1986, a set of coincidences led us to be offered a house of quite enormous proportions, and as we received the keys, a voice inside my head said, 'This house is given in order to do the work.'

Now we had decent accommodation, and with it, stability in knowing we wouldn't be moved with barely an hour of warning, I could find a job, and that was well timed too, because within six months, the top floor was vacated, and the landlord offered it to us at a very affordable rate. We took it and so ended up with a four-bedroomed, two-bathroom, two-kitchen house. If, as Shelagh stated when we moved in originally, it was given to us for the work, 'they' were proving to be very serious indeed about it. Such a large house gave us ample space to accommodate as many guests as we might ever need. We also had a room we could reserve as a refuge with no distractions. This could be used for meditation work, or as a study, which it eventually became.

It was in this room during the next four years, that Red Eagle furthered my education with an understanding of thought-form constructs, how powerful they could be, and to what uses they could be put. At this time, I was introduced to the remarkable power contained within even a single and fleeting thought. I had some inkling of what thought-forms were, because among Shelagh's extensive library I had read some astonishing stories about the subject. Alexandra David-Néel is just one of the names I encountered, but there were many more.

Tulpa

Alexandra David-Néel, born in October 1868, was a Belgian-French explorer, a Buddhist and a spiritualist. She is best remembered for her journey to Lhasa in Tibet, where she stayed for two months in 1924, and what is so remarkable is that this was at a time when the city wasn't usually open to foreign travellers. During her life, David-Néel wrote more than 30 books about her extensive travels and Eastern religion. However, of particular interest to me was that she studied tulpa creation from adepts; a tulpa being a very strong thought form created by effort of will and intense visualisation methods. Eventually, David-Néel set about creating a thought-form of her own, in the image of a plump and jolly Friar Tuck-like figure.

This began as a visualisation exercise, and as it became stronger, it became ever more solid as she continued to focus her energies on the construct. This 'friar', in fact, became so energised that her companions, who didn't know of its existence, began to report seeing a strange monk close to their camp. The problem that can arise with tulpa creation is the risk of the creator losing control as the form continues to feed and takes on a stronger, and with it, an increasingly independent form.

Now David-Néel discovered that if you allow a tulpa to exist long enough, it's reluctant to give up the life it's been given. You might argue that if this thing is an artificial construct, how can it struggle to maintain its existence, as surely that indicates freewill? Remember this much: an occultist is forming it from the very substance of creation, proto-substance, the subatomic formlessness of matter that our illusory universe - our holographic universe, is, itself, constructed from. Because the tulpa is essentially a part of you, an expression of your own individuality, that is going to be reflected in the thing. Which is why its deconstruction takes a great deal of energy, and is what David-Néel was to discover next.

It took several weeks for her to successfully reabsorb the creation; a process involving a very exhausting struggle of wills. The longer a tulpa is left to roam, the more challenging that struggle will become. I had the disciplines taught to me at night, followed by a chain of synchronicity that guided Shelagh to finding books on the theory and practice of thought-forms and a more complete history of Alexandra David-Néel. All this reading was good grounding for what I launched myself into next.

Red Eagle had, over the period of time he had been with me, created a morphic web, a kind of mental entanglement between me and the astral plane, just as he'd formed them to me and many other dimensions, which allowed me to visit them freely of a night. This morphic entanglement was the key to me being capable of building and disassembling thought-forms with such relative ease; it was as though I had been experimenting with them for years instead of months. How I recall this astral world is as me standing at the edge a vast and seething white sea, limitless, choppy and reacting to the slightest thought from every single living thing, to which it is inextricably a part.

I would wake remembering where I had been and what I was doing, and as such, developed an instinctive 'knowing' of what to do and what precautions were required. I would spend a single night in this astral environment, learning directly into my subconscious, what it would have taken years on the Earth to learn. Within a few short months I felt the urge to start building something.

Initially, I would sit in our quiet room and condense small spheres of energy in the palms of my cupped hands. Visualising that connection to the astral world, where energy could be manipulated by willpower and concentration. I focused a particle of this sea into a dense pinprick of energy, which with force of mind; I transferred it to my cupped hands which rested in my lap. Slowly channelling psychic energy, I built layer upon layer like onion skins, compacting the layers beneath. Building its density - willing this construct into physical existence; to shift from its state of existence to ours. I worked with this energy manipulation for about a year before feeling confident enough to move a stage further and create a simple servitor - an energised thought-form with a temporary existence.

By the third year of this and other training process, I felt ready to move to yet another stage; the creation of a tulpa in humanoid form. I had plans to keep it in existence for several months, programming it with my thoughts as I constructed it. I decided to build a Grey which I gave an invented name, one with no significance other than to the thought-form - the tulpa. It's important to give a name, it personalises the tulpa; helps the construct to identify itself, I guess in computer terms it is thinking up a password to use, and like any good password, the name must never be shared with anyone, and for the duration of it's existence, only you and the tulpa must know it; once used, it should not be used again. For this experiment, I used Shelagh as a backup psychic power-source, a battery to help focus and maintain the energy needed. In this way we contributed an equal measure to the project.

We, first of all, drew an image of what we wanted, important for a consistent visualisation; we decided that a copy of the beak-nosed Grey that Shelagh had seen was a good basic template because it didn't have a complex facial representation. The rest of the body was also easy. It was a typically slim, thin-limbed Grey standing four feet tall. This is such a basic, uncomplicated form, that we had little trouble at all in maintaining and strengthening the image.

The tulpa remained in existence for three months, and although we had invested a tremendous amount of energy into the entity, we had no realistic expectations of it becoming dense enough to register visually. In fact, when both of us could see it as a vaguely perceptible, misty apparition, we regarded that as a spectacular success. While it was being built, we were constantly programming it with instructions that would shape the world it was capable of perceiving.

For instance: It was forbidden to leave the room in which it was built, which means it was programmed not to register the existence of anything beyond those four walls. The room we used was one Shelagh used as her Wiccan temple, so even if we had guests, no one ever went into it except her or myself.

One Saturday afternoon our landlord arrived to empty the electric meter, and as he did so he remarked to Shelagh that he thought he'd seen a grey, bald person, with big black eyes watching him from the upstairs window before vanishing. He even mentioned the beaked nose, and the comparison he made was that it looked like Mr. Punch, from Punch and Judy. He had only spotted it for a fleeting moment as he glanced up, so assumed it must have been a pattern of reflected light on the glass; but it had certainly startled him for a moment.

We were happy for him to believe what he was suggesting, so we said nothing. However, I was amazed that the manifestation had been seen - an unexpected testimony to how powerful the tulpa was, and underscoring the warning of how, if neglected, a tulpa could easily become strong enough to slip from its creator's grasp. If the landlord hadn't made the chance remark, we would probably not have known it had reached a visual density, and maybe we would have felt sufficiently safe to keep it in existence much longer.

What might have happened had we not reabsorbed it when we did? If we had not been made aware of how strong it had become in such a short period of time? In only three months it seemed to have breached the programming by standing at the window and becoming conscious of the outside world, could it have left the room and investigated the world beyond? Might there have been reports of an alien creature being seen around the area, like David-Néel's monk-figure being seen by her companions?

You need to be cautions, because a tulpa acts as an energy magnet, it will attract and absorb energy compatible to itself, therefore, it will start to feed itself on any available energy it detects, allowing it to strengthen without your knowledge. That's when they can become uncontrollable even malevolent

My second tulpa creation was a large raven, that I decided to build by myself. I didn't want Shelagh involved in this one because I wanted to see if I could use it as an occult tool. I invented a name for it, and found a picture to use as the focus for its creation. Before I'd started building it, I had chosen a purpose for it; I was going to see if I could use the bird to travel. It's why so much of me went into the programming without Shelagh's help, I wanted to see if I could use it as a remote viewing platform.

Eventually, the tulpa-bird matured into a strong and consistent apparition. I could even see it from my peripheral vision as a faint ghost-like image, on an empty bookshelf which I had programmed the tulpa to think of as home; in other words, a default point where it would remain static when not active. This is important, since you can't leave a strong thought-form - one that you've created, and therefore, exists as an extension of your consciousness - to roam free and aimless. So with all this done, and my personal psychic protection in place, I lay on the bed and entered a state of relaxation and restfulness.

By now, I could quite easily step out of my physical shell while in a restful state and listening to shamanic drumming on my cassette player. This was another ability that I seemed to develop. I think I probably had a latent predisposition to mediation and astral travel, but it was enhanced by Red Eagle's continual occult training over the years.

So, once out of my physical body I stood looking at the raven. Instead of a hazy, ghost-image, it was now sharply defined and appeared perfectly solid. It stood out like a cut-out image, sharp and clear and black. It was only now I realised I wasn't sure how I should attempt to merge with the tulpa, I wanted my awareness to inhabit the thought-form shell; Then I had an idea.

I remembered my left eye being where my own shape-shift always started, so maybe that was my psychic doorway between states of being; I might be able to enter through the eyes of the tulpa. So I looked at it, staring hard, concentrating on its left beady black eye and willing it to look at me.

It took a number of attempts spread over several weeks, but suddenly during a session, and with no sense of movement, I found myself inside it - or at least, I had the sensation of looking out through its eyes - which meant that something of my awareness had transferred to that empty shell. I was still aware of standing as an astral form across the room, and the image of myself within the raven was in my mind. In a sense, I was in two places at the same time – bilocation.

Merging with a thought-form is a strange experience, I imagined that I would make it flap its wings, and it would fly, but that didn't happen. I looked at a sideboard on the other side of the room and willed myself there. I expected it to fly, but it didn't; it was suddenly at the new location with no sense of movement between the two points. One moment I was on the bookcase and the next I was on the sideboard. I was confusing a thought-form with a physical bird, and, of course, they don't operate the same way at all.

No doubt, had I persevered; I might have had some success in actually learning to fly like a living bird and soaring through the sky. Perhaps the tulpa would have been seen by observers on the ground, maybe they would have seen no more than the fleeting shadow of a bird in flight. Might this have been how witches flew, hundreds of years ago? After my experience with the raven, I am convinced this was one of the truths behind occultists and their animal familiars.

It's how a shaman can shape-shift into power-animals, an art which Red Eagle had now taught me. Then that ephemeral reference to Dead Crow magic came back to mind. I was pretty certain that this was exactly what I was doing now. However, my brief but exciting and successful experiment now concluded; I slowly and carefully reabsorbed the energy that had been the raven.

The Dreamer

While we existed in transient B&B housing we'd made friends with a young woman called Michelle. I say 'we', but Shelagh was the social animal of the pair of us and chatted freely to just about everybody and was unfailingly ready to put herself out to help. Michelle was twenty-one years old and married to Roger, a heavily built man of thirty-five; a drinker; a possessive husband and wife-beater. It didn't take Michelle long to start showing Shelagh some of the bruises on her shoulders and chest.

She described a life of being so controlled that she had to give him details of when she was going out, who she was seeing and what time she would be back home – and woe betide her if she was late and hadn't phoned to warn him that she would be. Such a lapse would have Roger on the phone ringing round all their friends and gradually spiralling into panic followed by anger.

Then, as often happened in the B&B environment, we went our separate ways, but Michelle remained in contact by letter because it seemed she didn't have many people she felt comfortable enough to confide in, and just talking to Shelagh helped her deal with things on her mind. When we moved into our permanent flat, we made sure we gave her our phone number, and it's just as well we did, because one day she phoned Shelagh and told how Roger had almost killed her and their three-year-old child.

Michelle had been cradling the child in her arms while having an argument with Roger at the top of the stairs, he pushed her backwards and both woman and child tumbled down to the bottom. Michelle crashed into a door which was little more than a sheet of glass in a wooden frame. Luckily, it only cracked, and didn't break in the collision. I hate to imagine what would have happened had it shattered into fragments. Thankfully, the child made a soft landing on top of her mother, but Michelle suffered a broken arm in the fall.

We told her she only had two choices, either find a safe refuge or report this to the police, preferably do both now that their child was caught up in his violence. We had told her at various times from then onward that she should go to the police, but she refused, she was too scared to do so, even begging us not to bring the police into it.

I wondered how we could be of any help if she wouldn't even go to the authorities.

Then I had an idea. Not a particularly nice one, but it was a desperate idea to help a despairing victim of violence.

I knew I could take my tulpa creation a stage further than I had done before. So after giving the idea much thought, I decided it was the only way to help Michelle if she felt incapable of helping herself, especially as next time she or the baby could be dead. I asked her if she wanted some of our 'special help', as I referred to it - she knew I meant some form of paranormal intervention - and she said 'yes please.'

So I set about creating a new tulpa. and on this occasion I decided to house the energy in something I could use as a kind of mould, making it easier to adapt to a form I wanted seen. We had a cheap plaster ornament portraying a Hindu Rakasha, a grotesque bulging-eyed demon; it would be a perfect image. I hung this on the wall in my workroom and began to focus the psychic energy; concentrating it into this template.

I'm not going to explain the sequence of what went into its creation and programming, because it was a long process that took a year of slow and methodical work, which included using something of Roger's that Michelle had sent us. This was to create a sympathetic link between the tulpa and what would be its target.

During the creation process I remained as relaxed as possible, not wanting to transmit feelings of revenge or satisfaction. I did this by only working on it after meditation. I needed this thing, which here we will call The Dreamer, to be as uncontaminated as possible. I chose to reinforce its connection by imbuing it with an attraction to alcohol around the target. In other words: when Roger went to sleep drunk, he would feed The Dreamer, revitalising it; Roger would sustain his own demon.

Eventually, The Dreamer was sent to its target and Shelagh explained to Michelle that she needed to keep an eye on Roger and let us know if he started to display any unusual behaviour, or mentioned anything about his sleep pattern. That way, we could monitor what The Dreamer was doing.

At some point Michelle phoned to say that Roger had begun having disturbed sleep; he'd been going downstairs to sit with the light and the TV switched on. I wasn't sure if this was a result of The Dreamer or not, so we waited to see how things developed. It was a further six months before we heard from Michelle again. Roger was unable to sleep a lot of the time, and when he did, his dreams were nightmares of being chased by demons. It was getting to a stage now, that when he woke during the night, he felt there was something crouching in the corner of the bedroom. She told us that this was leaving him exhausted by a day, and affecting his work as a builder. He was becoming forgetful as fatigue started to drag him down, and no matter what he tried, nothing could stop the horrible dreams that hounded him.

When I heard what was happening, I didn't whoop with joy, nor did I feel a sense of victory; I was simply doing what was needed to help Michelle. That woman and child needed help, desperately and it was taking an extreme measure to give them the opportunity they needed.

Over the course of a year, Roger was losing much-needed work through increasing fatigue and a deteriorating state of mind. He eventually went to his doctor for help, which, Michelle told us, led to sessions with a psychiatrist.

His increasingly debilitated state gave Michelle all the leverage she needed. Now with a husband who had virtually no work, weakened physically and emotionally, and under medical supervision, she took her child and left him. However, at least two months before that endpoint was reached I had withdrawn The Dreamer and re-absorbed the energy that had created him. Having existed for a full year in its operational form, the tulpa was very strong and wasn't easy to dismantle.

I had now discovered the terrifying power that was possible with directed thought-forms and the kind of weapon they could be turned into. This was more than enough for me.

The Dreamer was the last I ever created.

What I had done to help Michelle went rewarded by Red Eagle just a few days later while we were sat in a café having lunch.

'I can see Red Eagle is standing behind you.'

I glanced at Shelagh, but said nothing. I waited for her to continue, and pass whatever he wanted to say.

'He's braiding a second eagle feather into your hair, and putting a string of animal teeth around your neck.' She fell silent and closed her eyes.

I sat sipping my tea and waited, waited, then asked: 'What's he saying?'

She held up a hand. 'Wait a minute, he's telling me what this initiation name is all about, and I'm trying to find out what the teeth are.'

She remained silent a few moments longer, then looked at me. 'He says it is for what you did to help Michelle, without seeking reward; it is because you destroyed the thought-form and didn't try to keep it in existence. It's because you recognise your strengths and can control your weaknesses.'

'My weaknesses?'

She nodded. 'Yes, you knew when to bring back the thought-form and didn't allow ego to control you. He says your name is "Silverfox."'

All of this stuff: the increasingly tough shamanic lessons, shape-shifts, tulpa creation and journeying to parallel worlds; this was all being written in my journal. Meticulous details of what had happened over the years following Shelagh's hypnotic regression, which, itself, was treated as our start-point, rather than the incidents individually experienced in the years prior to it. As I sat writing the details of The Dreamer, I began to feel that a major part of our current work was nearing completion. I had been exposed to enough in order to comprehend features that suggested an alien operation of some kind. I was also beginning to understand the mechanism by which they contact humanity and deliver their information to individuals, and not only that, but actually work with and through us.

I was becoming aware of how they could conduct bizarre, and even what should be, impossible abductions of humans, Shelagh's own being the example to me. The enormity of what is happening only really becomes apparent when you consider the hundreds of thousands, possibly millions, occurring on a repeat basis. Not only had these beings validated their ability to shape-shifting imagery, but were also capable of conducting a manipulation, deep within the human unconscious; in light of this, I was looking at a theory that focused on what I thought of as mega-tulpa. What I have termed Artificial Intermediaries (AI).

These AI function between Earth's planetary species field and that of intelligences that came to the Earth an incredibly long time ago - visitors responsible for branching human evolution from the animal by encouraging agriculture and spirituality, acquired from AI by way of shamanic journeying to alternate realities, where communication could be established.

Many encounters throughout history have been with these Intermediaries, reflecting the hopes and fears of humanity, responding to the expectations of cultures and civilisations. By being observed as angels; demons; fairies; witches; and complicit in significant numbers of modern alien encounters - most often as Greys, Reptilians, and the very tall blonde aliens known as Nordics.

That isn't to say these AI are anthropomorphic entities; far from it, they are an energy pattern injected into the collective awareness, and interacting through the human species field. Following such reasoning, many encounters are through this symbiotic mask, morphing into a relevant context. In other words, the human is unconsciously projecting their expectation onto the intelligence so it would more likely be accepted rather than rejected. Because the contact is through the collective unconscious, it's why so many experiencers have bizarre, and, quite often wildly conflicting memories. This was important to me, because during recent OBE, I had been shown how that theory could relate to me directly. I decided I wanted to present my ideas of Artificial Intermediaries in a talk at a UFO group meeting, get some feedback and see what others thought of it. However, I wouldn't be saying anything much about the shape-shifting and how I saw that fitting in; I knew the shape-shifting was slightly weird even compared to some of the strange stuff that other people were saying.

Then my journals vanished.

White Knights

A couple of thousand pages documenting everything, had disappeared. One important file was split into two sections: the material on AI that I wanted to develop further, and the private stuff relating to the shape-shifting and how I saw it dovetailing into my embryonic AI conjecture. The worrisome thing is that I kept this material in the spare room - the one we usually locked. I searched through the desk drawers, the cupboards and the bookshelves - nothing.

I asked Shelagh if she had seen them, maybe she'd moved them, for some reason, and forgot to tell me.

'Why would I do that?'

True enough, why would she? I knew she hadn't touched anything, but you do tend to ask the obvious when there doesn't seem to be any other option. She hadn't touched them, and I certainly hadn't moved them, who else could it have been? We went up to the study together and turned the room upside down a second time, but still with no result. How difficult could it be to find three cardboard folders? Eventually, we did the only thing we could think of when mysterious things happened; we went for a stroll across White Knights, maybe hoping Red Eagle would enlighten us.

Over the years, we had continued to visit the White Knights campus of Reading University; it was where I had my own strongest connection with Red Eagle. We realised this heavily wooded area where UFOs and strange lights were often seen, was a portal, making the area a generator for much of what we were experiencing; where Shelagh had a direct connection to this intersection of dimensions which manifested itself to her as an alien abduction.

That experience resulted in a unique channel of communication being made between her and this portal. You could say she'd had a cable link installed, and is why clairvoyants were unable to detect them; all they could see was the front man; a Red Indian.

White Knights has a large lake we'd circumvent during our dog-walk, and whenever approached, the lake instilled a sense of trepidation within both of us. There was something old, perhaps even ancient about it. This encouraged me to look into its history, but I was to be disappointed when I found nothing sensational.

The site was the home of John De Erleigh II, the foster-son of the Regent of England, William Marshal, but takes its name from the nickname of his great grandson, the 13th century knight, John De Erleigh IV the 'White

Knight'. The De Erleigh (or D'Earley) family were owners of this manor for some two hundred years before 1365. St. Thomas Cantilupe, Bishop of Hereford and adviser to King Edward I, was allowed to live there briefly during the 1270s. In 1606, the estate was purchased by the nephew of Sir Francis Englefield, following the confiscation of Englefield House and its estates in 1585. The Englefield family in turn sold the estate to George Spencer, the Marquis of Blandford, in 1798.

Between 1798 and 1819, the estate was the scene of vast extravagance and 'wild entertainment', all at the Marquis' expense. 'Splendid gardens' were laid out, complete with the rarest of plants. During this period there was an incident involving a coach and horses that were passing over a bridge across the river. Something spooked the horses and in panic they ran off the bridge and plunged with the coach into the river, killing all on board. What makes this incident of interest is that it was only yards from where Shelagh was abducted. In 1819, the owner, by now the Duke of Marlborough, became bankrupt and moved to his family home to Blenheim Palace at Woodstock in Oxfordshire. The estate in Reading was sold off and the house was demolished in 1840, supposedly by a mob of the Duke's angry creditors.

But in all this I could find nothing about the lake except that it was no more than a couple of hundred years old, probably built by George Spencer as part of his gardens, so why we felt there was something ancient about it we just couldn't understand. Curiously, each of us would be getting random flashes of Arthurian-like imagery which - considering the history we were aware of, and Reading having no known connection with Arthurian myth - was a complete mystery. Nonetheless, the images continued to flash through our minds intermittently whenever we walked beside that enigmatic lake. On one occasion, I saw an arm coming out of the water bearing a sword - archetypal Lady of the Lake stuff.

But there *is* a history of psychic phenomena being witnessed there. A single account will serve as an example of the many I have discovered over the years. Late on a Spring Saturday evening in 1991, a man I will refer to as 'Gerry' felt an overwhelming urge to visit the lake, and so as dusk began to settle in, he went there with two friends. Standing by the lake, all three began to feel an anticipation, as though they expected to see something. Then, a short while later, they heard a splashing sound.

To their astonishment they saw a female in a flowing white dress running across the surface of the water! This woman was looking around herself, especially over her shoulder, as she continued across the lake. This image, as unsettling as it was, fascinated them enough to decide to return to the lake, the same time the following week.

The next Saturday, again, as dusk approached, the trio were at the lake, and all of them seemed to feel the area buzzing of static electricity. Then they reported seeing a cloud approach from across the lake. It resembled a snowstorm of miniature hexagons blending into a rainbow of colours. The hexagons were less than a centimetre in diameter and formed a single layer, somewhat like a snowstorm of energy. Gerry approached the cloud as it halted near the trio, and rather bravely, he walked into it. He spotted a flash of blue movement to his right, and as he turned, he saw a woman dressed in a blue one-piece body suit. She is reported to have had shoulder-length brown hair and stood about five feet six inches tall. She smiled a greeting; leaving Gerry feeling as though this woman was a friend he'd known all his life. The report goes on from there, but this is enough to demonstrate what a powerful psychic generator White Knights truly is, and the effects it has on people who go there.

Following the loss of all my written work, Shelagh attempted to contact Red Eagle at various points during our walk along the meandering paths. We even went and sat in the small sheltered glade where she found her contact to be at its strongest, but he wasn't available. She tried a number of times to establish communication, asking: Where have our papers gone? How did they vanish? In her mind, she could see his tepee on a rocky bluff.

She always saw this image when she contacted him, and he was usually sat outside the tepee or standing next to it, but if he wasn't visible, as was the case now, it signalled 'go away and deal with it yourself'. We accepted that we had to handle a lot by ourselves, otherwise we wouldn't grow and evolve. He had practically abandoned us to the almost unbearable B&B, but we had come through by using our own initiative and guile; the reward for that was the house we were now in. So the incentive was always there at the end, but the path we trod together was a rocky one.

Mistakes Made

I had now reached the point where I felt we needed to contact someone who might understand all this stuff. So much had been happening, some of it even crashing down upon us simultaneously from different directions, it sometimes left me wondering why it hadn't driven us crazy. Who to turn to; we had no connections with anybody and had no idea where to look. I did the only thing I could think of; I got hold of some UFO journals and went through them and considered who I might write to.

Obviously big-name organisations headed that list, along with a sprinkling of smaller organisations jumping out at me. But I couldn't decide between them all, so eventually went for the first one that stood out to me. I had come to the conclusion that no matter who I contacted; they would have the experience and background to be able to explain what was going on here.

So over the next few months we invited 'experts' to our home, all coming through this same organisation, and our only expectation was that we would be given a fair hearing. We hoped we would be offered a reasonable idea of what they thought might be happening, and just as importantly, where it all might be leading us.

Of course, I had my own personal belief in what was going on, a belief that Shelagh shared in an equal measure. But when you exist in a permanent high-strangeness environment, continued paranormal events isolating you from what other people refer to as 'normal life', how can you step outside of it and take an objective view? It's impossible, and this is why we were opening the door to these people.

I had been shown sufficient - even Shelagh and Julian had witnessed enough - to convince me that I was intimately connected to something so utterly different to what most people around me had any experience with. That much I was willing to share with these researchers, but that I have been entangled with this thing from a very young age? that was not something I was prepared to share with them, not unless they could demonstrate their sincerity and earn my trust. I'm glad I had that attitude because the problem, we quickly discovered, was that these people were so full of their own theories and ideas that they were unprepared to accept much of what we were saying unless it supported those ideas.

This left us bewildered, especially when three of them submitted us to a psychological test that, regardless of its searching and sometimes intimate questions, ultimately led to no conclusion. Our appeal was for understanding, even just a sympathetic ear. However, the harsh truth was that we had no support whatsoever. These armchair experts came to our home, drank our tea, ate our food, and then went away to portray us as deluded storytellers; one even suggested seeking treatment for 'fantasies fuelled by schizophrenia and a deep-set psychotic paranoia.'

These were the years of psychological damage to two confused individuals who had undergone experiences ranging from the strange to the downright terrifying. But our plea for help wasn't only being derided, we were treated at delusional if not mentally ill.

THE SILENCERS

The First Man In Black

The Men in Black (MIB) phenomenon as we recognise it, began with Albert K. Bender, of Bridgeport, Connecticut, who in April 1952, created The International Flying Saucer Bureau, an organisation which attracted an ever increasing membership, both at home and abroad, and this happened at a truly astonishing rate. But then with barely any notification he closed the Bureau down, and an air of mystery hung over this until eventually the truth was told. It transpired that Bender was visited by three men he described as wearing black suits and black Homburg hats, and with what he described as 'flashing' eyes.

Prior to the mysterious visitors, Bender's attic apartment had been subject to intense paranormal phenomena, accompanied by sulphuric smells. The MIB, when they arrived, told Bender to stop his investigations into the mystery of the flying saucers, they even claimed that he'd stumbled on the truth of why they were here. Bender was then taken on a journey to a secret UFO base in Antarctica where the few things he had not 'discovered' were revealed to him.

Make what you will of Albert Bender's claims, the really important thing is that since then, and from all around the globe, there have been thousands of reported encounters with strange visitors, typically clothed in black suits, and often wearing Homburg hats and sunglasses. They generally drive black vehicles reported as looking brand new. These MIB, more often than not, employ harassment, intimidation and outright threats to scare people who have had a UFO encounter, into silence. It does seem, however, they are not exclusive to UFO witnesses, researchers who have been involved with other paranormal phenomena, have also had visits from these people.

There is reason to believe that some of these visits are, in fact, from government agencies making investigations of their own, even though any official line is that they don't engage in such practices. There certainly is evidence that one of Albert Bender's encounters was FBI agents who undoubtedly were monitoring UFO groups, presumably in case the ever growing organisations were being used by Communists as a vehicle for subversion. However, not all these visits can be attributed to government agencies because alongside this, there's an even stranger breed of Men in Black who are attended by a number of paranormal effects, and leave those they visit, confused and puzzled.

I was in my study when the first Man in Black arrived.

It was a Saturday morning in August 1989. Shelagh had taken a walk into town to do some shopping and would as usual, soon be heading home laden with her charity bargains. I heard the front door bell ring, and muttered my frustration at having to break off what I was doing; I stopped typing and went down to answer the call. As I walked towards the door with its opaque glass, I could see the silhouette of someone standing on the other side. I opened the it to confront a man who stared at me with a broad smile on his face. The kind of expression you would expect from a salesman or a Jehovah's Witness.

He was about five feet nine inches in height, and at first glance looked as though he would have passed without attracting attention in the street. He was wearing a suit consisting of a dark, almost black buttoned-up jacket and neatly creased trousers. The tie was of the colour of his suit and might even have been cut from the same material, which made his brilliantly white shirt stand out in stark contrast. He had a dark trilby-type hat on his head, and he carried a briefcase, brown and looking brand new, by that I mean it had a high sheen to it's surface.

This was held in his left hand, and an odd characteristic about him was that he held it somehow awkwardly. His forearm was at something like a twenty-degree angle from his body, and the stance gave the impression that he was being careful not to let the briefcase touched his body. I thought it was a bit like a 'man's man' who might reluctantly hold a female handbag in public for his wife, but away from his body in such a way that says 'this is *not* mine.' in other words, he held the briefcase as though very self-conscious of his connection to it.

He communicated first: *We need to talk*.

This is where it all gets a little confusing for me; I'm unsure whether he spoke aloud, or if it had been telepathic. If I think of it as having been extrasensory, and I try to imagine him sending it mind-to-mind, something in me says no, it was vocal, and I can recall seeing his mouth moving as he spoke. However, if I think of his words as having been vocal and I try to imagine him speaking the words, the voice in my head says no, it was telepathic, and try as I might, I cannot recall his mouth moving. It is a very baffling contradiction.

Without further communication between us, I opened the door wide and stepped to one-side. He walked in and knew where the sitting room was, which happened to be the first room on the right. He went straight to it without hesitation. I closed the door and followed in silence. Then I stood in the middle of the room while this stranger, who was now sitting on the couch, fumbled around with his briefcase.

First, he placed it at his feet, but then, looking uncomfortable with it there so moved it to the side of the couch. However, that didn't seem right either so so he laid it flat on the coffee table. Apparently happy with it there, he turned his attention to me. I was feeling like a school child standing before a head teacher. I seemed to have slipped, without realising, into some kind of state that rendered me utterly powerless, and I still have no idea how it happened. I think it had been from the moment I opened the door.

Still not knowing if it was verbal or telepathic, I received the following words: *You need to stop all this silly shape-shifting nonsense. It's not the right thing to be doing. Do you understand?*

I nodded, and for no reason whatsoever I actually felt ashamed of myself! I was like a child who'd been caught with her hand in the cookie jar, because somehow he was stirring feelings of embarrassment and guilt within me, emotions that had no reason to be there. He seemed to be blaming me for the shape-shifting, and causing me to feel I was deliberately doing it to annoy him. It was ridiculous!

So you will stop it? Get rid of all that paperwork? There's no point to it. You need to stop making a public display of yourself.

I felt bad about it and at one point, I could even have cast my eyes down as shame swept over me. I felt that I was being reprimanded with good reason. It was an incredible degree of control as he played my emotions like an accomplished musician.

Apparently having completed all he'd set out to do, he stood and picked up the briefcase, and as soon as he did so, he appeared to be uncomfortable once again. I watched him walk out of the sitting room, and as soon as he left I felt myself slip out of that 'Stupidity Zone' which had gripped me for the duration of his visit. As my own thought processes seemed to start working again, I was left wondering why he had felt a need to invite himself into the house to deliver what turned out to be just a few sentences. Like everything else, it was a puzzle.

I waited for the sound of the front door to announce his departure. After what had to be long enough, and still not having heard the door either open or close, I left the room expecting to find him standing in the hallway, which wouldn't have surprised me. However, he wasn't there. So thinking he might have gone elsewhere in the house I went to check each room in turn. Maybe he'd gone to my study, but no; he wasn't there either. So he'd definitely left the house, but it hadn't been by the front door, and I know the back door was locked.

The Second Man In Black

Because we felt we had suffered at the hands of individuals who took it upon themselves to judge our truthfulness, I decided I wanted nothing more to do with them. I even told Shelagh; 'If we are to co-operate with any of these people, they'll need to come to us; I'm certainly not going to look for them.'

Shelagh agreed. She too had had enough of them; like me, she wasn't angry, just very disappointed.

In January 1990, I re-subscribed to *Awareness*, the magazine of

Contact International; the organisation I'd joined shortly before The Man came into the electrical shop, in 1975. I made this fresh subscription, in the hope of discovering reports from people who were encountering anything similar to us. If we did, perhaps we could learn by reading their accounts, and if we were very lucky, maybe we could even write to them.

My thinking was that if researchers couldn't handle what we were telling them, maybe people who experienced similar, would be able to. Then in the second issue of my subscription, which I received in July 1990, I read an article called *Alien Contact or Armageddon?* It was written by a researcher from Leicestershire, his name was Clive Potter. The article looked like a fair and balanced report that focused on the unusual claims of several people. I read the article twice, then turned to Shelagh: 'Do you remember a few years ago, when we were told we'd be brought into contact with a UFO investigator?'

She nodded.

'I've found him.'

I showed her the article which outlined five people; each described some element of what we were familiar with from our own history. I was impressed with the fair treatment the author had given these people and decided I would write to him. I wasn't breaking my own oath about contacting someone, because his address was conveniently supplied in the article, therefore, so far as I was concerned, he had literally come to me by dropping on the doormat. I wrote this letter to Clive the very next day:

10-7-90

Dear Mr. Potter,

I read with great interest, your co-written article, 'Alien Contact or Armageddon?' in Issue 4 of Awareness, as I have had similar experiences to those cited in the case histories. I will not, in this letter, describe the ongoing experiences of eight years, but I will make this available if you wish it.

What I do particularly want, is to contact others who have, (or feel they have), communication with 'alien' beings. With many, there seems to be a need to talk to others. I also share this feeling. I would like to contact a few of these people so that we can discuss our experiences, share our feelings and communications. I really do think that much can be gained through open discussion, rather than a one-to-one with an investigator. (I have had difficulties with investigators who have put me on my guard a little).

Please make my address available at your discretion, to people such as those in your article. A kind of 'self-help' group would be very beneficial; I know it would be help to me.

That's an innocent enough letter, one that anybody might write. However, not only did it seem that something else knew that I'd found Clive, but it obviously didn't like the fact I'd written to him. One week later, the second Man In Black arrived, just eleven months after I had opened the door to the first one.

On this occasion, I was at work, so didn't hear about it until I got home at around six in the evening. Shelagh was in the kitchen at about 2pm and was preparing herself some salad lunch when the front doorbell rang. She headed along the hallway, and what puzzled her straight off was that she couldn't see any silhouette the other side of the opaque glass in the door, so assumed whoever rang the bell had left.

Nevertheless, when she opened it, she was confronted by a man wearing a black suit, a white shirt, and black tie. She told me how struck she was by the immaculate suit; its fit being absolutely flawless. When she related this all to me later that evening, she remarked on how perfect the cuffs and trousers were, and that the tailoring was so impossibly precise. She said, perhaps cynically, that she'd never seen a man with such razor-sharp creases in their trousers.

Then a further observation struck her, although he wore a pristine white shirt and tie, and it was a very hot July afternoon, there wasn't a single bead of perspiration on his face nor were there any sweat stains on his collar. His hair was black and combed back over his head and shone like it might have been coated in gel. But as Shelagh looked, she felt there was something artificial about the entire scene.

This man carried a black briefcase, and as with everything else about his appearance, it looked new and unused. Then her eyes wandered to a button-badge on his lapel. She looked at it, but try as she might, she couldn't seem to focus on it. The white shirt dazzled her, and the button-badge seemed to hold her hypnotically. Then she became aware of what was going on in the background, or more precisely, what *wasn't* going on in the background.

Even though the house was on a busy road and it was early afternoon, there was suddenly no traffic or pedestrians passing by. Oxford Road is a main arterial road into town so was heaving with traffic no matter the time of day. Not only was there an inexplicable absence of life, but everything else behind the man had now blurred out of focus; Shelagh told me that she was only able to focus on his badge. This hallucinogenic effect with its ability to shift her focus and hold it in place, and the empty street, was perhaps his way of saying:

I'm talking, so pay attention!

He then asked her if I was home. Shelagh told him I wasn't.

He smiled at her at that point, displaying perfectly white teeth: 'That's OK; I will come back another time.'

The house was above pavement level and reached by eight concrete steps. Then, as if things were not already strange enough, the man was suddenly two steps down from the front door, having made no physical movement at all. It was like a jump in film continuity.

He was now looking up at her and said: 'You both need to stop what you are doing, you really do.'

Still with no observable movement taking place, he was instantly on the pavement, and continuing to smile at her, He said: 'You need to stop it.'

Then, with the first physical activity she could recall, the mystery man turned and walked along the pavement. At that point, the spell was broken and she realised the street had returned to normal with it's familiar flow with traffic and pedestrians. It was only now that she also realised she hadn't heard a sound while the MIB was standing in front of her; this, she later described to me as 'dead silence'. Maybe this effect was similar to what we had experienced when the dinosaur appeared, but because that had happened during the early hours of the morning, and not mid-afternoon, it hadn't been as noticeable.

Shelagh walked down the steps wanting to see if he got into a car, because if he did, she wanted to memorise the license plate. But when she reached the pavement, he was nowhere to be seen. There was only one other road he could have gone along, just a few yards away and running alongside what was then a snooker hall. She went to have a look, to see if he had gone down this road; but no, he had vanished.

What struck me about this doorstep MIB, was his being invisible through the glass until she opened the door. Does this mean he would be unseen by anybody passing the house? Perhaps becoming visible only to Shelagh when she opened the door? Whatever the case, her perceptions were clearly being manipulated, perhaps because she was a psychic, and maybe this was being used against her. The sudden absence of local activity is often a signature for impending paranormal experiences.

The 'Oz Factor' is a term invented in 1983 by British researcher, Jenny Randles, to describe an altered state of consciousness commonly described by witnesses of paranormal and UFO phenomena. She has noted the strange calmness and lack of panic exhibited by witnesses, and they describe this 'Oz factor' as 'the sensation of being isolated, or shifting into an alternate state of reality. This reality is slightly different to normal, as in 'The land of Oz.'. This describes perfectly, the environmental characteristics when we saw both the dinosaur and our Men in Black.

I also felt that: *you need to stop what you are doing*, referred to the documenting of our experiences and publicising them to Clive Potter. However, the Man in Black's warning did no more than encourage a reckless streak within me, regardless of any consequences.

A couple of weeks after this encounter, we stumbled across a rather disturbing consequence to Shelagh's meeting with the MIB. I was curious about those inexplicable jumps he'd made to reach the pavement. That, as well as the hypnotic effect could indicate some kind of manipulation of her memory, so maybe her conscious recall was only part of the story. I was seriously starting to wonder if something might have happened that we were unaware of. Unfortunately, Shelagh hadn't noticed the time before and after his visit, so couldn't offer anything to support the suggestion.

These thoughts continued to nag at me until I suggested we contact Len - the man who had uncovered the abduction memory - and see if he could go over the MIB encounter with her. Shelagh had got to like and trust

Len, so it shouldn't have been a problem. Following the abduction regression, he gave her a number of sessions of relaxation therapy using hypnosis and gentle music, so she was no stranger to the process; in fact, she enjoyed the therapy, and always felt good for it. However, when I mentioned the MIB as a target of regression, she went into a state of near hysterical panic. For no reason she'd suddenly developed an inexplicable and paralysing fear of hypnosis. She believed - and I mean really believed - that to 'play around with it' would cause her permanent blindness. Prior to the MIB encounter, she had never once associated hypnosis with blindness.

To go blind was Shelagh's single fear in life. It was a terror she'd had since childhood, and as in the last couple of years she'd developed type-2 diabetes, the fear of blindness lurked very near and was a real threat. She couldn't even watch films if any of its characters were portrayed as blind. But where did this connection between regression to the MIB incident and her biggest fear come from? Had the MIB seeded the idea in her mind to prevent her doing the very thing I was suggesting?

A few months later, she did pluck up enough courage to attempt the hypnosis, and it took me a lot to convince her that she'd be safe. Len wasn't so sure, but went ahead as she was now insistent that she tried She knew she needed to combat this inexplicable fear regardless of the horror when she thought about it.

On his first attempt to put her under, she developed a migraine as soon as he started his countdown, so the session had to be aborted. The punishing migraine lasted days, and no amount of painkillers would touch it. The second attempt was a couple of weeks later, but this time she started crying as soon as he began the count. Nothing we said could stop her tears, and yet again, the session was halted; this time Len advised us to abandon the effort.

His guess was that somehow there were blocks in her mind, and that they were impossible to break through with Shelagh's fear before even starting. If he did manage to get through, he wasn't sure she'd like what was found on the other side. That chilling thought was enough for me to forget the whole idea. The MIB had beaten us, but thankfully that was the last we had seen of them for now.

Around this time, there was a development in my capabilities as a healer, and the Grey made itself seen to yet another witness.

The Healing Grey

From the time I started working within the Spiritualist Church, my healing ability increased significantly, and within just a few months. Some of this development was due to the training of what must have been latent abilities. However, this was fortified of a night by Red Eagle offering me alternative routes to heal, unorthodox even by Spiritualist standards.

Initially, I was of the belief that I was connecting with the patients' unconscious and 'hard-wiring' a positive healing suggestion into them, in a sense 'supercharging' their mind over matter. In conjunction with that, I was also connecting to the ailment through their astral bodies and healing them from the inside; detaching a fragment of my healthy energy and setting this within them to generate the healing. Somewhat like fitting them with a healing implant.

Shelagh comments:

As Red Eagle has been initiating Lucy as a shaman, her healing powers have developed significantly. In 1991, I spilt a cup of tea onto my bare feet, and received serious scalds to both, leaving me almost crippled. Lucy began healing, and within three weeks, my feet were virtually healed. The burn unit at the hospital were astounded at what they saw; the specialist even commented that such healing is a miracle. Lucy has progressed beyond 'laying-on-of-hands', now able to heal in a 'dislocated' state.

She can detach a fragment of her astral form, which will meld with the patients, and she will then heal by that means. A friend of mine discovered that she had cancer, and Lucy used her system to contain the disease, my friend is now very healthy. The same friend had a cat which was almost dead. Lucy brought it back from the edge, and it regained the health of a young cat. On another occasion, someone Lucy doesn't know, not even met, had a serious skin complaint with her face, a lot of bad sores. Lucy commenced her shamanic healing, and within a week or two, the skin was cleared. The doctors had told her it was incurable. In fact, the woman said the healing had started that very evening Lucy had been told about it.

In July 1991, Shelagh made a visit to a charity shop, and she noticed that the woman behind the counter wore a dress with a very high neckline. Because of the weather, this made her look hot and uncomfortable.

'Why are you not wearing anything cooler than that?' Shelagh asked.

The woman pulled her neckline down to reveal a scar that ran from throat to cleavage; it was very red, and prominent enough to warrant a high neckline, even in the summer heat. She then explained the heart operation and that perhaps having to wear high-necked tops were little price to pay. Shelagh mentioned knowing somebody who might be able to help with distance healing, and the woman was overjoyed and readily agreed to any help she could get, even just to ease the inflammation. Shelagh came home and gave me these details, and that very evening I commenced a procedure that Red Eagle had taught me. One week later, Shelagh returned to the shop and could see, by the expression on the woman's face, that there had been some improvement.

'Look!' she said without Shelagh having to ask. She pulled down her neckline and Shelagh saw the scar was no longer a deep angry red, but it was now white and not so prominent. It looked as though months of natural healing had taken place, compared to how it was only a week before. The lady told Shelagh that it was no longer irritating and uncomfortable, and that was what had been making her so very depressed. Shelagh asked for, and received, a signed testimony from the patient, and her daughter also added a handwritten comment to it:

At the beginning of the year, my mother was a very ill woman, but now is so much better.

It was because of encouraging results such as this, that I began regular healing activity from our home. This was offered free and was eagerly taken up by a number of people from the Spiritualist Church, which I still attended, but not as frequently as I once had. Three ladies came to me for regular sessions, a couple of times a week. Elizabeth Framley was a middle-aged lady; a widow, who had lost most of the use of her left side due to a stroke. She had attended the Church for healing, and had done so since the condition had struck three years previous. Now she stopped attending the Church and came to me instead. I felt this placed a tremendous sense of responsibility upon me, especially when she told me she came because her guides directed her to: 'I just felt I needed to,' she said.

The healing progressed remarkably well, even I was surprised it's speed, and yes, she also recovered some use of her left arm and hand, whereas her doctor had told her, she never would again. According to him, there was too much damage. It was during my healing sessions with Elizabeth that I learned something interesting from her. Opposite the chair in which my patients sat, was a wall mirror, and by chance rather than design, angled so patients could see my reflection as I stood behind them. After around eight sessions, Elizabeth told me that when my hands connected with her aura, she could see a change take place.

At first, she thought she was seeing an ET spirit guide. She said it often happened about ten minutes into the healing, and at a point when she began to feel a significant amount of heat from my hands that spread across her arm and left side. On the first occasion, she happened to open her eyes and glanced at the mirror, and instead of me, she saw a 'little Grey alien' healing her. I was unsure how to respond because I didn't want to frighten her away, so I agreed that it was probably working with me as a guide.

It was after a number of sessions, and having seen the Grey several more times, she told me in a rather matter-of-fact way: 'I don't think what I see is a guide, I think it's you. Something very profound happens when you heal.'

Elizabeth was a Spiritualist, in her 60s and like Shelagh, had experienced a great deal of phenomena in séance circles, so didn't seem unduly concerned that her healing might be courtesy of an ET source. In fact, I think she found it a refreshing change.

As for me, it was another indication that this particular Grey, whatever it was, had a desire to help humans. I remembered the first indication being when it showed its glowing white face to Shelagh, and I felt its affection for humanity. Affection and a desire to heal humans are not in the profile of a typical Grey, so was this one different? It was beginning to seem that way to me.

Plant Consciousness

Holding meaningful communication with plants might be a slightly more contentious subject, but maybe the following will serve as a good example: In my bedroom, there was a large palm plant, floor standing in its twenty-four-inch diameter pot, and standing a head taller than my five feet seven inches. This plant dominated the room in a literal sense, because it had been the only one there for a long time. Whenever we had to move house, I was sure to place it in my personal space.

Then one day I decided to move a smaller plant into the room where it might benefit from the better sunlit position. However, even as I picked the pot up, I sensed something brush against my mind. It could have been a flicker of resistance, perhaps a protest, but it had been so weak and fleeting that I chose to ignore it. Then, within just a few days, I noticed the once healthy and thriving new arrival beginning to wither at an alarming rate. This went on until eventually by the end of the third week it had dried out so much that I thought it might be dead. I had a feeling as to what had happened, but it was a ridiculous thought: plants displaying territorial aggression? However, by the end of that third week, I knew that if I didn't take the small victim out of the room, it would surely die. So back it went to its original spot in the dining room, and although it didn't receive quite as much sunlight, within days it revived and thrived as its former self.

What was the reason for the smaller plant's Near-Death Experience? The large plant that had dominated the room had been my near-constant focus of attention and I would even lie in bed of a night and talk to it. Having been the central feature of my room for so long, it had felt threatened in some way when I brought its cousin in. The palm plant had somehow been killing the smaller one. Was it draining the life-force? I had no idea at the time, I just knew the facts as I have described them. In our world this simply cannot happen, plants cannot express themselves. Or can they?

If that isn't crazy enough, try this: I was sitting in an armchair reading a book, and, of course, when you are sat comfortably, your mind is open and receptive, especially if you are listening to music or reading, which is probably what made this experience possible. Suddenly, I developed a rather bad taste in my mouth, as though there was a liquid that I wanted to spit out but were unable to. Opposite me, on a window ledge, a small pot plant seemed to draw my attention. As I looked at it, there was a bright spark of colour that flashed around it, just for a moment. That flash must have carried information, because as soon as I saw it, I knew that Shelagh had started adding something to its water - but the plant didn't like it and was appealing for it to be stopped. I asked Shelagh about it, and she confirmed it was true, she was adding a liquid that was supposed to aid growth and health, so I suggested she stopped doing it and to go back to plain tap water. The plant didn't disturb me after that, so presumably it was content once again. In our illusory world this simply cannot happen. Plants don't have deductive reasoning; they cannot make distinctions and pass that information on. Or can they?

One obstacle to my story being acknowledged as even remotely possible, might be that I was a White European living in a Berkshire town in England. I wonder how more acceptable it would be if I were a Native American, a Siberian or African shaman? It shouldn't matter, but it matters a great deal to the masses immersed so fully in this artificial and mechanistic reality, in which communication with the greater universe has been so nullified it might as well be switched off. To re-establish these channels, you first need to cultivate an elementary belief that you can extend your senses beyond this illusory world, and that you can develop both a clairsentient and clairaudient bridge between yourself and other life-forms. If you work to this end, and learn to trust your intuition, it's possible to share a communication with the life-forces around you. As with the case of pet owners, this empathic communication will evolve naturally over time. But at least it can be said that animals possess a brain through which they can define imagery and thought. Plants, however, are a whole different kind of evolution. It's without a brain, which places the process of communication at a most basic and rudimentary level of clairsentience, which means you are needing to sense their energy fluctuations, and learn to interpret that.

SHAPE-SHIFTING

Meeting Others

My correspondence with Clive Potter was intermittent and cautious to begin with, and it wasn't until December 1990, that I wrote him any detailed letters. It looked like things were going to move forward positively as over the course of several letters I explained our experiences, and he replied with questions that carried a genuine desire to know as much as we were willing to share. I even committed a lot of our paranormal history to cassette tape, I found that method to be more conversational and allowed me to express myself better than by letter.

I finally met him in January 1991, when he travelled down from Leicester to stay for a weekend of relaxed and informal chat. In his thirties, he topped six feet tall, slim build, and always smiling with a quick wit. Clive was Regional Organiser in the Midlands, for a major UFO research organisation and he seemed to have a genuine passion for the subject.

As he listened to us, he didn't make any remarks that questioned our sanity or made me feel like a fraud or a liar. That in itself was a breakthrough. We learned that Clive wasn't only continuing to investigate the experiencers mentioned in his article, but that he would like to try getting us all together, just as I had suggested in my introductory letter. This was the opportunity we needed, to meet others and end the isolation imposed by that lack of mutual contact.

By February 1991, meetings between us and one of those mentioned in the article had been arranged. This man, along with two of his female friends, who were also experiencers, travelled down from Coventry for a weekend visit that Shelagh and I had been eagerly looking forward to. However, as things turned out, we didn't have a great deal in common, and we mutually agreed that further contact wouldn't prove particularly constructive.

In focusing on communicating with other experiencers through Clive, it never occurred to me that he, rather than contact with other experiencers might be the reason for the MIB visits. Maybe I was underestimating Clive's value without realising it, as over the next few months, more experiencers came and went, and with each meeting we discovered our experiences were too diverse – in some cases contradicting each other - to find co-operation worthwhile.

Nonetheless, we continued with the meetings: an individual from Northampton, and others from various locations that I cannot now remember, all came into our home and spent anywhere from a couple of hours to a full weekend with us, but to our disappointment, as well as to Clive's mounting dismay, none of us found common ground on which we could cooperate. None of us felt we could achieve anything productively. Thus it went on, and it was soon realised that many of us seem to be compartmentalised in what we were doing.

Clive then decided that a wider audience should be hearing the ideas we were formulating, so he booked me to speak at a Northampton UFO conference in August that same year. I was excited and anxious now, things were starting to move forward rather swiftly.

When we got to Northampton, we found it was in a small hall with an equally small attendance, and as I had never spoken in public like this before, it was a comfortable situation for me to be in. I don't count the Spiritualist Church as speaking experience because that is guided by the disincarnate, not me. I was happy with how the talk went, and it seemed to be well received; with only a single hitch. One member of the audience planned to film my talk, so had brought a good-quality video camera with him to do just that.

Before my talk, I'd stood chatting with him and watched as he unwrapped and loaded fresh batteries into the machine, he then set his tripod in place and do a few tests to check everything was functioning as it should. I had rewritten some of the AI material, and although this content was nothing close to the originals that had vanished - too much had been lost for me to recall - fresh ideas had spilled from my mind and even read slightly better.

However, as good as it all went, and with many questions from the audience to follow, the camera failed to record anything, and I was very disappointed as I'd been anxious to get a copy of it. The mystified cameraman examined his equipment and found the batteries that he'd unwrapped and tested before use were completely drained. He managed to capture no more than ten seconds of film before it died. I heard from the cameraman a few days later; He said when he got home, he put another new set of batteries in and on testing the equipment found it was, once again, working properly. This effect on electrical equipment has happened to me on a number of occasions.

After the meeting, I went back to Clive's home for the remainder of the weekend. When I'd settled down with a mug of coffee, he told me he had something he wanted me to hear. He put a cassette tape into his player and I sat listening to a band who called themselves *Alien Agenda*. I had a variety of musical tastes, but rock music wasn't one of them. However, I was impressed with what I was hearing, and I could tell they were a bit different. There was something in what I heard that attracted me and this music managed to hold my attention all the way through the album. Clive said they were based in Gillingham, Kent.

Around the time of the Northampton meeting, I found some of my habits making an inexplicable change. First of all, It was smoking. I wasn't a heavy smoker, but had smoked regularly since the age of fifteen. About a week before this meeting I'd woken one morning and simply didn't want one. This continued from hours, into days and then into weeks. There was no withdrawal and it was as though I'd never smoked to begin with.

Alcohol went the same way. I wasn't much of a drinker, apart from socially; nonetheless, what little alcohol consumption I had also suddenly ceased. I also went vegetarian and my food intake became both minimal and healthy. I hadn't made plans for any of this to happen, and it all started in the same week. This new regime remained in place for the next ten years, aside from smoking, which never resumed.

I was undergoing a detoxification. I know this is because Red Eagle had said some time before, that I would need to undergo a 'purification' but had refused to tell me why or when it would happen, so it was only a couple of weeks into abstinence that I realised what was actually happening.

The Recording

Later that same year, the British UFO Research Association (BUFORA) and the Independent UFO Network (IUFON) were holding their Sixth International Congress in Sheffield. I initially decided not to go as I had a hospital appointment that would prevent me from being a speaker, which had been my original plan.

Then from the advertising I noticed that *Alien Agenda* would be performing their first gig in the North of England, even at this stage it had not yet hit me that this might have been the band that the Grey had identified some years before. With prompting from Clive I was encouraged to make a last minute decision to attend the congress. It was only after I had made the decision to go that I felt a frisson of excitement as, only now, I recalled the information gleaned from the Grey eight years previously.

I had told Clive about my advance notice of him coming onto the scene, and had also mentioned the unknown band. He now nodded in silent wonder as I watched this group perform live on stage and told him this was *definitely* the band we needed to speak to before the weekend was over. So at some point during the two-day congress, Clive made his acquaintance with them and in turn introduced me as an interesting contactee with a history of original and consistent experiences.

So sitting quietly outside the conference centre, I told the band some of my history. I remember John, the vocalist and lead guitarist shaking his head in wonder and remarking that it was all very heavy stuff. Nevertheless, he found it fascinating, especially when I went on to tell them about my seeing them come into play some years back, and that it surely must mean *Alien Agenda.* Somewhere in this conversation John said they were looking for another band member and asked if I could play guitar. I smiled at the sudden image popping into my head of me playing rock music. I told him I definitely wouldn't make a rock musician and so ended the shortest interview in history for a new band member.

John's Testimony

We remained in contact over the next few months and it was one of Lucy's letters that revealed she and Clive were doing a paper based on her experiences. This would probably be in the form of a talk at a conference or as a series of articles in a UFO magazine. The paper was almost complete by late 1991 and had also included the experiences of a close friend of Lucy's. The important contribution made by Shelagh will become apparent as this record of events unfolds.

During the correspondence I began to wonder if this paper could be applied in audio and include the witnesses speaking of their experiences, with sound effects and music where appropriate, added in our own time in the studio. It would be intriguing to work with the witnesses and certainly an interesting medium to put across their experiences.

I put this idea to Lucy around Christmas 1991 and she was very interested and, along with Shelagh and Clive, were eager to go ahead as soon as possible; So we began working out how it could be done. We would have to meet to get various voices recorded and this would have to be a time that suited everyone. We all agreed it would be started around February 1992. We continued to correspond and work out what recording equipment we would need to take with us.

I and the other band members, Terry and Andy, left Gillingham on a chilly but sunny Friday morning. In the Transit van were the four track recorder, microphones and other essential recording equipment. The idea was to tape the individuals on Saturday and leave by Sunday afternoon. On return to Gillingham, we would then mix and insert effects and music where required. Through past correspondence we knew they had their scripts spot on and we had been sent copies.

We arrived in Reading just before lunch and were greeted by the trio who were extremely happy to see we'd made it having had little problem with traffic. We unloaded the van and Lucy showed us to our rooms, one of which was to be used as a small studio. So after some much needed food we began to set the gear up and all agreed we would start recording around lunchtime on Saturday, hopefully being finished by teatime. The rest of Friday afternoon and evening was spent chatting about various subjects and downing a few welcome beers.

My personal impression of our hosts was that they were all seriously involved and very knowledgeable on the subject of UFOs and the paranormal in general. Clive was businesslike in his approach. He emphasized his eagerness to get this material out to the public and how seriously he viewed this particular case. Clive, like the rest of us, relaxed more as the evening went on and was soon discussing the various processes involved in recording.

Shelagh was a lovely, kind woman. She freely discussed her various strange experiences connected to the paranormal and the effects it had on her life. All of Shelagh's experiences were extremely interesting and very believable. She would relate these events in her life in a very matter of fact manner and lots of what she said was parallel to our own experiences with the paranormal. She seemed to accept these incidents as a normal part of everyday life. Shelagh was a very genuine person.

Lucy was so obviously different from the others. She had an inquisitive mind and would move easily from one subject to another, wanted to know about our gigs, the instruments we played, the song writing, how and why we did it all. She was also very interested in our own UFO and paranormal experiences and was a good listener who could maintain an intellectual conversation. We questioned her with regard to her talk on the album we were about to make and she would always reply in detail. Lucy left us in no doubt that she was completely sincere in what she was going to state on the recordings. Meeting all three in person, helped our confidence and made the long journey with all the equipment, more satisfying.

We woke quite early on Saturday and after breakfast, Terry took Clive and Shelagh into the room for some test recordings. I remained in the lounge with Lucy and Andy. Chatting away with regards to how the recording would go. It was during this relaxed conversation when Lucy asked me had I slept OK. I replied I did and had a good rest. She then asked if I remembered sitting in the lounge around 3am with her and an Indian spirit guide.

I have to say, I burst into laughter. "No, I replied, I don't remember that at all!" She said we had discussed various aspects of life, both here and elsewhere; the Indian guide was also very interested in what we were doing. I have to say that although I believe a spiritual side exists I do find it difficult to comprehend; nevertheless I took great interest in what Lucy was telling me. Maybe I was visited in the night by Lucy and the entity, if I was, it's relevance was to be made shockingly clear to me within the next few hours.

I had taken loads of photographs, both on the journey to Reading and at the house, the camera battery was now getting very low. So before we started the recordings I decided to go into the town centre to search for batteries; Lucy, Clive and Andy joined me. The batteries were a special type and before we could find a specialist camera shop, I wondered if Boots department store might be worth a look, and as it turned out they did have them. Although I had the camera with me, I chose not to put the batteries in there and then, I would do that later at the house. This means I had a useless camera around my neck as we walked out onto the street – probably the only moment in my life when I really needed it!

On leaving the store, Clive held the door as Lucy, then me, followed by Andy, began to head out into the street. There was nothing particular in my mind at this moment apart from the fact that I had got the batteries and would be able to get more photos later.

The next moment can only be described as a massive shock to say the very least: As Clive held the door and Lucy began to exit the store, I saw her body 'break' at the waist and the top half fall over to the left. Although I could still clearly see her torso, a definite image of a small Grey took shape in the place it had occupied before 'breaking'. The grey torso then also fell over to the left as if overcome by gravity, before suddenly shooting back into an upright position. It was visibly smaller than Lucy and I was looking down at it. This was immediately followed by Lucy's lower body suddenly vanishing and being replaced by the lower half of the Grey.

This creature took a few steps round Clive and into the street. I immediately followed it and as I entered the street it had returned to being Lucy's body as normal. The Grey was visible for only six to eight seconds.

As he let the door go, Clive fell behind me and I made a wide berth around Lucy as the sights and sounds of Reading suddenly came crashing in around me. Only at that point did I realize that everything had gone quiet and very still when I was staring at the Grey. Lucy was talking about Reading in general and acting very normal.

I couldn't concentrate on where we were going and just kept thinking: Did I just imagine that? Is she aware of what just happened? *I moved in front of her and kept glancing back at Lucy but she still appeared oblivious to what had happened. I think I had hoped for some reaction from her – anything - but there was nothing. My expression of shock must have been more obvious than I thought because she asked if I was OK, I replied that I was fine and just a bit tired. But, of course I was far from fine and I wasn't tired at all.*

As we continued to wander around Reading I became deaf to the conversation and blind to what was going on around me. I was deep in my thoughts as I continually cross-examined myself. Did I really see that happen? And if I had, why would it occur as we left a department store and entered a busy street? Why did it not happen in the house some other location where it would have allowed closer examination? Did it wish to be seen? Why did no one else see it? My mind constantly interrogated me for the remainder of our walk.

As the reality of the busy street became more apparent and my mind exhausted, it began to feel comfortable to dismiss this unexpected and bizarre incident as imagination.

Of course, I couldn't do that. I had seen this monstrous little Grey in perfect detail, and its darting movements were quite menacing and deliberate. I admit it, I was scared to accept what I was seeing, but I still took in as much as possible. In hindsight, I'm glad I didn't turn away.

I recognized the Grey through sketches and reports made by many UFO witnesses over the years and accepted immediately that this was what I saw. If I didn't recognize it as a Grey, its movements and appearance would have had been convinced I was looking at some form of demonic materialization. On the way back to the house I resolved myself to confront Lucy with what I had seen. I didn't feel comfortable putting such a preposterous idea directly to her, so decided to question her in a roundabout way.

 Upon arrival back at the house, Terry suggested that he and Lucy get some recording started, so they went to do that while Shelagh, Clive, Andy, and I retired to the lounge. After a few minutes I plucked up the courage to ask Shelagh and Clive. "How did Lucy do that trick?"

Both of them gave me a strange look. Clive replied with a question of his own: "What trick was that?"

I knew what I saw and just told them that I felt they knew

something about Lucy that me, Terry Andy did not. I could now see them becoming increasingly uncomfortable by the moment, and that's when I knew I was onto something. Shelagh said she would go and make a pot of tea while Clive said he would call Lucy to come down and deal with this. When Lucy did arrive in the room, I asked her how she had done what she did in town, how did she change.
Lucy turned to Clive and simply said "tell him."

'"Are you sure?" Clive seemed cautious, but turned towards me and asked me outright, "Did you see Lucy's body change?"

I replied yes, I had. He then asked, "Did she change into an alien?" I again replied to the affirmative. Clive's face remained very pale as I asked him why he should immediately think of something so bizarre. He ignored my question and became very excited. He grabbed a pen and notebook and started asking me to describe exactly what had happened. While taking notes, he told me it had happened twice before. Two other people had also witnessed Lucy's transformation in recent years and although recorded, was never made public or mentioned within the UFO fraternity. Seemingly it was the same creature I had witnessed, although on both occasions it had ended during transformation

I certainly hadn't heard anything about this and I must admit that had I known, it may have affected my stay in the house. I learned Shelagh too, was a witness to this shape-shifting, and she related her experience telling me that while retiring one night, Lucy sat on the edge of the bed and with her face just inches from hers, her face transformed into a shining Grey alien. She seemed content that I too had witnessed a similar event. The difference was that I had seen a full body Grey, it had totally transformed from being a human. After the initial excitement died down I was ready to ask Lucy some serious questions, and my approach was like that of a prosecutor in a courtroom. I had to ask everything now, while the incident was still fresh in my mind.

Lucy was fairly relaxed and as we all listened, she pieced together the jigsaw that was her bizarre life. I asked what she felt while walking out onto the street and she said she was aware that it was happening, and that she had found it difficult to breathe the atmosphere. Apparently during those few seconds of transformation, she had been hit by a light-headedness, and her lungs felt as though they were burning. I asked, did she feel she was being used? Her reply perplexed me even more when she said "To a certain extent". Her knowledge and seemingly interactive involvement with these beings had surely unlocked a doorway and allowed them through. She agreed this was very possible and through recent dreams and flashes she knew they were close.

She was particularity interested that the metamorphosis was now a full-bodied Grey. I believe Lucy knew what was going on and was calmly accepting her strange existence with these creatures. She knew exactly where her future lay and that her entire range of experiences were shamanic in nature. I asked about her past, but this, too, was clouded in mystery. Clive sat in silence and continued to take notes as part of his ongoing investigation into this bizarre case. He seemed surprised at some of Lucy's replies and admitted the discussions with Lucy and myself were extremely productive to his investigation. I gathered Clive had usually kept his questioning aimed at Lucy's particular case and not her past life in general.

Sometime during the evening Clive asked me to sign a paper to confirm that I witnessed Lucy's transformation, and I did this without hesitation. I fully understand the reliability problems in relation to witness testimony so was happy to oblige, and would do so again if necessary.

Terry broke up the chat by asking Lucy to return to the studio where serious recording now began. All three had their separate scripts and were cued when to come in. Terry handled the recordings very well and after checking through the results, we finished around 8pm. The recording, for us, was fairly easy and the real work would happen back home in Gillingham, where we would add everything else.

During the recording there was the chance to watch each individual as they spoke their piece. Sincerity and confidence showed in all their faces, yet the more I watched and listened, the more I wondered exactly who was doing the talking. Who conjured this deep, meaningful mind boggling talk? A strange feeling of someone or something utilizing them came to mind.

Up until now it was good fun; it was what Alien Agenda did - meeting with UFO witnesses, gathering info and expanding our knowledge of the subject. But this was proving to be something a little more than just that. All the band members agreed there had been an eerie atmosphere during the recording sessions.

Lucy, Clive and Shelagh easily accepted that other uninvited guests, alien or spiritual, were within the room, listening and watching the proceedings. There was a strange presence in that room. I felt a presence of some kind throughout the house. Was it the same presence that moves into and out of Lucy's body? I have to admit that I had a problem sleeping on the Saturday night! We woke quite early on Sunday and after breakfast we discussed promotion and packaging of the project.

Various ideas were put forward with regard to the cover design and advertising the album. When everything was ready, we would send Lucy copies from master tapes and they could make up their own from these.

After packing all the gear into the van, we sat for a while talking about the weekend and hoped it was worth the input. The conversation inevitably drifted back to the spiritual and alien side of things. I'm still not convinced of exactly what was *present in the room during recording, or of what I witnessed in town, but I'm certain there was a presence of some kind.*

Clive's Testimony

We found a department store with a photographic shop, brought what we required and then headed for the street. I opened the door and this caused me to turn at an angle away from Lucy. Lucy than followed through, going round the back of me to leave the store.

It was at this point, to John's utter amazement, that he saw Lucy's upper body bend sharply over to the left until it was parallel with the ground. As the torso hung at this angle John could suddenly see the image of an alien body, also leaning over with her own form, it's left arm hanging limply as if in response to gravity – implying that this image had mass.

He said he couldn't see the right arm, so presumably it was hanging limply as well, therefore hidden by the body. He also noted that the head was hairless and the same dull grey as the body. Up until this point, the lower half of Lucy's body remained normal. The Grey was sucked swiftly to an upright position in one movement, and as it settled onto the waist and legs, John now noticed that the lower half had now changed to match the Grey alien form. The now complete transformation was, by John's judgement, about four feet tall.

By now all John can see is the Grey entity and me. To all intents and purposes Lucy has disappeared from existence. Remember, the way in which I opened the door forced me to turn at an angle, so the consequences of that means the entity passed my back – it was totally in my blind-spot. As the entity passed my back, it took a sharp right, thereby passing my left side.

Going out onto the street and then passing on my left side, caused it to be obscured momentarily from John's view, because he was several feet behind the Grey, but when he got out the door and had the thing in view again, he found it had turned back into Lucy's human form. As soon as John was clear of the shop doors, he took a wide berth around both Lucy and me.

Having left the department store, we then headed for a music shop because John wanted to compare some prices, but for the remainder of our walk John stayed ahead of us. This resulted in Lucy and I having to call ahead to give him directions as he didn't know Reading at all. During later questioning, he said that he felt he'd been manoeuvred into having to observe the transformation, and that he didn't have any control of the situation at all. So he stayed ahead of us, not wanting to chance it happening again!

It wasn't until we got back to the house that John broached the subject of his experience in town. Remember, I already had on record the previous experiences of what Shelagh, Julian and Elizabeth Framley had seen Lucy turn into, so when I did eventually hear what John had to say, it didn't hit me with the same kind of impact it would otherwise have done. John's caution at raising the subject is apparent in the text of his testimony. I quote:

"I chose to approach Shelagh and Clive with the incident at a time when Lucy was doing some recording with Terry, because I felt this would be less embarrassing than putting Lucy on the spot with such an experience delivered without warning."

John then started to speak with some caution, so much so that the inevitable cryptic statements were made, starting with:

"I saw something very unusual happen with Lucy while we were out."

At this remark Shelagh and I must have given meaningful looks because John noticed this and leapt on it immediately:

"Two of you know something that two of us don't!"

Meaning Shelagh and I knew something between us as opposed to him and Andy. This went on until, in the words of John's own testimony:

"I then realised that we could skirt what we wanted to say all night, so I thought, To Hell with it, come out and say it. I then told them what had happened."

So John told us what he'd witnessed, and as an investigator this was almost a 'Holy Grail' experience for me. Here I was observing an independent witness grapple with his own emotions and feelings as he attempted to explain something completely without parallel in his past – for me it was an almost unprecedented moment. I was getting a spontaneous account of Lucy's shape-shifting – at a point where a witness is dealing with the experience at a personal level – usually before they even start thinking of reporting it to whoever they consider may be appropriate.

Shelagh and I really would have preferred Lucy to deal with this herself, so with her consummate skill as a hostess, Shelagh managed to get out of giving any direct answers to John by suggesting she go and make a fresh pot of tea, while I called Lucy down.. In later testimony, John knew through this singular act that he was onto something. Shelagh and I had got out of the room to decide how to handle it. For me, without any doubt, this situation supported Shelagh's claims, and to some extent offered substance to claims Lucy had made in private to me about herself.

With the tea made, I managed to get Terry and Lucy away from the recording for a break. Almost as soon as Lucy was in the room, Shelagh told her that John had something he wished to tell her. So, John, knowing it was all or nothing, launched into his experience. At the end of his dialogue, Lucy didn't offer any input – but I know that this is how she normally reacts. Instead, she told me that I could tell John what Shelagh had seen happen to her.

I interviewed John several times following this experience and his testimony remained absolutely consistent with the original. In fact, in the interviews John was able to demonstrate his keen and accurate memory for facts, recalling many small and irrelevant details. Therefore, I am more than happy with these more extraordinary observations he made, and about the smallest details he claimed he could take in about the incident.

From my own point of view, I had some idea of what was happening, it was a stage further in an 'acclimatisation' process evolving from that which Shelagh and Julian had witnessed previously. What I remember of this latest incident is as follows:

We were about to leave the store and walk out onto Reading's Broad Street when I suddenly felt a thought flick through my mind that it was going to happen. I foresaw the entire sequence happen within the space of a moment.

My response was: *no, not here, not in the street!*

My concern was that a mass of people might see the Shift taking place and I imagined all kinds of panic. Of course, nothing bothered to tell me that only John would be able to see it.

As I reached the doors I was overwhelmed with light-headedness and pressure hitting me from all sides and squeezing my body, but not like the 'trapped in amber' effect. This was a lighter effect that still allowed movement. After the discomfort that accompanied the previous Shifts, I was convinced there were serious issues with the atmosphere, and because of that, it was difficult to both maintain the Grey for any length of time and assure the safety of my human form.

In fact, now it was happening outside, I felt I would die if this had been sustained long-term, I was finding breathing so painful! I passed behind Clive who at that most crucial moment had his back to me. Poor Clive! He had been with us a few years now, monitoring us and steadfastly accumulating data, but this one experience was eluding him. However, as you see from his and John's testimony, Clive was able to glean a great deal of valuable information from this experience.

Our production of the tape went on to do reasonably well, especially as advertising wasn't particularly well achieved. Although the production had been intended as a limited edition, we did end up selling close to a thousand copies.

Final Conference

In September of that year, I attended the BUFORA Sheffield UFO Congress once again, but this time Clive had arranged for me to be a speaker, as he had continued to do at a number of other smaller venues. I really felt I had undergone experiences that might be of value for others to hear, so was always eager to get out there and tell it. So for my first major venue I had chosen to describe Shelagh's MIB encounter; the talk fitted nicely into a one-hour slot and could be explained well with slides we had produced in order to depict the events graphically.

We also went armed with several dozen copies of our recording, and I was very excited about taking these tapes with me, it was the first public exposure of it and I had visions of it selling by the thousands! The conference talk went well and I was both terrified and excited at being on that platform in front of a packed conference of hundreds. I also felt apprehension for a different reason, suppose that as I at stood under those glaring lights I shape-shifted? How would everyone react if it happened here and now?

But I need not have worried, since no such thing happened and alas the cassette tape didn't sell well. I think we sold two from a stall in the foyer, and that was handled by a renowned sceptic who would have done nothing to promote our product. Nor did the band themselves do anything much to promote either ours, or their own work. I don't think advertising is a strength that any of us possessed or had even prepared for. I think we assumed it would somehow sell itself.

I know that although we had sat and discussed all this with the band, little was actually done in our run-up to its launch, so all the effort put into what had been a very promising period of teamwork, didn't come to much and the project effectively died soon after its birth. Looking at it with hindsight, I find much of the production boring and unenlivened. I think the only part that had an edge of tension was the reproduction of Shelagh's abduction, taken from our notes at the time and re-enacted. I am kind of glad it didn't do too well, since I know so much more now and many things are different to how I viewed them then. I was still in a process of growth and my main work still wouldn't even begin for a few years yet. I thought it already had - but I was very wrong.

I enjoyed the conference, and even made contact with an author, who I had been specifically seeking for some months. I sat with him to discuss initial ideas for a joint writing venture, without any realisation that this conference was a turning point, and was to be the end of my very brief public speaking career, and this in turn would lead to the end of my relationship with Clive.

There were to be severe repercussions for talking openly about the MIB visits, and the next fourteen years of my life were to be the most testing of all; ultimately turning me into something very different. Something capable of fully interacting within a truly alien environment.

THE DESCENT

The Spark

On July 25 1993, Clive did his own début talk at the 7th BUFORA International UFO Congress, held at the University of Bristol. For his presentation he chose to describe the shape-shift in Reading town centre. Armed with his notes and a series of slides that he'd prepared from the photographs take by John, he gave a concise account of what took place. This talk was the spark to the tinderbox.

I have watched the video recording of his talk and when you consider he had never stood and spoke before an audience before - nerve-racking experience even for many established speakers - it went extremely well. In addition, it's risky enough to defy Men in Black by ignoring their warnings; worse still to stand up and tell the world precisely what they warned you to keep quiet about.

That really is inviting trouble!

However, Clive talking about shape-shifting Grey aliens in a Berkshire town centre was obviously a bit too much for most of his audience to swallow, and so far as I could tell, regardless of the fact he had witness testimony from John as well as the historical records from Shelagh and Julian, most of the remarks made to him were either sceptical of the whole thing, or so full of questions that Clive was left floundering for answers.

One of the audience asked the usual question regarding whether I might possibly have mental health issues, and I find it astonishing how often my own mental stability comes into question. When the talks were done for the day and everyone socialising in the bar, Clive was all but ignored, even by the conference organisers who bypassed him with barely an acknowledgement. There were one or two curious members of the public who did speak to him, but with the negative reception Clive's talk received, plus what was to follow as a result of him speaking out, it wasn't worth the price we had to pay.

Final Threat

In September 1993, six weeks after Clive's presentation in Bristol, I woke during the night with a feeling of somebody in the room. I could feel eyes watching me. I was still quite euphoric from the previous September's conference and as a consequence, had met a couple of researchers with whom I'd made initial plans to work with, there was also still interest from the author regarding a joint project, and I was very optimistic about this because his previous book had been on a similar theme to my own experiences, and had even helped support the authenticity of what we were dealing with.

But by the following morning, everything would all change.

The feeling of being watched persisted and eventually I eased myself up onto my elbow and peered into the gloom, but saw nothing. I squinted a moment longer before falling back onto the pillow, but the sensation of something continuing to watch me became strong enough to force me from bed and walk cautiously towards the corner of the room. I could sense that there was something wrong and I couldn't figure out what it was. My curtains were slightly parted, allowing moonlight to bathe most of the room apart from the obvious shadows where the lunar glow didn't reach.

Then I realised what seemed to be wrong - the corner of the room that I was walking towards, should have been in moonlight, but it wasn't; nor was it in shadow. It was plunged into blackness. In fact, it was more than just blackness, it was as though that part of the room had been erased and nothing but a black rectangle remained. It was like a black doorway. I walked towards it with that feeling of being watched becoming ever stronger.

Then I saw him, a man stepping out of that darkness. I rationalised that I hadn't spotted him because of his black suit – but it didn't cross my mind for one moment that he shouldn't have been in my bedroom to begin with! It might have been the same man I had opened the door to, and if it wasn't him, it was his twin. Also, as with the first MIB I encountered, I cannot say for sure if this one spoke to me, or if it was telepathic.

At this point I realised that it wasn't shadow behind the man but rather it was some kind of portal, a doorway like the 'Event Void Singularity' I had encountered on my bedroom wall in Shelagh's marital home years before. Back then, the emptiness had urged the Grey to step into it, but this time, it wasn't a swirling black-hole; it was clearly defined doorway through which he'd stepped. But from where?

You really have gone too far now. That thought pounded into my mind.

'What do you mean?' I whispered back.

You have been warned not to keep doing these things. To not tell people. Now you need to pay the price for ignoring the advice you were given.

'I don't understand.' I shook my head, but I couldn't take my eyes off him. 'I don't understand what you mean.'

Those who are connected with you and all this, will have to pay for your stupidity.

Although encounters with Men in Black can often assume unreal and dreamlike qualities, I am absolutely certain this wasn't a dream.

Immediately after being informed that people around me would pay for my folly, I found myself waking with early morning light filtering through the curtains. It had been as a dream, yet I didn't believe it was a dream. I could still feel that thing touching my mind, and to just think of that strange encounter filled me with dread. For the first time in my adult life I was very scared. What worried me was that the contact had just 'switched off' and in the next moment I was waking up in the morning. What might have been said or done that I couldn't remember? How had I got back to bed with no memory of doing so?

I got dressed and went downstairs to find Shelagh, and coffee. She pointed at the table where envelopes were waiting for me.

'Post,' she said. 'There's a letter for you.'

I saw one of the familiar bulging envelopes, a trademark of the constant mail communication between Clive and myself. I always enjoyed getting my correspondence from him. It was the highlight of my week to sit and read them through several times over. But today I felt a chill shudder its way through me:

Those who are connected with you, and all this, will have to pay for your stupidity.

Had it meant Clive? I took my coffee and sat in an armchair, leaving the post on the table. I just didn't want to touch it. I couldn't.

On reflection, I feel there was more to the MIB communication than just the statements I could recall, just as we thought was the case with Shelagh's recollection of her own visitor. I sat there with an irrational thought that to even touch that envelope could be passing a death sentence on my friend. This might have been a subliminal warning lodged into my subconscious by the MIB, but I also remembered how a colleague of Clive's had been attacked a couple of years previously. It had been so sudden, and so swift that we could do nothing to prevent it. The speed of her degeneration had been horrific.

I had only known her for five months before a malignant entity took her to pieces mentally and emotionally within the space of just three weeks. So it was, that as I sipped my coffee and stared at the post, I recalled the shocking demise of Sylvia.

Shadowman

Sylvia was an associate of Clive's and training to be an accredited investigator for a UFO organisation. She was in her mid-40s, single and living in Birmingham with her German shepherd dog. Clive wanted to get her involved in our case as some fieldwork experience, and so, with our permission, started bringing her along when he visited. In fact, as she drove a car, Sylvia made transport much easier for Clive, who until now had been getting the train to Reading.

Sylvia took great interest in our experiences and everything went along fine to begin with. She did seem rather fanatical about conspiracy theories and was utterly convinced that, among many other things, she was being subjected to eavesdropping on the phone. Allegedly this was because she knew things that 'they' would rather she didn't, so there was a tendency towards paranoia from the outset and this may have been a weakness that was to be exploited.

Then one day Clive suggested that Shelagh, Sylvia himself, and I, meet another experiencer who lived in the Midlands. Not only was this experiencer going through things that might have connections with what we were doing, but he was another of those mentioned in Clive's *Awareness* magazine article.

Clive's idea was still that a number of experiencers should gather together and throw their ideas into the ring and see what happened. Maybe something could be learned from it, maybe not, either way, it was a good idea and we were enthusiastic about it.

We decided on an appropriate weekend, which would be sooner rather than later because we were due to have a visitor from the United States. Her plan was to spend a week with Shelagh and me, then go to Leicester for two weeks with Clive. He was going to take her on a sightseeing tour of the North of England and Scotland. So the arrangements were made and Shelagh and I travelled up to Birmingham on Friday 18 April 1991, to stay with Sylvia for the weekend. On Sunday 20th, we'd meet up with Clive and go to the home of the experiencer, called Tom, for an afternoon of chatting and sharing experiences.

I began to feel deeply uneasy about this meeting from the moment we arrived at Sylvia's home, and as the Friday evening progressed, that feeling intensified. For some reason I was starting to feel that this meeting was a 'trap', but that thought just didn't make any sense and I even wondered if some of Sylvia's own paranoia was beginning to rub off onto me. But very soon I had reason to believe my concerns had some substance to them after all, because on the Saturday evening as we sat watching television, Shelagh suddenly saw we had a visitor standing in the room. A protector making herself known.

Back in her witchcraft years, Shelagh had worked with a coven member who became a very close friend. Like Shelagh, Doreen Simmonds was a psychic and Spiritualist, and The friendship between this pair lasted from 1962 up to Mrs Simmonds' death in 1976. But it didn't seem to stop there, because Mrs Simmonds attachment to Shelagh was strong enough to draw her as a spirit guide, a kind of guardian angel, and she would always be around if there was likely to be a traumatic situation.

So when Mrs Simmonds suddenly appeared to Shelagh on this Saturday evening I knew my unease had substance, especially as up until now, I hadn't voiced my concerns about a 'trap' to either Shelagh or Sylvia.

'Oh, that's most unexpected; Mrs Simmonds is standing in the corner of the room.' Shelagh suddenly stated as a very matter-of-fact comment.

Sylvia asked who she was talking about, and Shelagh explained. Then when she'd finished, and without giving a thought to what I was saying, I said, 'I think she's here because there might be an attack made against us.'

This threw Sylvia into spasms of laughter, and I had to get a glass of water to help calm her down. For Sylvia, the funny side of things was over how this 'dead human' could possibly stand between us and an 'alien attack'. I tried to explain that I never said there would be an 'alien attack' but I could imagine it being a non-human consciousness using psychic energy against us, and that we really ought to be prepared, regardless of whether we chose to believe it or not. I then told them how I'd been feeling all through Friday and for most of Saturday, and that I could not pin-point any logic for my trepidation. All I knew with some certainty was that 'something' would be passed to someone in a way that would cause a state of irreparable damage.

Sylvia spent the remainder of that evening, having a great time cracking jokes about this dead old spiritualist confronting dark occult powers, and there was little that either Shelagh or I could say that would stop her mirth. I even told her she should consider taking it as seriously as she did her conspiracy theories, but I was wasting my time and I am certain that her flippant attitude contributed to her subsequent undoing.

We arrived at Tom's home early Sunday afternoon, and as soon as I walked into the room I saw what the threat really was. There was a 'something' standing behind the chair which Tom went across to sit in. I never had an opportunity to find out enough about Tom to try understanding where this thing might have originated from, or why it might have wanted to target our little group. But I knew for sure it wanted to break us apart and to do as much damage as it could.

The seating was arranged so that when we sat on the couch and armchairs, we were all lined up like ducks in a shooting gallery, while Tom and his wife sat in armchairs opposite us. I had the unnerving suspicion that this thing was poised to launch an attack on each of us. How and why, I had no idea.

All I could see of this thing was a black featureless outline of a human torso which was very tall, well over seven feet and close to the height of the ceiling, and it was a solid block with nothing to distinguish arms or legs. But the single feature that did stand out was two blazing white dots where eyes would have been.

I could sense this thing scrutinising each of us in turn. Its searchlight glare swept past me without pausing and settled on Shelagh. Then I saw what I perceived as a pair of extremely thin, steel needles about three inches long on the end of a hair-thin silver filament lance from its forehead, aimed straight at her. It seemed to be deflected by something I couldn't see. Glancing just several inches from Shelagh's own forehead, I saw the 'harpoon' fall to the floor and vanish. Then the eyes of the Shadow Being moved to Clive, pausing on him for just a moment before moving to, and remaining on, Sylvia.

The reason I assume it couldn't penetrate Shelagh is because over the years, we had built a substantial protective wall around the both of us, and then with Clive's arrival on the scene, we worked at putting some shielding around him as well. I decided we should do this because if I had been able to anticipate his arrival a number of years previously, it placed a value on him that might require looking after, and he might need that protective wall at some point. Unfortunately, Sylvia had been with us for just a couple of months and we had no time at all in which to put any kind of help in place, nor had we suspected any reason why we should, and this made her a weakness, especially with her obsessive paranoia.

The Shadow Being fired its 'harpoon' at Sylvia and I watched helplessly as it embedded itself into her forehead. I couldn't react as I wanted to, because Tom's wife and children were in the room, and I certainly didn't want to scare them. As soon as the 'needles' penetrated Sylvia's forehead, she clutched her head and winced in sudden pain.

I knew she couldn't see the Shadow Being, nobody in the room could, apart from me, but Sylvia's physical reaction was evidence that she had felt the assault take place. I sat feeling useless as over the next ten to fifteen minutes Sylvia became increasingly distressed, her expression being an indication that the pain was worsening by the minute, and getting so bad she could barely remain still in her seat.

Eventually, I thought of a possible way of escape for her, I asked if she wanted to go get some air and smoke a cigarette. She said that was a good idea, it might clear her head. I doubted that it would do that much, and I knew what we really needed to do was get her away from the house as quickly as possible. But I I just smiled and accompanied her from the house.

As we rose from our chairs, the needles disengaged, fell to the floor and evaporated. When we were out in the fresh air and she was puffing furiously on a cigarette, I explained what had happened. As I expected, she confirmed that she'd seen nothing, but had suddenly developed a blinding pain across her forehead. Now that she knew about the Shadow Being, I asked if she'd like us to make our excuses and leave, which I fervently hoped and even expected her to agree with. Imagine my surprise when she said she'd be OK and would like to stay longer. I knew it wasn't a good idea even as I followed her back into the house.

As soon as she sat down, the Shadow Being fired another harpoon which again embedded deeply into her forehead - where the Third Eye chakra is located. I had no way of knowing what this thing was doing to Sylvia, aside from giving her a dreadful band of pain across her forehead, but I knew it had to be doing more than just that.

Another fifteen or twenty minutes passed before I suggested she go for another cigarette. I went with her and again, the Shadow Being broke its connection. When we were in the daylight I could see how pale Sylvia had become, and knew this wasn't doing her any good at all. So I insisted that we drew things to a close and go home, reluctantly she agreed as she scrunched her cigarette butt into the driveway.

We went back in and with hurried excuses, ushered our very puzzled companions to their feet and guided them towards the front door, leaving an equally puzzled Tom behind us. As we drove back to Birmingham, I spent the journey explaining to Shelagh and Clive what I had seen and Sylvia backed it up with what she had felt. Arriving in Birmingham to the tail-wagging welcome of her dog, we thought we'd had a lucky escape.

We were wrong.

Usurpers

In the first three months that we'd known Sylvia, she hadn't shown signs of any psychic ability, and most certainly not mediumship. So imagine our astonishment when, just a week on from the Shadow Being attack, I received a letter from her telling me she could see an Egyptian Pharaoh in her house!

This Egyptian was described as adorned in ceremonial head-dress, or head crown, and wearing bracelets, armlets and anklets, all of gold. He apparently explained to her that he was there to help her rise to prominence in the group, whatever that was supposed to mean.

I was eager to go see her and find out what was really going on, and a month later we were able to pay a visit. This revealed that she'd been busy going round the charity shops and now her whole house - and I do mean all of it, upstairs and downstairs, every room, even the bathroom - was filled with cheap Egyptian ornaments and pictures. Most of them, like the four-inch soapstone bust on top of the television, portrayed Akhenaten, which, Sylvia explained, was the identity of this entity hanging out at her place.

Akhenaten was a Pharaoh of the Eighteenth dynasty of Egypt, and ruled for 17 years, dying in, perhaps, 1336 BC or 1334 BC. He's noted for abandonment of traditional Egyptian polytheism and introducing monotheism, centred on the Aten. But it would not be accepted, and following his death, the traditional religious practices were restored. This in turn led to the discrediting of Akhenaten and his immediate successors referring to Akhenaten as "the enemy" or "that criminal".

It wasn't long before I was getting letters from Sylvia daily, telling me everything that this entity was explaining to her, and how important it was that I listen to what she said. It was during this time that the American contact, Lisa, came onto the scene. Lisa stayed with me and Shelagh for a week, then went for the planned two weeks with Clive who, being the eternal gentleman, was happy to ferry her around the country in a cheap little car he'd purchased for the occasion.

While all that was happening, Sylvia and 'Akhenaten' set to work on me through an increase in the frequency of the her letter writing. Sylvia was now insisting that 'Akhenaten' - through her mediumship, which you need to remember, until a month ago, didn't even exist - was taking over from Red Eagle, and Sylvia had been instructed to replace Shelagh as my clairvoyant companion. Sylvia was making them both redundant.

As for Clive, he definitely had to go. 'Akhenaten' decided he needed to be sidelined because of the 'duplicity' and 'evil lies' he was telling Lisa about me. It was all made very clear to me, I had to stop working with Shelagh and everything had to be 'channelled' through Sylvia, who now spoke as though she had been a clairvoyant all her life.

I tried everything I could think of to help her break this unhealthy obsession, but it became too much for me and I was finding myself beginning to believe what I was reading in the tirade of letters which now often came at a rate of two a day, as letter followed letter. They were so prolific that she must have been writing one after the other. Sometimes a lengthy, rambling three-page letter would be followed by one with a single sentence written on the page, because she'd forgotten to add it to the main body sent by the previous post.

These were becoming a meaningless jumble of instructions from 'Akhenaten' and most were scrawled, barely legible, emphasised with upper-case, and underlined with two or three slashes of her pen, depending upon the strength of The Egyptian's 'instructions' to me.

In the end, sad to say, her letters were totally unreadable and incoherent. With reluctance, I had to begin distancing myself from her. At one point I thought I'd made a breakthrough when she actually listened to me and said she understood how deeply obsessed she'd become. This was followed by a promise to rid herself of the Egyptian-themed ornaments that filled her home. But I doubted that she had the strength or willpower to accomplish it.

The Shadow Being had done something that bent her to its needs, which was making her receptive to the entity, and now she was just lying back while it massaged her ego. I have little doubt that the Shadow Being and the 'Egyptian' were the same entity.

I made one last visit to her home, only to discover that she'd brought even more ornaments, and when I reminded her that she'd promised to break herself from this entity, she rounded on me with hatred burning in her eyes and accused me of jealousy because 'The Egyptian' had chosen her over me.

I was still shocked at the speed of which this Shadow Being had taken a head full of paranoia and egomania and turned it into something so efficiently self-destructive, transforming someone who had become a friend into a complete stranger – and an unpredictable one - I still wonder what might have happened had this thing managed to penetrate Shelagh, its first choice for attack.

What if it had got to each of us in turn?

So that, in detail, is why I felt as I did with the situation I now faced. The occult forces pursuing me - and I am sure it was me they were set against – had shown time and time again, that they were resourceful and would exploit any weakness they discovered. I think the apparitions in the bedroom were one attempt to send me senseless, and the EVS might well have been an attempt to remove me permanently. So why attack others?

Images of Shelagh and Clive crowded my mind. These were the only two people I dared have around me, and I couldn't bear to think of anything bad happening to them through my own doing. Just thinking of Sylvia was enough to force a decision; I knew what I needed to do.

Shelagh picked up the mail and brought it over. 'You usually open Clive's letters as soon as they arrive. What's wrong?'

I had to stop myself physically recoiling as she held them out to me. 'I can't take them. Put them away or destroy them.'

She still held the letters out to me. 'Why? What's wrong?'

'I can't open them. If anything else comes from Clive, you must never let me have them… destroy them.'

'Have you fallen out?'

'No, we haven't fallen out. I had a visit last night and Clive might be in danger if I involve him any further. It all has to stop now. We have to finish with everything.'

She dropped the letters to her side and asked me to explain, which I did. At the end of my recollection she said she'd keep the letters in a drawer in case I changed my mind, but I told her that wouldn't happen. I needed to keep Clive safe and that could only mean that everything between us would have to stop from that very moment. To open just one letter would be a show of defiance.

When I look back now, it does seem to have been a remarkably fast retreat, considering the MIB had, so far as I can recollect, only put a single thought into my mind. So I have to assume there was more that I cannot remember. I was scared, petrified, even though there was no immediate threat to justify such a fear.

So it was that the Men in Black appeared to have won by causing me to withdraw from my only associate. The one person, aside from Shelagh, I had bonded to. It was a friendship that until this moment, I had assumed was unbreakable. I didn't know if they could have carried out their threat, or even if the threat was real. But could I take any chances?

The one person I thought was safe, completely untouchable, was Shelagh. I didn't believe for one moment they could get to her. Besides, how could I possibly separate from her?

The Purging

So it was that I began my withdrawal from all involvement in what I had been doing. That last threat had beaten me into submission and the only action I could take was to seal myself off from everybody. If I isolated myself the problem would be contained, and those around me would remain safe. Having made this decision, I set about removing from the house every item and scrap of paper that pertained to my now aborted life.

I built a bonfire in the garden and all my ufology books - around three hundred of them - were burnt. All my paperwork and notebooks were shredded and the remnants also consigned to the flames. I had to burn everything as an act of ritual cleansing, and I hoped that it might indicate to the MIB, or what forces controlled them, that I had, indeed taken them seriously, and that whatever threat they felt I had posed was at an end. Maybe they could feel safe taking their attention from me.

Perhaps they would leave my friends alone.

I now switched my life completely and focused my efforts on being human. I didn't know if the real target for the Darkness was me or the dual consciousness that had been with me for so many years, and it was to this that I addressed my decision to tear up whatever 'contractual obligation' it felt I was under. This wasn't a case of taking *back* my life, it was *claiming* my life, which was something that hadn't been entirely my own from the age of eleven. With how my life had been directed, the last thing I had was any sense of free will. Always having been navigated in one direction or another, if I deviated, I found myself heading back to it by some alternative route.

I focused on my job and began trying to construct a social life of some kind, regardless of how difficult that might be for me. In fact, for the first time ever, I tried to assume a completely mundane life. But it wasn't for me and I just couldn't find any traction within a typically human existence. I think some of it was because of my experiences both in and out of the body, I knew what lay behind the illusion of matter and I couldn't fall into the same blinkered existence as the people around me.

I had written a manuscript some years previous, a part historical and part mystical work that I had wanted to keep. For some reason that I cannot now recall, I had given Clive a copy and asked him to keep it safe for me. I don't remember giving it to him and it would have been long before the third Man in Black had appeared, so I guess I'd followed some unconscious forewarning and got a copy to safety before I embarked on the burning.

Soon after I'd met him, I had told Shelagh that he would serve as a sort of archivist, keeping and monitoring material, and is another reason we worked protection around him. But it wasn't until 2012 that I'd learn just what kind of archivist he really was.

In 1986, Shelagh developed diabetes. She was always careful with her food intake, and had her regular medical checks because diabetes is linked to blindness, and blindness as we have already noticed, was her great terror. She had always been healthy because she'd taken herbal supplements and vitamins over a period of many years, which probably contributed to keeping her young and active well into older age. But she began to suffer as ill-health closed in on her. This broke her heart in two and over the months we found a strain placed upon us both. She was soon talking about dying, frequently suggesting that her days were now over.

I had tried desperately to talk her out of this way of thinking, but mortality had a louder voice than mine, and slowly declining health continued to creep up on her like a predator, But we limped on together, as soul-mates do. She tried to cope with my rather inept attempts to be as human as possible, and I was trying to handle some of her blindingly fast mood swings that were induced by her deteriorating health. In 1997, she had got herself into a council-run sheltered housing. It was a nice place, a comfortable, modern flat with 24-hour warden on call. But by 1998, it was clear that we were finished.

I had seen it coming for about six months. She was getting forgetful, and I was starting to retaliate against her mood swings. It was bringing us both down. Eventually I could no longer be around her as ill-health continued to put distance between our relationship which, no matter what happened, we knew could never be truly broken. We made some final attempts to get things right between us, to maybe hang in there a little longer, but it was to no avail as Shelagh helped make that final decision.

I protested, but fate stepped in and my job had me transferred to London. I would commute the short distance by train from Reading of a day, but it left me short of any free time. I delayed as much as possible, but I could see it was finished. I was devastated, but at least I knew she would be OK, and with nothing else we could do, I walked out of the door for the last time.

An amazing partnership was at an end.

I thought it was all finished as I left her on that spring afternoon and went to White Knights to stroll around what had been our dog-walking paths for so many years. I communed with the ghosts and echoes of all that we had done and discussed. It was a haunted gallery of memories as I reached the lake and sat on a fallen tree by its edge, and fixed my eyes, glassy as they filled with tears, on the smooth water's surface.

I had entered White Knights with the thought that I would need to find a new path in life that everything that had gone before was now at an end. But as I gazed at that lake, it almost became the surface of a scrying mirror, and I knew, there and then that I was wrong. Something reached out to me, telling me my work wasn't over, but was moving towards a second phase.

Something about that lake, a place we had always found enticing, spoke to me It whispered of a future I had yet to understand, and of a soul-mate I believed was lost to me. I sat there and cried late into the afternoon.

Shelagh passed from the earth in January 2000 and I wouldn't see her again until November 2004.

NEW LIFE

Hospital Encounter

2004 to 2011 was a time of renewal and reorientation, it was also the period in which my long-endured shamanic initiation process reached its climax. This phase started during the last week of November 2004, when I was in hospital for an operation following an assault at work.

I had been employed as a store detective in department stores since 1996, and on this November afternoon I had been monitoring a man who was acting decidedly suspicious. He kept picking up an expensive duvet and then after glancing at the people near him, he'd put it back down, walk away for a while before returning to it. Typical behaviour that told me he was going to try making a run with it.

These items became a target for the street-people as winter drew in. If they were sleeping rough it was often the only thing that supplied them with a enough warmth. This man, however, was a known face and I knew that he didn't need it, he was going to sell it on to one of the homeless and would probably cost what little Social Security money they possessed.

I radioed for backup as he lifted the box and walked towards the nearest exit. I followed, maintaining surveillance until my colleagues arrived.

The store had three floors and there were just four of us on duty, so it took them a little time to arrive. Then the thief got to the door and ran.

I gave chase.

For our own safety, we were not supposed to apprehend a shoplifter when alone, there should be at least two of us in case the thief turned hostile. But I forgot this basic rule because the adrenaline kicked in as soon as I began my pursuit, besides, he didn't look as though he would be able to make a fight, and also, I glimpsed one of my colleagues a few steps behind me. So thinking the moment was right, I lunged forward and clawed at the fleeing shoplifter's shoulder.

He may have been shorter than me and overweight, but he had phenomenal strength and I suspect he was high on drugs. As soon as I laid a hand on him, he dropped his box, twisted sideways and grasped my wrist; then swung me round and slammed me into a brick wall.

My right shoulder caught the corner and I crumpled to the ground with sickening pain coursing through me. Two of my colleagues piled onto the assailant and held him down while another two joined them shortly after. It took all four to hold him to the ground while police officers were called.

I limped back to the store cradling my shoulder and with burning pain dripping through my nerves as the shoplifter was taken away by the cops. After sitting for half an hour and having a coffee I decided that apart from the shakes - which I assumed was shock - at worse I probably had a dislocated shoulder. Besides, I could move my arm, only just, although it was incredibly painful to do so.

My manager told me I should get to A&E and have it checked out, but thinking I knew best, I decided to wait and see if the pain subsided through the day. It didn't, but I still didn't go to the hospital. I couldn't sleep at all that night because of the pain. So the following morning I phoned in sick and walked very slowly to the A&E.

It turned out that the assault had not only damaged the rotator cuff, but my shoulder was broken into four separate pieces and required surgery rather quickly. I had worked all afternoon and slept all night with my shoulder in this condition!

On waking after the operation, I was told that four pins had been put into my shoulder and it had all been clamped back into place. After peering at a wall clock which showed 6pm, I became vaguely aware of tubes in my arm, one of which was morphine. This meant I couldn't have gotten out of bed, even if I'd felt well enough to do so. I drifted back to sleep and wake again until about 3pm the following day. But it is what happened during the twenty-one hours of sleep that is of interest.

I woke up - or think I woke up - sometime in the night, because something had disturbed me, but aside from the gentle snoring from other patients, the six-bed ward was still and quiet. I felt an urge to climb from the bed, so slipping my legs over the side, I sat on the edge for a moment before standing upright. Then I looked back at the bed and saw my body lying in its morphine cradled sedation. I seemed to puzzle over this for a moment before turning my attention to the corridor at the far end of the ward. I gazed at it with an inexplicable curiosity. I can't understand exactly what I felt, except to say there was something out there I *needed* to see.

I sensed a presence out there and it was tugging at me for attention.

I left the ward, walked into the dimly lit corridor and turned to the right. Then I stopped. Ahead of me and standing about thirty feet away I saw a Grey looking back at me. It lifted a hand, and beckoned me forward with a single movement of a long slender finger. Beyond the alien, and just round the corner to the right was the night nurse's station. I knew there were two of them on duty, and I could hear them quietly chatting to each other, accompanied by the sound of cups and saucers.

It all seemed rather anachronistic, this alien creature standing in front of me but with a very earthly brew and a chat going on in the background! Although the night-duty nurses were talking and sounded at ease, I didn't doubt for one moment that they weren't alert and would respond to even the slightest sound in the corridor.

I remember thinking: *I hope they don't come out and see us.*

Nevertheless, I walked towards the Grey and as I neared the being I realised it was standing beside a doorway. A message was put into my head, instructing me to step into the room; I obeyed with no inclination to even ask why.

Implant

This room was no part of the hospital that I recognised. There was no distinct light source, everything was illuminated by a soft glow that seemed to come from everywhere. Perhaps the walls themselves emitted the glow; that's how it seemed to me.

In the middle of the room was a white table that looked as though it was moulded in one piece from the floor. It might even have *grown* from the floor since I saw no joints or fittings to suggest it had been manufactured and put into place. Three Greys were standing beside the table, and then a moment later the one from the corridor was also in the room with us.

I was urged, by a thought in my mind, to lie on the table. I did as instructed with no resistance. I didn't know what was happening or why I was there, but perhaps the morphine had such a deadening effect and made me so compliant that they had no need to exert control as I obeyed their every command. Maybe the NHS had done the job for them!

I lay motionless as the creatures crowded around looking down at me. At first I thought there was a good deal of chatter passing back and forth between them and that it was too fast for me to grasp. But then I realised it wasn't chatter between them. Their large black eyes were all fixed on me, like they were oblivious to each other, even though their heads were almost touching. This chatter, I realised, was from all four simultaneously and was aimed at me. I had no idea what they were saying and oblivious to that fact, they continued making the noises.

This chatter wasn't words and certainly nothing we would recognise as language, but rather a very rapid monotone clicking. There was a tumult of this high-speed clicking from all four, but they gave nothing to indicate what was happening. There did seem to be a familiarity about everything that was happening, as I was having a deja-vu experience, so maybe I had been taken when I was younger but am unable to remember. I still have no idea if that is true, but I certainly had that 'been here before' feeling.

After some minutes of this 'chatter' I was urged to lie on my right side: One of the Greys put a hand on my left shoulder and applied pressure to indicate that I should roll onto my side and curl into a foetal position. As soon as I had done so, and with barely a pause, I felt a shock in the base of my spine.

Years ago I was given a lumbar puncture which had felt like a knee jabbed into my back, an almost paralysing agony that left me gasping. This was similar to that experience except that the shock and pain was numbed as soon as it started. Something had been put into my spine. I was undergoing a similar experience to that of Shelagh in 1975.

I was then told - via communication taking place in my mind - to climb off the table. I stood and faced a second door which I hadn't noticed when I came in. It slid open, Star Trek style, and I stared dumbfounded as a familiar figure walked into the room. I was confused and in shock because my existence was, yet again, turned on its head.

The figure stepping through the door was Shelagh.

How could that be?

She smiled, walked across to me and took my hands in hers. She felt real and her hands warm, just as flesh and blood should. But this just didn't make sense, how could she be here? How was this possible? Was this real or an illusion created for me? She moved closer, almost as though we were entering a lover's embrace - that's when I woke up to find it was 3pm the next day.

I was still heavily drugged with morphine, but I didn't go back to sleep, and at first I had no memory of the bizarre events that took place during the night. But as the evening progressed more of the encounter came back to me. It was a patchy and hazy recollection at first, vague and dreamlike. But by the next morning I could remember everything that had happened. I also knew that Shelagh was close to me. Very close indeed.

Soon after Shelagh had passed, I had wanted to believe she was with me in spirit, perhaps as a guide and operating somewhat as Doreen Simmonds had with her. So I waited patiently for many months, hoping she would make herself known through clairvoyant vision, or at night in my sleep, or maybe through an independent psychic. But there was nothing.

But following that encounter in the hospital, I was convinced she and I now operated as a single entity. She's not a walk-in and neither is she a spirit guide. I don't know what they have done, but in the environment with those four Grey aliens, they fused us as one, which is what my last memory is, when we moved towards each other in what my mind perceived as a lover's embrace.

It was a fusion of souls.

I have absolutely no idea if this entire experience was induced by the painkillers. I do not know if this was a real experience in any way we might understand it. But its inclusion is because of how very real the entire sequence felt to me. I know how lifelike Shelagh's hands were. I was also left with an indelible impression that we had been 'fused' as a single soul.

It took me almost five weeks following this experience to remember that during my first shape-shift in front of Shelagh, many years before, they Grey had put the thought into her mind:

Two beings of a single spirit that can never part. When one leaves the flesh, they will return to be one flesh. Reunited as a single spirit.

GRS And Open Doors

I remained away from work over the next six weeks with my arm and shoulder immobilised in a sling to allow the injury to fully heal. My left hand wasn't the hand I favoured so doing almost everything was clumsy and difficult, so to preserve myself from having to watch television constantly, I turned to more and longer sessions of mediation than I had done before.

So I set about constructing my own pathworking: these are often conducted as a series of self-induced out-of-the-body journeys that are usually a pre-planned route through the astral realms which often lead to some kind of interaction with archetypal entities or mythic figures.

Also, and aside from the OBE element, pathworking can also take the form of intense inner journeys of enlightenment within your own self, or a series of lucid daydreams which take you on a voyage through your inner mind. Again, this can culminate in meetings between your consciousness and your own set of archetypal imagery. In either case, these encounters often leave a profound effect on the traveller, whether they be a lucid daydream or OBE.

Many of my pathworkings were set in a White Knights environment because of the emotional and psychic links I had to the place, but often - and this is where pathworking gets really interesting - I would find concealed doors or vegetation-covered stone archways that would lead to other places that do not have a physical counterpart, and that's where my journey starts to become an exploration.

I spent my weeks of convalescence pursuing both astral and inner-mind journeys, and with much of the symbolism I encountered being of purely personal meaning, I won't need to describe it here.

On one occasion I found a new archway. I walked through it without hesitation and found myself walking towards White Knights lake. At its edge, and standing beneath the shade of a tree, I saw a tall, slim female wearing a dark hooded robe. She was standing beside, and stirring, a large cauldron that was set over a small fire. Although this figure never lifted her head to acknowledge my presence, I knew who this was.

In my earlier years when I was practising witchcraft under Shelagh's tutelage, my principle deity was Cerridwen, the Welsh Goddess of magic and transformation. Interestingly, the legend of Cerridwen is loaded with shape-shifting that I never related to myself when I adopted her as my patron goddess. It was during her epic chase of Gwion, that they both change several times into animal and plant forms. This chase is part of the Mabinogion, a series of eleven medieval Welsh legends.

The tale relates that Cerridwen's son, Afagddu, was so ugly that to compensate for this, Cerridwen decides to brew a potion in order to make him the most brilliant and inspired of all men. The cauldron is significant in that it's an ancient feminine symbol of renewal, transformation and rebirth.

Cerridwen then puts her servant, a youth named Gwion in charge of guarding the cauldron and to continue stirring it for a year and a day. It is said that the first three drops of this brew granted wisdom, while the remainder would be poison. But three hot drops spilled onto Gwion's thumb, burning him. He instinctively put his thumb into his mouth, and so gains the wisdom and knowledge Cerridwen had planned to give her son.

Knowing that Ceridwen would be angry and seek revenge, Gwion abandoned the cauldron and fled. Ceridwen gave chase. Now that he had abilities endowed by the drops of liquid, Gwion turns himself into a hare, and in response, Cerridwen becomes a greyhound. He then becomes a fish and dives into a river. With no intention to abandon the chase, Cerridwen turns into an otter. He turns into a bird and she becomes a hawk. Realising now that outrunning her isn't an option, he turns into a single grain of corn; but she becomes a hen, finds him and eats him.

When Ceridwen later becomes pregnant, she knows it is Gwion and decides to kill the child when he's born. However, he's so beautiful that she can't bring herself to do it, so sewing him inside a leather-skin bag she throws him into the ocean instead. The child did not die, but was rescued by a prince named Elffin ap Gwyddno; the child grew up to became the legendary bard, Taliesin.

This encounter was profound because I had least expected it. I had not worked with Cerridwen for some years, but then suddenly there she is; at the end of a pathworking and in a location that I had a connection with.

As I stood before her, I received a message, most of which I will not share as it isn't directly relevant to our present story. However, there was something in the tree that Cerridwen directed my attention to, something with a significance that I immediately recognised.

A large butterfly.

As a totem animal, the butterfly is a symbol of freedom and creativity. The butterfly has the gift of transformation, shape-shifting and soul evolution; requiring a degree of courage to carry out the changes required in order to grow. Cerridwen had drawn my attention to this creature in the tree above her head, and as a symbolism, it wasn't lost to me. I certainly agree that the path that had got me this far had, indeed, needed a certain amount of courage.

The whole theme underlying this most extraordinary pathworking seemed to be shape-shifting and the evolution and enlightenment of the soul.

But it was only as the weeks went on that I felt something different within me. I was becoming increasingly uncomfortable with who I was. I had never once felt any sense of gender dysphoria: the feeling or knowledge that one is born into the wrong body, but that is what I soon recognised I was now experiencing. That butterfly suddenly took on a whole new meaning.

As things progressed, my own body told me the direction I needed to go, and by early 2006, I started the National Health Service system to prepare me for male to female gender reassignment surgery. Oddly, the fact that I had only had this condition for two years didn't seem to bring anything into question, and I was son getting the go-ahead from the doctor.

But then things were postponed in October 2006 when, through social networking, I met the man who was to become my new partner. I left my old life in Reading behind me and moved to Manchester in January 2007. This change of location meant I had to begin that entire process again before I finally became Lucy Palmer following the medical procedure in September 2009.

Some weeks after I came out of hospital, I started having the same dream time and time again, it was of a very big black bird at the top of a gigantic tree that reached almost to the clouds. I would always be standing at the base of the tree staring up at the bird, and the entire scene was under a dark and overcast sky. I had this same vision over the next six weeks, until one morning I woke with two words in my mind. They were carried on a voice that I heard in the very instant I woke up. It had been so clear that for a moment I thought someone was in the room:

After weeks of seeing this image in my sleep, I now knew what my third and final shamanic name was to be, and rather appropriate as I favoured wearing black:

'Dark Raven'.

I looked into the shamanic symbolism of the crow and raven and found that they are:

Shape-shifters; carriers of souls from darkness to the light; They work in darkness without fear; are guardians of before existence; have an ability to move in both space and time, and able to move freely in the void.

As a carrion eater, the raven mediates between the living and the dead, and as a bird, it mediates between the heavens and the earth, and embodies the shaman's ability of magical flight. I found this interesting and very relevant to me. But not as relevant as I found it to be one night in mid-March 2010. This is when I began an entirely new dimension of experiences that seemed to qualify my final shamanic name. Following the transgendered stage, and quite likely as a consequence of it, I stepped out of my body and into an entirely new state of existence.

I was now familiar and comfortable with going OBE in a Grey body and experiencing reality through a Grey consciousness. It had happened on a number of occasions in the past, such as when I encountered the Event Void Singularity in my bedroom wall, at Shelagh's bedside, and even more spectacularly, in the street. But with all of these shifts, there had been various problems, or the shape-shift had been in response to an emotional situation.

This time it was nothing like that. This felt comfortable and completely natural, And this time it eclipsed everything that had happened in the past.

This was the night I first went aboard the ships.

I don't know how this change of agenda was decided, but I know it was linked to the implant of 2004 and the transgenderism of six months earlier. Just as Shelagh's implant had been linked to the communication she later had with Red Eagle.

From the time of its initial placement, I knew this implant was both a tracker and a data relay of some kind; serving a dual purpose. The first is to monitor me - which I have no problem with - and the second is to record and relay environmental and social information gathered from around me. But this is not exclusive to me; it is the case with many who have undergone an abduction and implant procedure.

On this night in March 2010, and immediately after realising I was out of the body as a Grey, my environment switched from the familiar surroundings of my bedroom to a circular and featureless room. It was about 20 feet in diameter and glowed with a brilliant white. This room, for all its size, was virtually absent of any contents. All I could see were two long console-like structures against the wall with seven Greys standing attentively at them; they had their backs to me and were focused on their tasks which seemed to involve little more than monitoring coloured lights of reds, blues and greens. None of them looked round at me when I suddenly appeared, and it's odd to say, but I hadn't expected them to. They knew I was there, and I was aware they knew. There was an incredible sense of complete awareness between all of us.

I woke up very soon after, and nothing had happened when I was on that ship, and I think it was nothing more than a connection being made for the future. But I came back from that ship realising that I 'wear' a Grey body as a kind of 'space suit'. I always find this very difficult to describe, but I will do my best. Imagine a space suit of an advanced design, with memory circuits in the helmet that contain information on the environment in which you work. It also holds all the data required for a mission in that environment. Now imagine that 'Jane' is a person with her own life and history, and is the one person for whom the suit has been modelled, no one else can wear it.

Imagine, she steps into the suit and the memory chips activate at the moment she is suited-up, and the contents of those chips override her own thoughts. This floods her mind with the data and information from the suit, and suppresses her own identity to such an extent that while she is in the suit, she has no memory or even any knowledge of the 'Jane' she is, outside of the suit. She ceases to be the individual she was and instead, has become a living component of the suit.

She is the suit's power-pack. But it goes even further than that: Although the suit has on-board programming, Jane is able to modify that programming to some extent, but is not able to operate beyond the programmed parameters. In other words, there is an objective and Jane can modify the programming to achieve her goal, and that goal is known from the moment she is suited up.

So, as clumsy as that scenario is, that was my situation as I stood there staring at the backs of those Greys, working almost mindlessly at their consoles.

This was now a period of personal enlightenment, as over a succession of nights I had the mysteries of much of my life revealed to me. I was to bring this knowledge back to waking consciousness and compare it with historical and traditional records. It seemed to answer almost everything from the first day when Red Eagle had told me I need to 'learn and be ready'.

This was now my time of revelation.

ALIEN SHIPS

Chinese Bases

As a likely consequence of my final shamanic initiation, a great deal of what happened now took place at night and in a Grey form. Most important of all is that this was to extend as far as having a direct impact on the lives of other people. My experiences around this time offered convincing evidence that a tremendous amount of contact happens within an alternate reality. A conscious existence in which human and alien meet. One in which nocturnal extraterrestrial and terrestrial activity takes place on a regular basis.

I was now waking of a morning with a clear memory of regular nights away aboard what I still thought of as 'alien ships', but that conception was to change over time as I became accustomed to them and came to understand them as something more like 'environmental generators'.

Like everything else in my world, these 'environmental generators' could shape-shift, they could appear as anything from a ball of light, to an aircraft or helicopter – even a motor vehicle! The interior also has the same morphing ability. However, to minimise confusion to a minimum, I will continue to refer to them here as 'ships' or 'craft'.

As the frequency of my activity increased, so did the clarity of recall. Everything that follows is what I woke of a morning remembering without having used hypnosis or meditation to aid recollection. But there is one curious aspect throughout, I rarely ever have any memory of my human life during my time aboard the ships. Originally, when standing in the bedroom as a Grey, or shape-shifting in front of the earlier witnesses, I retained a complete awareness of my human life, although when I looked back at my sleeping body I would feel distanced from it, I still knew I was connected to both it and its memories. But when I started going on the ships everything changed: When I am there, it's as though this earth identity had never existed for me.

Since the hospital implant, the spiritual entanglement between Shelagh and myself, and the transgenderism, I had some certainty of what I needed to do. My life was now energised with a fresh sense of mission and the new direction that it would take me. This certainty and invigoration also carried with it something else that *was* a puzzle to me, and that was a need to reach some unspecified short-term objective.

It was strange to feel I was moving towards something unknown that had a deadline. How can you achieve something within a specific time frame if you don't know the target or what that time frame is? But that's what I faced.

It became a little clearer when the first tangible step towards that objective surfaced on social networking.

I have never been particularly interested in online communities, but in 2007 I did create a social networking account. It fascinated me for a while, but after that initial enthusiasm died I deactivated that particular account, but kept one active which was to advertise the shop I opened in 2011.

But in early 2012, I reactivated that former account with the sole purpose of re-establishing contact with someone, and to make an initial contact with someone else I didn't yet know. All I knew is that I needed to find them soon. So I started with what was realistically achievable; I went searching for Clive Potter.

If he was on social media, then finding him would be easy enough. The difficulty might be in explaining the dramatic changes that my life had undergone over the last nineteen years - I wasn't sure how best to handle that, especially the issue of my sudden disappearance from his life. I knew Clive to be a tolerant and forgiving man, and he had always recognised the authenticity of what I said, so I anticipated a sympathetic ear. Of course, there was always the chance that he might not understand, and to be honest, I wouldn't blame him for that.

But I *needed* to re-establish communication with him - although with no idea why there was such a need - so didn't feel I could leave it to chance. It was because of the possibility of him not understanding, that I thought the best way to initiate communication would be if I could reach him at night, communicate with his mind while he slept.

As unlikely as it sounds when I came up with the idea, I thought I might be able to 'walk into his mind' and show him everything that had happened over the years. I could transfer everything, including an emotional content and hopefully there would be a subconscious acceptance that would bubble to the surface when I made actual contact.

I guess you could call it subliminal conditioning. It isn't something I had ever done or even attempted before, however, I knew I could do it.

By now a pattern had established itself: I recall drifting towards sleep, then suddenly finding myself standing beside the bed and with my room dissolving and then reforming into a new environment. I am Grey-Shifted at some point during that transitional state.

That sequence occurred in June 2012, when I made a couple of extraordinary shipboard trips to China - of all places.

When the environment reformed around me, I found myself standing beside five other Greys who were manoeuvring what I sensed was a very big craft. I was aware of more Greys on the ship, along with a large human cargo. Referring to humans as 'cargo' is such a dispassionate term, but I'm trying to give you a feel of how the Grey feel towards humans, especially when dealing with a large number of humans. I just don't think the concept of 'passenger' exists.

I seemed to join this ship in mid-flight and the humans were already on board, selected from various locations in Europe. I also seemed to know that most had been taken during their sleep, and would remain asleep until they were returned. Greys ensure humans are treated with as much care as they are capable of; humans are of extreme value because we exist in a three-dimensional world but can quite easily exist just as comfortably in theirs, plus many more besides. They find us quite remarkable.

We also exhibit a vast range of complex emotions and expressions that they don't possess – either have never had, or have evolved along an alternative path that have taken them beyond such things. Even now in human society, our technology and it's miniaturisation is racing headlong at blinding speed towards what is known as 'The Singularity'.

The Singularity is an event predicted to happen within a few decades time, and is the moment when artificial intelligence will overtake humanity intellect and ability. Coupled with nanotechnology advances, this could ultimately see humanity become an artificially enhanced being with amplified abilities, thoughts and mental processes.

So if we are as close as three decades from this becoming a reality, imagine what the product would be after millions, if not billions of years of development. This is what the Grey might very well be and would explain why they are so interested in humanity as it is now and explain the value we hold for them.

I was only on this ship for a brief time, in order to create a three-way connection between myself, the Grey intelligence mentally entangled with me, and humans on the ships. There were around two hundred humans on board, and coming back to earth with this knowledge was when I realised the staggering number of humans who are taken on a regular basis.

I now know that those who step forward and talk about their experiences are but a minute fraction of the multitude, vast numbers have absolutely no memory of these events happening. I wouldn't be surprised if every human on earth hasn't had at least one encounter during their lifetime.

The humans on this ship were lying on couches a deck below me, so although I never saw them, I could sense them. I could even see through the floor at any moment to where they were being held. But more than that, I could sense their minds. As most of them were asleep and unaware of what was happening, their thoughts washed over me like gentle, undulating ripples.

Several others were near-conscious and I could feel their thoughts jabbing me like pinpricks. Their semi-consciousness was causing them to have bad dreams which created a disturbance in the otherwise gentle undulation of the hundreds of sleeping minds.

The Greys could not interpret these spikes for what they actually were: trepidation and anxiety. I think outright fear would have been evident if the sleeping human minds hadn't been subdued. The Greys can predict some human emotions, but only broadly, such as joy and fear. Consequently, they prepare for it. But there are different degrees of joy and fear, and also different humans might display them as reactions to different things.

I was on this ship because I was able to understand the humans easier than the Grey crew could, as with shaman throughout antiquity, Red Eagle had trained me to be a mediator, an interpreter. In fact, I was performing the same kind of role I had assigned to Artificial Intermediaries - my so-called 'mega-tulpa'. So is that what this Grey form was? A tulpa? Was this no more than an extremely advanced version of the raven I had built and inhabited with my consciousness? Was it inhabited by both me *and* an alien consciousness together? This whole idea is something quite extraordinary, but as unique as it sounds, I don't think I'm alone in doing this. I suspect there are many others who are mentally entangled, or 'twinned' with these intelligences.

One other question remains: how did I know this happened over China? I didn't at first. It took another trip to realise that this was where a lot of large quantity human cargo was taken. I cannot say what became of these particular humans, because I returned to earth before they had reached their destination. I was there to establish that initial bonding, a process that was to strengthen over a period of time. What I do know is that all these humans were returned to their original locations unharmed, and most likely unaware that anything had ever taken place. There might have been some who recalled strange dreams. That would be those who had spiked with fear and apprehension as some of this reality bled through into their consciousness. But most would not remember a thing.

Something became immediately apparent to me after I returned to Earth and re-acquired my human emotions. Unlike being Grey and being unable to identify with a human life, when I return to human, I *do* usually remember the ships and what happens while I'm there, but it's like having the memories of something else entirely. I believe this is because I still carry something of my humanity with me aboard the ships, but perhaps, submerged within the Grey subconscious.

That is when I began to have a vague idea of what I was, and what was happening. I had known that no matter what was occurring in my life, I was not from another planet. That's a common assumption I had rejected from an early age. But I did believe that I was intimately linked to either another dimension, a reality that lay just beyond human perception, or that my Grey-self was from the future. Perhaps my human body was a kind of 'base-camp' and the Grey construct was something the future-consciousness used as its identity to interact in our time. Maybe all true-born shaman worked with these beings, and like fairies, appeared in various guises throughout local tribal history. But more often than not as animals.

My second trip to China was an important one because it revealed a co-operation between humans and Greys. This happened in September 2012. I was Grey-shifted and on a ship racing at a tremendous velocity east to west, across a landscape on a bright sunny day.

The ship was as large as the first I had been aboard, or it might have been the same one. I was standing with three other Greys, and facing a wall that displayed a view of our direction of travel, but this display wasn't on a screen. We were looking *through* the hull, but it wasn't transparency. It reminded me of when I ejected from my body on that first occasion in my bedroom and was capable of seeing through the wall where the EVS had been. I think if a human had been watching us, they would have seen four Greys staring at a wall of their craft.

Then I sensed a sudden 90-degree turn to the left which combined with our phenomenal speed, should have plastered us across the walls, but we weren't. Although we were doing what must have been several thousand miles an hour, judging by the speed of the landmass flashing past beneath us, there was no sensation of speed within the ship itself. The sudden turn we made had felt little more than a slight jolt to the left, even though in reality it had been a sudden mid-flight turn. I think gravity within the ship was somehow being manipulated to nullify effects of our violent manoeuvres.

Then we were suddenly over a long structure that, on my return to the human mind, I was able to recognise as China's Great Wall. It's because we took a 90 degree turn left and then raced along the line of the Wall that makes me assume our initial direction had been east to west. But I could be incorrect and this is just an assumption on my part.

We followed this for some distance, still travelling at a phenomenal pace and then came to an abrupt halt, no deceleration, it was a dead stop. I could see people on the ground, and although we were at a great height, we could see things around their necks and in their hands. These items were cameras, and the people were tourists. One of the human males looked up and pointed at our craft. A camera was raised and I can assume that in 2012, there was a multiple witness sighting at the Great Wall, possibly with photographic evidence.

We were very high, so I suspect the image was, as many are, distant and indistinct. Possibly just a strangely moving and hovering light in the sky. But we could see the humans clearly because our means of observation had a facility to magnify down to whatever scale we required, regardless of our height or speed. It was in the same way your eyes will adjust to its distance and bring an object into focus, this operated in the same way. Whatever we looked at was brought into sharp clarity and high detail, regardless how far distant the object was.

Then an entire side of our craft vanished and we were looking over a much wider expanse of this landscape, as from some location beneath the craft, a robot was released and sent down, and this *was* a classic robot form. Remember those blocky walking robot toys we had? Square heads with flashing eyes, rectangular arms, stocky body and legs, often with a plastic flashing gun protruding from the chest? It was a life-size version of that which flew down from the ship.

But the humans didn't see it, because not only were their eyes locked on the UFO hovering high in the sky, but they were almost completely frozen, as their perception of time slowed to a crawl. I don't know what the robot went down for, but I know it was a research data gathering unit. Then I became aware of the unit being observed by one of the group of four humans.

The other three continued to stare unblinking at the UFO aside from this one female had been left unaffected in order to observe the remote unit. So in among this conflicting sighting is a female who will swear she saw a robot leave the ship and approach them. The others will swear they saw nothing but a hovering UFO. This is planned manipulation to sow doubt and confusion in the minds of those who witnessed it. I suspect this manipulation is played out in a lot of scenarios, so what is seen by one witness isn't necessarily observed by a companion.

The robot returned from its mission and we continued on our way, still following the Wall. Then we had mountains in the distance, high, snow-capped peaks across the horizon. We eventually landed near a large, very flat and desolate expanse, and then I was outside of the ship and walking towards large open doors set into a mountainside. A human dressed as a Chinese military officer stepped from inside. I approached and then stopped, looking up at him as he looked down at me. He then made noises with his mouth, in a language I was unfamiliar with. But noises I could identify and understand as speech, he said:

'I am speaking Chinese, can you understand me?'

My response, sent as a thought aimed at him, was immediate: *Yes. I am not speaking, can you understand me?*

The officer smiled and nodded.

He was expecting me and for some reason I was not the least bit surprised to see him. All this suggests that there is a relationship between the Chinese and the Greys, an alliance or agreement of some kind. But the introduction also made me realise he thought I was an alien. I don't think he knew I possessed a human body that at that moment was asleep on the other side of the world. He probably assumed I was from another planet - unless the Chinese are engaged in research with time travellers or parallel dimensions and thus have a clear understanding of what I was.

From here my memory gets a little foggy, and I don't think I was able to bring much memory beyond this greeting, back with me. Through my hazy recall, I do know I went with him deep inside the mountain. There I saw a base several levels deep. I saw children, but these were human/alien hybrids, and were operating as a workforce.

I also know that as they mature, some of these Chinese hybrids are on ships as helpers. But the children I saw had vacant-eyed expressions and appeared to be little more than biological machines. I also recall transparent, clear liquid-filled tanks with bodies in them, many hundreds of hybrid children. It strikes me that in the mountains, the Chinese military are busy people, or at least, a covert operation is. At the time, I had no idea where this base could be, especially as I was completely ignorant of Chinese geography. The only thing clear to me was the mountain ranges, the vast open space, and the border between China and Tibet, or China and Afghanistan.

CONNECTIONS

Reconnection

In July, a month after that first trip to China, I found Clive on social media. I naturally remained cautious about suddenly contacting him after all these years. Do remember that so far as he was concerned, I had vanished without any warning. I had been filled with such fear from that last MIB and pulled the plug so fast it had even caught Shelagh off guard. Feeling as uncomfortable as I did, I decided I could do with a little support in this.

So I began conversing with a mutual friend about approaching him. Paul assured me that he would be fine with it. I gave this a lot of thought, but still favoured making some kind of mental contact initially, if that was possible. A week later it happened. I don't recall leaving my body, but I suddenly became aware of standing facing my bedroom wall, and walking through it.

I found myself in a public park on a sunny afternoon. I think this environment was seeded with imagery from Clive's mind because I could see him sat on a bench watching children at play, and possibly a recollection of his youth. I sat alongside him and told him everything that had happened, as an instantaneous thought transference. The warmth of the sun, the children at play, the entire scene of tranquillity was an inner expression of peace, acceptance and understanding.

This park is a familiar one to me, as it's where I have many astral encounters with both the living and the recently dead. Because this is all in the mind there are many layers of symbolism to these encounters, and this was no exception. There was one sight I wasn't prepared for, however. Red Eagle was in the park! I recognised the dark-skinned man who threw a stick for his dog. I was thrilled because I had lost my connection with him ever since losing Shelagh.

I then realised that he had probably helped arrange the meeting. In fact, he might have organised the whole thing from the very first moment I had decided to do it. After all, connecting with Clive in his sleep-state, had been very easy to achieve, and as someone who had never done a mind to mind connection at night, it had been ridiculously simple.

When eventually I did connect with Clive on Earth, to say he was surprised, would be an understatement. But because his subconscious had already met me, and the explanation was nestled in his subconscious, he didn't take the changes with as much impact as he might otherwise have done. It didn't take us long to get back into our stride and start playing catch-up, especially with the internet replacing our formidable quantity of mail correspondence.

So that was the first contact established, and as I chatted with him, I was starting to look around social media for my second, and still unknown contact. There was one lead. I had been out of body as a human in recent weeks and had been talking to a female who I was beginning to feel might be that elusive second target Then, within weeks of reconnecting with Clive, I started commenting on the social media posts of a woman called Denise.

She and I got on well with each other from the start, and it didn't take me long to realise this was, in fact, my second contact. I knew this was the case because that persistent sense of urgency suddenly left me for the first time in a year. I don't think she had any recollection of nightly meetings. If she did, they weren't ever mentioned. When I saw Denise's profile picture, it matched the face of the night-time connection. From that point the pressure was off and I relaxed, as casual chat replaced urgent searching. Within a month of our initial communication, we were on each other's regular contact list.

That's when it all kicked off.

Mind Entanglement

Denise Lane is a mother of two living in St Albans, Hertfordshire, an experiencer with a long history of paranormal and UFO activity. With much joking and banter through our random comments on each other's social media postings, we quickly bonded as close as any two people could ever do on a networking site.

This bonding was artificially accelerated, however, because those nocturnal meetings of consciousness between us not only continued, but intensified to a frantic pace. In fact, they became an almost nightly occurrence from July through to the end of October, and five of these meetings were so emotionally intense that I would wake of a morning with barely the strength to climb from bed; the curiosity from her was incredible.

I subscribed this to her overwhelming interest in me, but later, I was to learn that she had emotional issues which would have added to that obsession. I seemed to make such easy contact with not only Clive and Denise, but also others Since my experiences at hospital, I had been moving through dimensions with considerable ease compared to what had gone before.

In previous years when I had travelled with Red Eagle, he was guiding me and showing me what I could connect with, somewhat like I was doing with Denise over the first few months before and after we made each others acquaintance. But since that implant had taken place, I had become self-sufficient and didn't sense Red Eagle's presence in the way I used to. In fact, I was now able to access places previously denied to me, or that he would have needed to open to me, such as interacting with humans directly in their sleep.

Then at the end of October 2012, I received an email from Denise that signalled not only a change in our relationship, but an intense confrontation:

Hey, you...are you OK? I had a dream about you the other night. You were sat opposite me. There was a man standing behind you. He looked like he was trying to look like someone I knew but hadn't quite pulled it off. He had his hands on top of your head and his fingers were on your forehead. I was looking at you and your face changed for a split second, like a projection had failed and I saw you change. You turned into a Grey for a split second. I said to him, "Oh my God! Her face changed!"

He said "Let me have a look." He stepped out from behind you, and that's when I realised his eyes weren't right either. They had a white dot at the top of the iris. He walked out from behind you and took a step forward and he just lunged his face into mine until his forehead was on mine and his eyes were right in front of mine. There was a blinding flash, and my eyes hurt and I woke up.

I knew what she was talking about because I had woken in the morning with memory of this encounter. I could recall observing Denise as she sat cross-legged before me and wearing an orange robe that even to this day she couldn't understand the significance of. She said that she would never wear a robe, and certainly not orange! But unlike her, I didn't view it as a fashion statement, but representative of a state of mind. The robe would have signified her supplication, perhaps analogous to a Tibetan Buddhist pupil about to have *maya*, the illusions of reality, stripped away, to be shown what lay beyond.

We were discussing elements of the alien abduction phenomena, and of special interest were events from earlier in her life. So that was the significance of the robes she wore. It was a moment of truth. But first she needed to cut through her own confusion and loss of direction, because I could feel the exasperation radiate from her in waves. With someone like

Denise, what was needed was a climactic moment of revelation; something that would deliver an impact that she could take back to her waking consciousness and remember - something she could hold onto that might act as a lantern in the darkness, to help her find the direction she had so desperately asked for.

But I needed her to be receptive for this to happen, and that just wasn't the case. As she sat staring at me, I could feel a defensive shell around her that needed to be breached. I put into her head images of me shape-shifting into a Grey, and along with it I told her that I was here to give her what she had been asking for. This broke through, because although she continued to glare challengingly, she stabbed a thought, as sharp as a dagger, deep into my mind. 'Go on then! F*****g prove it!'

That was the moment I needed. Her mind, for just a very brief moment, was receptive. I shape- shifted in order to 'f*****g prove it.'

That is when she received a download from the intelligence which she saw as a second entity. But this was more than information being put into her mind; it was the beginning of repairs to her long-term ill-health. If she wanted to achieve the things she aimed for, she'd need good health. Whether she actually achieves her desired goals is down to her, but she was about to start on the road to health, motivation and understanding in order to accomplish it.

Not long after this experience, Denise told me that she had indeed reached a crisis point and had sent a personal plea to the universe, that if they wanted her to work, she needed some proof, or a sign of some kind. I suspect that is what triggered the race within me to find her.

Over the following year, Denise spent a considerable amount of time with me OBE. Sometimes I would be perceived by her as a human, and other times as a Grey, and at times I would be a mix of the two. So far as I can understand, these three perceptions of me were dependent upon what she needed to know or what her inquiry was about. Some information would be accessed through me as a human; other information would only be accessible to me as a Grey. Occasionally this need for information would be what I knew as a Grey, but needed to be translated to her in human concepts, hence the hybrid appearance.

I was her mentor, leading her through a personal 'awakening' process. This woman was re-orientating her awareness towards other realities, but that isn't to say she didn't already possess an intuitive understanding of them, because she did. This was a mind-expanding trip to a more complex reality than she had previously understood. During these fact-finding mission of hers, I was also experiencing something very new, as I was hammered night after night with her insatiable curiosity. Often I would message her the following day and tell her that even though my body had slept well, I was waking mentally and emotionally shattered.

This was all new to me. Not only had I been teaching someone in OBE, but I was waking with physical and emotional effects from the encounter. So I started fortifying myself as best I could, using relaxation techniques, and while this did take the brutal edge of the emotional drain, it didn't go quite far enough, and for weeks I would feel like a zombie for the entire day. However, as the months passed I did begin to adapt, until eventually, I started to wake feeling less like I had crawled from a train wreck. I had now begun linking to the emotional states of the humans I interacted with, bringing some of their pain back to earth with me, but within just a couple of years, this fact would deliver quite a crushing blow to me.

CHILDREN

Towards A New Humanity?

Throughout 2013, the focus of my 'time away' had turned towards children and expectant mothers, this has taken place in an environment. I refer to as the 'Natal Ship'. As an example: on one occasion I was aboard the Natal Ship and as usual in these circumstances, Grey-shifted. I was with four other Greys plus two humans helpers, (there are a surprisingly large number of humans who assist the alien agenda).

The room itself was round and everything gently curved, including the floor. I don't recall any angles or edges to anything. In fact, it may as well have been the inside of a large egg. This room was a nursery, with many dozens of identical cribs holding human babies. I think they were all about two-years-old. Suffice to say, when I am Grey, it is nigh on impossible to even begin to guess human age.

Then the bizarre happened. I lifted my arms and the children began to levitate from the cribs. As they lifted into the air some began chuckling and kicking their legs, enjoying the sensation and treating it as a game, which was fine as it made them receptive. Within moments dozens of babies were suspended in the air, their chuckling and giggling almost a musical tinkle that filled the room. Then, I set them swinging in gentle arcs from one side of the room to the other. At the end of a swing, they would gently turn to face the opposite wall, and then swing back to the other side. They were so close to each other that their hands reached out and brushed those of their companions as they passed. The babies are the only humans I have seen on the ships who have openly expressed pleasure.

I don't recall the swinging as anything other than a distraction to keep their minds relaxed and easy to access. I remember that when I had them gently sailing back and forth, I began implanting imagery in their minds, that they were special because they were *our* children. I don't know if that means they had been bred on the ships or whether they had genetic modifications, but I knew they were bonded in ways that make them exceptionally gifted humans.

Because of this fact, they were given warnings that they had to keep this knowledge to themselves and not to tell people. That they should not try to explain that they were children of the Star-People. They were to carry buried knowledge of being gifted with understanding that other people around them - even their parents - might feel uneasy about if they knew. They received imagery suggestive of a superhero secret identity. This was embedded deep into their subconscious and not just the once, but layer upon layer of it buried behind the security of screen memories. This is a small part of the child preparedness program that they have been conducting on increasing numbers of infants. A bridge between the species.

A more recent event involving children occurred when we were somewhere over the U.S. I joined the Natal Ship when there were already six females on board, but there was one in particular I seemed interested in, inexplicably. I was there just for her. I had never been on a ship to see a single individual before, so I was gaining new insights all the time.

With a single mental command she stepped out from the group and stood before me. I knew this was her first time with them as an adult. She had been taken aboard several times as a child, as had her mother before her. Maybe it was her childhood memories that were surfacing now, because her eyes were glazed with terror, and the fear emanated from her in palpable waves. She was here because she was pregnant, and a lot of that fear was for her unborn child rather than herself. I needed to try convincing her that they weren't going to harm her; that the child was just as important and would not be damaged in any way.

I was putting telepathic images in her head that she was not in any danger, and that it was her child that was of special interest to them. That might be true to some extent, but the Grey mental processes could only see human females as incubators nurturing genetic stock, and this is one of the things I find disturbing when I wake in the morning. Greys appear incapable of expressing adequate sympathy or compassion for the terror that grips the humans they take, and it makes the them seem ruthless, if not evil. Although able to express rudimentary surprise, bewilderment, puzzlement and curiosity, they are in some ways programmed to perform as they do.

My memory is edited when I return, it's like a black pen ruling through sensitive details. Some of this is a defensive measure, my human mind rejecting entire sequences of memory that it wouldn't be able to cope with on waking. But occasionally this fails and something will slip through that probably shouldn't have done. This happened not so long ago, in a circumstance very much like the one just described. A female who had been taken several times during childhood (her mind had buried these bizarre 'childhood nightmares') now faced the reality of those former nightmares.

She was recently pregnant. In fact, so recently that I'm not even sure her waking mind was aware of it at that point in time. The moment I woke up I was aware of her name. I also knew that although not taken since a young child, she'd been monitored throughout her life. But abductions had now resumed because of her pregnancy.

This woman's name was unknown to me, and it isn't the name of anyone I have encountered subsequently. She is just one of many thousands of humans, but unique in that I know her name. While speaking of thousands of humans, when I am Grey-shifted, humans all look so very much alike, and it's difficult to put an individual description to any single one. Major ethnic differences are clear: Caucasian, Negro, Chinese, and so on, but closer distinctions get confusing until I awaken and the memory clarifies.

So all I could say for certain about this woman is that she was a white female and her head hair was indistinguishable from her complexion, which means she was either bald, (unlikely) or had short blonde or fair hair. So how *do* they make individual distinctions? They do it by means of the implants. Among their multiple functions are the unique signatures they emit. There is a unique signature for every one of the billions of people with implants in their bodies.

An encounter with Denise took place on the Natal Ship in mid-April 2013, but because I was Grey-shifted, she didn't show any sign of recognition, and I only knew it was her because of the implant signature. At the time she had been 'travelling' with me, I have been more often than not, a true hybrid, part human and part Grey. This was so she would feel comfortable as having some element of familiarity. But this time, here on the Natal Ship, she was denied any such comfort. To her credit, unlike many others, she didn't emit fear, but I wouldn't have expected her to because she has witnessed plenty, and experienced much, even before her 'travels' with me; more than enough to be able to handle it, especially with the more recent revelations I gave to her.

What I did sense, was ripples of apprehension radiating from her. When I was Grey-shifted, I knew why this was happening, but when I woke the following morning, it had been stripped from my consciousness. There was some knowledge they didn't want me bringing back to earth, but I had no idea what it might have been. I didn't think she was pregnant, but neither did I feel she was there as a maternal helper because she lacked the freedom to act. It seemed like she was waiting for something, and I was especially puzzled because as I woke, it was with a piercing thought, like an instruction punched across my mind.

Do not tell her that you have seen her

So I didn't, and I kept this encounter to myself for almost a year. When I recalled encounters with her, it was usually my habit to send her an online message starting with something like: 'Do you remember last night?' That became a signal indicating that something had occurred, but rather frustratingly, although I had a near perfect recall, there was usually very little or no memory on her part. But then, in early July 2013, she sent me a message:

'Want to know a MEGA secret?'

I fired back without even thinking; 'You're pregnant?'

'No.'

The warning came back to mind:

Do not tell her.

I withdrew into silence and hoped she wouldn't question my response. She didn't, and the subject moved in another direction as she told me what the 'MEGA secret' was. But I was now left wondering about my almost instinctive reaction: so *was* she pregnant? Or was she about to become pregnant? Was that why I saw her on the craft? It could explain her apprehension. But I chose not to think about it any further and pretty much forgot the encounter after brushing it off as an anomaly. But later, in September, I got this simple message from her:

'I'm pregnant.'

So that *was* why she had been on the Natal Ship, and it explained my earlier slip-of-the-tongue. My Grey-shift would have known about it, obviously, and it must have been held in my memory block, but managed to slip through. Nevertheless, even though she was now telling me of her pregnancy I still I didn't tell her I'd seen her on the ship because the original command still held me in abeyance:

Do not tell her that you have seen her.

That mental command still stands, and even to this day I have not mentioned it to her.

Paula Elisabeth Green is an abductee from Bradford who has had alien encounters on so many occasions over the years that she's formed relationships with them and admits that if they left and never came back she would miss them, even though they cause her some considerable distress, it doesn't seem to be what they do to her that causes upset, but their sudden arrival and the sometimes rough handling.

I have had a Grey-shifted encounter with Paula and uniquely, Paula is the only person with whom I have experienced being in two places at the same time while *awake*. This particular incident falls squarely in with my recent activity with pregnancy and children. On this occasion I have far from perfect clarity of memory, and is possibly because I was bi-locating.

I was in my shop in Manchester in early December 2013. It was particularly quiet and there hadn't been much custom all day, so I spent most of it sat in my office area reading a book. Then I began to feel drowsy and kept losing concentration in my book. Rapidly, I slipped into the throes of a daydream, but still fully conscious and would have been aware had someone come into the shop.

In this daydream I found myself standing in a room and everything was blurred, like looking through glass in a steamed bathroom. All I could detect was a bed and a wardrobe. I think they were my focal points to the exclusion of all else because of their mass. To one side of the room, I could sense a human presence, but I also realised that I hadn't arrived by myself. At my side was another being, a young hybrid female.

I want to see my mother,

the child put that thought into my mind and I then knew that the human was this child's mother, and the human transmitted a signature I recognised as Paula.

Animals don't only sense an alien presence, they see it and respond to it. They register any alien presence, and the hybrid child was the first to realise we had now been sensed an animal staring at us. It seems that Paula's cat knew we were there and that it wouldn't take Paula long to focus on where we were standing. Having been around Greys for extended lengths of time, she was easily able to either see or sense their presence in her home. But for some reason the hybrid child didn't want to be seen by her mother, and I still do not know why that would be.

She's a beautiful child, with wide, dark, elongated eyes, and even with her alien characteristics, you can see her mother reflected in her. In human years, she would probably be in her early 20s. She's about five feet six inches tall and very slim. 'Willowy' comes to mind as I write this. I can see no reason why she would want to be unobserved, so can only guess that she'd been ordered to, and maybe that's why I was there, as a chaperoned.

Paula was now becoming aware of something in the room and was looking towards us, we knew we needed to deflect her attention. So I 'thought' a Grey into existence, a fleeting tulpa mirage to draw her attention in the opposite direction to where we were standing, and as she was distracted by its movement, we disappeared. I assume the child went back to where she originated from. Me? I stirred from my 'daydream' and it took several hours for me to feel grounded again.

I don't think for one minute that I was actually in that room with Paula. Too much about the picture seemed wrong for that to be the case, not least of all the mistiness of my vision. I think my Grey body was being used as a remote-controlled avatar and maybe I went into a semi-trance because I was required for it's activation. This would put me into a remote-viewer mode. Why was I used? That I cannot answer. I knew Paula, so perhaps the child trusted me or needed that link, but I cannot say for sure.

The following day Paula posted a message about what she had seen which tied in with my bi-location experience, and just one month later I discovered the likely reason why the hybrid wanted to see her mother. At the beginning of January 2014, I learned that Paula's daughter was expecting her first child and had been pregnant for four to six weeks. So maybe a proud daughter wanted to visit her Earth mother. Well, why not? She was going to be an aunt!

This is a situation, one of many, in which I have acted as a conduit between alien and human, and this has established itself into a regular pattern. Maybe the alien/human maternal link is possible because of the entanglement between Shelagh and I. Previously I could have been regarded as a soldier, confronting the darkness that ranged against us. But since I've had Shelagh's deep maternal instinct on board as part of my new programming, I have felt privileged to be helping bridge alien and human parents, and their offspring. I soon came to realise that as with any shaman, I was operating at various levels of reality and mediating between the star-people and the tribe of humanity. I walked between humans and aliens without being one or the other.

DREAMWALKING

Source Of Inspiration

Not all of my OBE is conducted Grey-shifted, nor is it always associated with the Greys.

©2009 Lynda Julie Richardson

Nor do all of them work out as planned. Lynda lives in Yorkshire, England, and channels images that she manifests as artwork. This art is very abstract and loaded with significance and symbolism.

I met with her and looked through a portfolio of prints and found them intriguing, I told her that I felt there was more to them than the surface material we could see.

I wanted to see the originals rather than copies and so told her I would try to OBE one night later that week, I would go to her house and see them for myself. Lynda took that remark in her stride and even said she would lay out all her pictures across the room and on the couch so I could get a better view of them. Mind you, I wasn't sure if I could do what I had suggested, not any more than I was certain I could meet up with Clive, but having managed that, I was going to give this a try. It so happens that later that week I *did* OBE to her house, but there was a big surprise waiting for when I got there.

The moment I walked through a wall into her house, I was 'bounced back' by a force that was hanging over her house. I had no idea what I had collided with, but knew it had some connection with her images. I did get a little information in the moments that I was there, but not much. Something repelled me with such ferocity I that I was left with a dull and throbbing headache for a week. I didn't feel malevolence from it, so I rather suspect it was an energy of some kind being generated by the imagery.

The next day I told Lynda that I'd discovered enough to know that her images required a second component; tones and sound in order to make them a complete composition, and that in their true form they would extend and resonate at a frequency beyond the dimensions that we recognise.

Ian, from Newcastle, is another channeller, his medium is music. I met him via social networking through Lynda and some of his initial remarks to me echo conclusions I had reached; including:

I'm thinking collective consciousness... I basically came to the same conclusion as you, about manifestation of entities that are reflections of ourselves....then with Lynda telling me about you manifesting as a Grey....that led me to you.

Manifestations of entities that are reflections of ourselves,' is a reference to the AI that we discussed previously. Then something most interesting emerged as Ian's next statement brought things full circle:

If we recognise that sound is holographic we can use sound in the moment...to collectively project love...heal the planet...ascension, etc.

I suspected that Ian's musical inspiration was doing precisely the same as Lynda, but with tones rather than image. Thus it was now with some caution I suggested to Ian that I could try making a visit to him in OBE. My caution was because I still remembered that strange repulsion effect when I went to Lynda's home, and it had me wondering if that effect would be consistent around people who channelled art. But feeling he had an important source channel through which he derived his music. So I was enthusiastic enough to try.

He went on to ask. "So are you going to visit me in my sleep?"

'If I am allowed to, yes, I will. But I'm not entirely free to roam as I wish. I'm not sure, I think it has to be a mission target. I can't just walk into anyone's reality.'

Nevertheless, that same night I found myself outside a towering, monastic-like structure, its dimensions and architecture reminding me of Notre Dame Cathedral, but vastly bigger. This edifice gave a sensation of being fluid, and not maintaining a uniformity as in my mind it seemed to twist, turned and shifted through colours in subtle ways that made me think it had a life-force, or even *was* a life-force all of its own.

The shifting had a holographic quality, as though I were looking at different parts of it through layers of glass, and it was uncertain in which form it wanted to remain from one moment to the next. I climbed a set of wide stone steps leading to the open doors of the building that sat under a strange, pinkish sky. As reached the top of the steps I was met by a man coming out of the building and who seemed *very* enthusiastic that I had arrived. I assumed he'd been expecting me as he certainly didn't seem surprised to see me, even though I hadn't guaranteed being able to get to there.

As I entered the building, with my host leading the way, he was smiling and pointing enthusiastically around the interior. I was overwhelmed with the impression this building gave as being a very spiritually-orientated construct, but without religion attached to it.

The walls, ceilings and floors of the main room, itself a single vast chamber, were soft pale colours, creams and beige that were alive and emitting a soft, warm glow that seemed internal. Interlacing the walls and ceiling, were delicate tracings of unrecognisable symbols and interconnecting lines, none of which I could interpret, nor did I feel it was my place to even attempt to do so.

Placed around the chamber were formations of fluted columns that were rather like the Doric order of classical architecture, but these were of varying heights, as short as a meter, to as high as four or five meters. Some were on the marble-like floor; others seemed to be suspended at various heights in the air, some of them impossibly high and close to the vaulted ceiling. I was told these were illustrative of sounds and tones, but I could not understand the concept, but Ian seemed to, well This was his construct after all.

Ian walked at my side along the central walk-way, his ebullient enthusiasm now tempered as he explained that this is where he came to form the essence of what would become the conscious inspiration for his music. He continually referred to this building as his 'Centre of Being', a creative cosmos of his own design, and formed over the course of several incarnations. He told me that his 'Centre of Being' wasn't used through every one of his lives, although the experiences of every incarnation fed into it. It was only used during his artistic lives, of which I could tell he'd had several. I am tempted to suggest he was one of the great classical composers, or had a spiritual link to such, but that would only be speculation based only on what I felt. The corridor leading from the main chamber had many doors leading off of it, and all uniformly plain and featureless.

Without even having to ask, I knew they were locked and inaccessible to me, perhaps to him as well. Now it was beginning to dawn on me what all this represented. This building was his collective lives. Sometimes called 'The Halls of Knowledge,' or the 'Akashic Records.' It's a Spiritualist and Theosophical concept that is said to hold the knowledge of the universe and our individual incarnations. It is said that everything we do, good and bad is stored for us to account for between incarnations. This building was a link to his 'Akashic,' and is where Ian tapped some of his inspiration. That explained his use of the term 'Centre of Being'.

At the far end of this corridor, which was about two meters wide and with the same high vaulted roof, he led me into a second chamber, which was almost a copy of the first except at the far end there was a raised area. It wasn't replicating a physical construct, such as a platform or a stage but it was a coalescence of vibrant energy.

Standing on this raised area of near solid energy, I could detect five figures, but figures that were not actually there, it was an afterglow from their presence.. Each afterglow wore pure white monk habits with hoods down. They each had white beards and all could have passed for Old Father Time, especially with the sense of great age that hung about them. Attached to each of their corded belts were a large gold key. All was composed of an energised afterglow that denoted their presence.

Ian told me they were the Source from were where his music came. They offered him the components of each composition, but was much more than just music. What was being produced were gateways of consciousness

Most of my visit to this 'Centre of Being' involved Ian talking very animatedly about what I could not see. He was rebuilding things in his mind and internally he could see everything as though it were there at that moment. I knew that nobody except Ian could ever see what the mechanics of this musical inspiration was, and it It was as hidden as Lynda's source, just as it should be. But the common bond between them was plain for me to see.

The source of Ian's inspiration isn't entirely unique. There are accounts of people dreaming what would become world famous musical compositions, poetry or novels. Even mathematicians are able to solve problems in their sleep that they were unable to while awake. We all have this 'Centre Of Being,' our own personal retreat of inspiration, and it can take any number of forms.

Descent Into Matter

When I travel of a night, be it human or Grey-shifted, I have a connection to everything. An intimate bond, not only with this planet and its inhabitants, but with the entire universe in a way that is quite profound, and finding words to adequately describe it defies me. It is the same as that I described earlier, when my face was inches from Shelagh's, only many, many more times stronger

This inadequacy to describe it often leaves me with a wish to explore the connectedness further, try to understand it better and pass that understanding on. This became an all-consuming desire after experiencing Ian's 'Centre Of Being.' I had perceived the universal connectedness while there; it seemed to ooze from the walls of that construct. So I did the only thing I could think of, I set my sights on exploring the source of this total connectedness at night.

Eventually I managed it, but it was very different to anything else I had experienced to date. I didn't leave my body in the usual way. There was no stepping out, and no melting of one world into another. I simply became aware of being nowhere.

I found myself in nothingness. I had no form, there was no time, and there was no existence beyond my own consciousness. I was part of the totality of pre-creation. I was everything, and everything existed within me. Everything expressed as the energy of an awakening potential. Then I sensed something. It was not a desire, because desire, will and intent didn't exist. Instead, I sensed the state of timeless consciousness shift very slightly. It was minuscule, but created the existence of an impulse to explore itself through acquiring a more complete sense of an awareness that didn't yet exist.

Consciousness within the nothingness began to explore itself via an infinite multitude of concepts. Within those self-creations, the consciousness poured itself as consciousness within THAT consciousness. So exactly the same sentience became the life within the creations it made of itself. We know that all life is made of star-stuff, but this was having me experience that everything inert is made of the same conscious-matter as the very life that exists within it.

This made concepts such as Karma much clearer to me. By harming and damaging anything – anything at all - we are hurting and damaging ourselves, any display of aggression is reflected back upon us. It was brought home to me at a very deep level that there is no separateness, not even across other dimensions of existence, not in the past or future, all of which exist as a single dynamic moment.

It seems that humanity has forgotten this, lost its way as it's immersed itself deeper, and isolated its senses in a physical framework. It's a trap that not only humanity, but all life has created for itself. I guess that what

I have described in my woefully inadequate way is an echo of the Biblical Fall, perhaps as portrayed through the Kabbalistic doctrine. It's an astonishing revelation when you are immersed within it.

This has made me and question many of the earthly values I held in human form; values that are somewhat different to when I am Grey-shifted. I guess that is why I experienced it, so that my humanity can understand why I have that sense of connectedness. Does the Grey have a living memory of that pre-creation? It's through the Grey-shift that I first felt this profound connectedness, and I think it re awoke that thirst for knowledge within my humanity. I suspect it is a continuation of the entanglement process that the intelligence had me engaged in.

This dream-walking, that takes me to Lynda's home, to Ian's Source and to the origin of consciousness, is a consequence of the shamanic training I've had for most of my life. Over many years it has forged deep bonds between not only humans and myself, animals and myself, and between the universe and myself.

Animal Afterlife

Here is my most beautiful experience with an animal soul. In mystic lore the 'Rainbow Bridge,' is a passage taken by animals between this life and the next. It's a transitional state that our companions take as they embark on their own journey to the afterlife and on towards rebirth. I have been privileged to stand at this side and see my animals set off across it, but as with most humans, I had never been allowed to step onto it. Not until now.

One of the most moving experiences was when my humble hamster passed on. She had been with me two and a half years, which made her quite old for a hamster; so old that she was almost hairless when she left me in the early hours of that cold New Year morning in 2011. We buried her in a small, wooden Turkish Delight box, accompanied with a little food and her favourite toy. I buried her body beside a waterfall feature that dropped into the fish pond.

That night I stepped out of my body and it was one of those occasions when I remained human. I found myself standing at one end of a very long bridge that arched across nothing but mist; not a cold winter mist, this was cloud-like and looked as soft and as gentle as a duvet. This was astral matter, but not choppy and violent as the human astral sea, this was the surface of a lake compared to the surface of a wild ocean. I looked down into my hands and saw that I was cupping my hamster. Demie, who now lay so small and young compared to how she had left our world.

I knew we were at the edge of the Rainbow Bridge, I had seen it many times. But here I was being invited to take her halfway across, that is a privilege granted to so few. So I started across and as I set foot on the bridge our minds made a connection and a transfer of thoughts took place between us. It sounds nonsensical in conversation-form, but do understand, all this happened in a fraction of a moment and was more of an awareness of each other than an actual conversation,

Communication at any level with a rodent would seem an absurdity unless you are freed from the restraints that has seen humanity alienate itself from the life force of the planet and the universe, as it plunges ever deeper, ever more blindly into its materialist state of existence. This is an idea of what passed:

Thank you.

For what?

Looking after me.

I didn't really do much looking after; you slept most of your life away. I told her.

But if I didn't feel safe and secure, I couldn't have. I needed to finish that cycle and now I can move on.

At first I didn't realise what the animal spirit was telling me, but as we moved on towards the centre of the bridge a transformation occurred. The hamster changed her form suddenly became a small baby ape in my arms. Then the strangest thing of all, across her new simian face was a smile as human as any I have ever seen. Then with a final *thank you*, as we reached the centre of the bridge, she faded and disappeared from my arms.

This is a memory I will carry for the remainder of my life, that small creature ending one cycle of incarnations as a rodent and preparing to begin another as an ape.

I just hope that when she comes back to this world there is still enough jungle for her to enjoy.

HARASSMENT

Plans Awry

On Friday 21 2012, I went to visit Denise Lane in St Albans. There was a plan which had been in place for two or three weeks, was we were going to be guests on an internet radio show which would go out live at 3.30am on Saturday morning; it was at such an unearthly hour because the host operated the station from his base in the USA. So I caught the train on Friday afternoon, Denise picked me up from the station and we went back to her flat.

After tea we relaxed with a film and chatted, then in the early evening Denise explained how she did things when she had been on his show in the past. She told me that with little to do for now, we could go to sleep or just rest if we didn't feel like sleeping. Then she would get a phone call from the radio station and they would discuss what she was going to talk about. We would then hook-up on air at 3.30am for the broadcast.

I decided I could do with a couple of hours sleep. It had been many years since I had discussed my experiences with anyone, so was nervous and thought a refreshed head would probably do me some good. I didn't bother setting my alarm, after all, Denise had been through this before on various shows - so what could possibly go wrong?

At 4.15am I was woken by Denise. We'd overslept!

I went downstairs, following a bleary-eyed and puzzled Denise as she told me that she couldn't understand what had happened, and went on to say that she never usually sleeps before a show since her mind was usually running over the questions that she might be asked. She looked glassy-eyed and said that she felt as though she had been drugged or sedated. I certainly wouldn't go so far as to suggest that, but we felt very sluggish, probably due to waking up abruptly.

Denise then checked her phone believing she would find at least a few missed calls from her American link-up, nothing. That was puzzling to say the least!

I went to my laptop, intending to log into the show's website to see if there was anything on there. Maybe something had happened and the host couldn't make it and had cancelled the show. But I couldn't even find the website! It had been the last thing I had accessed before switching the laptop off, so it should have featured on start-up .Of course, all this is disregarding the fact we had overslept, which would have had nothing to do with a show cancellation.

I hit the desktop icon but the result remained obstinate: 'Website not found'. I went to the search engine and typed the shows' address in full. Same result. 'Website not found'. So no phone calls and no access to the page meant we were not only finished as far as contact went, but in doing the show, as well! One thing that never crossed our minds was for Denise to simply phone him, it was just not even thought of. I've no idea why she didn't.

Denise wandered out of the kitchen without a single word to me. and I assumed she'd gone to find her laptop. After about fifteen or twenty minutes I realised she'd actually just gone back to bed - that puzzled me as much as anything else - It wasn't like Denise to beat a silent retreat without making some inquiries first. At this point I could do no more than finish my tea and go back to bed. Oddly there was little mention of it throughout the rest of Saturday and Sunday, even though I even found I could now get onto the show's website with no problem. However, with little said between us, it left me in the dark over any future prospects of doing a show.

The rest of the weekend, we both agreed, had a very strange feel about it. There was something hanging over the day that just didn't feel right and neither of us could identify it. However, we shrugged it off and spent the day visiting St Albans museum, and then taking a stroll through the one hundred acres of Verulamium Park. I went home Sunday morning, and still with almost no mention of the 'lost' broadcast.

Throughout the following week I had the feeling that I was being followed and watched, I even began to wonder if I was going to face a recurrence of the Darkness that had played with my head after Shelagh and I had been to the cinema. By Thursday of that week, and with that paranoia still clinging to me, I even began to think that people I encountered were going to suddenly turn nasty without cause. It was completely irrational and is probably the most uncomfortable and uncertain I have felt in my life. I found I was going through every hour of the week cautiously, and with great concern for my safety. It was a week of constant anxiety as I waited for something to happen that never did.

I phoned Denise and discussed these feelings with her, and she said she felt exactly the same, and like me, for the entire week.. But what I was to learn the weekend after the St Albans trip was that on the day we were at the museum and park, something bad was happening to someone I knew, but who was unconnected with the show.

While in St Albans I left my assistant, Alan, in charge of the shop, and didn't speak to him until he came in for his usual 11am shift on the following Saturday, as he settled down he asked how my previous weekend had gone and I explained how it had been a very strange non-event. Alan has an interesting background, having worked for more than thirty years as a psychiatric consultant, and in that time had garnered a wide ranging knowledge and experience of mental aberrations and disorders.

He was also deeply interested in the paranormal and his own spiritual development, so not only had he read extensively across a wide and diverse range of subjects, but also set about learning to read runes and tarot cards, which he became very competent at. But there was no interest in UFOs and aliens, which reminded me of Shelagh's own situation when we had met. So with his lack of interest I never found any reason to tell him about my 'other' existence.

Going back about three months before the show was even planned, Alan became aware of me one night in his sleep when I was engaged in extensive OBE travels with Denise during those first months after she had witnessed the shape-shift. I can still remember this journey quite clearly. I created a 'world' through which Denise and I passed on the way to our specific destination, which seemed to have a social rather than mission objective. It turns out that we went to visit a family; we sat around a table eating while Denise was talking to them. But it wasn't English being spoken, I was able to identify the tongue as German. I never did ask Denise if she knows how to speak German, but during that night, sitting at that table, she was fluent.

There were two follow-ups to this experience. The next morning, I sent my usual opening line to Denise: 'Do you remember last night?'

She told me she could remember having a dream, and that it was something to do with eating. I told her about the social gathering, and the food we'd eaten, and her response was that some of her family are German, so I assumed they were the ones we went to meet. But as with many other things I seemed to get up to, I couldn't understand why many of these trips were specifically for her since I was generally around her as a confidence builder.

But, during our transition through dream-states to our German objective, I spotted a change in the environment. I recognised what this change was. It became a road familiar to me, but I hadn't caused it, and it would remain a mystery until Alan explained that he'd had a dream in which he'd been in the street outside our shop in Manchester, and then suddenly saw me pass by on the opposite side of the street.

He told me I was following a woman dressed all in black, and that she seemed in a hurry to get somewhere. Alan tried to attract my attention, but received a shock when I turned my head to him and he saw my eyes were 'large black alien eyes' that wrapped around the side of my head. This was interesting for three reasons. The first, I have already mentioned, I had not, until this point, said anything about my Grey existence. Nor did he know Denise and her involvement with me. The third point of interest is that after that single appearance in an orange robe, she has always worn black. Sometimes a black jacket and black trousers, at other times she would wear a one-piece black jumpsuit. I put this imagery of hers down to The Matrix and it's theme of facing the reality behind the illusion. So I was dumbstruck that on the very night I had been OBE with Denise, Alan had not only seen us, but had seen me partially shape-shifted and had accurately described what Denise had worn.

Perhaps this is what had drew unwanted attention to him on the day I was in St Albans.

Stalked!

Having told Alan about the non-event and how my plans had come to nothing in the strangest of circumstances, I asked him what his weekend at the shop had been like. What he told me came as a shock. He said that the Saturday was one of the most frightening he'd ever experienced.

He left the shop at his usual time of 6pm and on the way home decided to stop for a takeaway, and as he returned to his car with his meal he noticed a black 4x4 parked behind his little smart-car. I asked Alan what had made him notice this vehicle in particular, and he said it's pristine condition stood out in stark contrast to his own car.

As he pulled away, he glanced in his mirror and saw the black vehicle was close behind him. Alan sped up, wanting to break the almost bumper to bumper, but try as he might, the 4x4 remained close behind. When he slowed down, so did the 4x4. When he accelerated, so did the black vehicle which, by this time, was giving him the distinct and uneasy feeling of a pursuit. Alan approached a set of traffic lights and moved into the left lane which offered the option to go straight ahead or to turn left. He came to a stop as the lights changed to red.

The 4x4 pulled into the lane next to him, this only permitted a right-turn, so at least Alan knew they would be parting company. Alan had his window open because it was a warm afternoon, then from the corner of his eye he saw the 4x4's passenger window roll halfway down. I asked him if he saw the driver, but he said that wouldn't have been possible because he didn't look directly at the vehicle, not wanting to risk antagonising the occupant. Then the most inexplicable happened, Alan heard a man's voice from inside the vehicle, which, so I am told, seemed to be little more than a whisper:

'Mr smart car driver.'

Alan described the tone of voice as 'hushed and soporific', he still puzzles over this; How could he possibly have heard a whisper from vehicle-to-vehicle at that time of day? Surely the amount of traffic and other noise all around him would have precluded this? He is also convinced the driver muttered something else but he was unable to make out what it was. Then the lights changed to green and Alan drove on, while to his immense relief, the 4x4 turned right and headed away from him.

He told me there had been no threats or antagonism, there had been nothing apart from this quiet voice uttering those four words. But it left Alan with a most uneasy feeling for the remainder of his journey home. He even began to wonder if something had been said that he had only registered unconsciously, perhaps a threat of some kind.

What most intrigued me is that the man sat telling me this bizarre experience is a former psychiatric consultant!

Alan continued: how when he got home, and lasting for several days, there was an uneasy sense of 'presence', as though something ominous was stalking him. With it, came a pervading sense of dread that he couldn't rationalise. I asked him if he was aware of such things as 'psychic attack' and he said he was familiar with such things, but this didn't seem like that; it was a feeling of being constantly watched. Accompanying this paranoia was a headache that started as soon as the 4x4 pulled alongside him, and it too persisted for days, not even dulling when he took strong painkillers.

Then things got even stranger for him. While I had been sat in St Albans on the Sunday morning, still wondering what had gone wrong with the show and while watching a film – which happened to be *Men In Black III* - Alan started seeing a bright red Chrysler car. From Sunday through to Wednesday, this vehicle was everywhere he went. Alan says he has a habit of going to places at very short notice, such as suddenly deciding to visit his mother or a friend, or making random trips to the supermarket. But for those four days, no matter where he went or who he went to see, or how randomly he decided to go, he would encounter the red Chrysler waiting at his destination.

On the few occasions he attempted to drive close in an attempt to see who was in the car, it would move and park further away, or leave the area completely. I asked, what made him think it was the same vehicle? Alan explained that it was a new model Chrysler only recently available and there wasn't many on the road at that time, a fact which made the vehicle all the more distinctive; even more so as the colour was a shade which appealed to Alan and drew his attention all the more. Everything about it suggested the driver *wanted* the vehicle to be seen by him

During this conversation I noticed Alan constantly referring back to what he heard from the window of the 4x4, and although there was nothing threatening in what was said, the initial impact was as if someone had attacked his car with a brick!

'So your reaction to him saying "Mr Smart car man," was as if you'd been victim to a road-rage attack?'

'Yes, as though I had been assaulted.'

I was astonished at hearing this, but I was also now certain that something subliminal *had* affected him. It had to be, since there was nothing else left.

This is his opinion of the entire experience:

After the events of that Saturday evening, and the subsequent uneasiness, I reflected on any potential issues that may have contributed to feeling this way in my personal life but could not think of anything causing me distress or even the slightest angst, and as I have over thirty-five years' experience working in mental health, I'm aware of the many aberrations that the mind can produce. But I had no reason to suspect I might be deluded or suffering any other syndrome, nor have I ever used recreational drugs. So I cannot offer an explanation for the way these events made me feel, or for the way they impinged on my consciousness.

This experience and its aftermath coming from the mouth of a mental health professional is astonishing testimony, Alan even stated that had someone reported this episode to him, he would have seen it as an indication of early stage paranoid schizophrenia, the elements were in place and would have been very easy to diagnose.

Perhaps this is how they operate? Disguising their footprint by playing with the fragility of human sanity, and the illusion of paranoid schizophrenia being an easy camouflage to hide beneath. Think about it; who's going to take too much notice of someone who feels they are being watched and followed?

But how could any of this linked to the failed radio broadcast? I don't know, but I believe it was. The 'coincidence' of ours and Alan's experiences happening at precisely the same time are simply too much to be anything else, especially if you remember that all through the week that Alan had a feeling he was being 'watched', Denise and I felt exactly the same.

But I don't know why Men in Black - if it was MIB - would intimidate someone who works in my shop, has no knowledge of the UFO subject, or indeed, has any involvement with what I do, aside from seeing us in his dream-state. However, this encounter was enough to scare him into selling the smart car - a vehicle that stood out from many others on the road - simply because he didn't want to remain a potential target.

The encounters with the 4x4 and red Chrysler left Alan fearful and uneasy for many weeks, even six months later when I raised the subject again while gathering my notes for this book, he still felt sick and edgy whenever the black 4x4 was mentioned. In fact, he distanced himself from the subject entirely and said he wanted nothing to do with it, and if I recount his experience he wants his identity hidden. This is a man having had an encounter that has scared him half to death.

But then it returned.

Two weeks after he recounted details for this book, Alan suddenly had two further encounters with the mysterious 4x4. He's a car park warden at the privately-owned flats where he lives, and one of his responsibilities is ensuring that non-residents don't use the residential parking bays. On this particular evening, he went out to have a look round, as his duty calls for, and he noticed a vehicle on the opposite side of the car park which he didn't recognise as belonging to a resident, so he started towards it. He knew a driver was sitting in it, perhaps waiting for someone, because the engine was idling and the headlights were on. But as he continued towards it he began to get a bad feeling, maybe it was the way the vehicle gleamed under the car park lighting. Then he recognised it, the immaculate condition and those black tinted windows were unmistakable.

It was the 4x4!

Without any warning the vehicle revved its engine and lunged across the car park, its headlights switching to full beam in a deadly attempt to dazzle him. Alan shifted to one-side and the vehicle sped past, narrowly missing him. It swung onto the road and disappeared into the night. Was this a deliberate murder attempt? I found it difficult to believe that it was in any way associated with me asking him to recall the original 4x4 incident, and although sounding like something from a Hollywood thriller, I know Alan not to be a liar.

I questioned him over possible reasons for what appeared to be an increased level of intimidation, maybe he'd upset somebody enough for them to seek revenge; but he was absolutely positive that he hadn't. I know Alan to be a very gentle man, there's nothing aggressive about him at all and it leaves me unable to imagine someone displaying such a rage against him.

I could see he was as baffled as me, why had the mysterious red vehicle been waiting for him? It seemed to know where he would be in advance. Had the 4x4 and then the red Chrysler been driven by the same person? I didn't know.

Alan was getting so paranoid that he started looking through my office at the rear of the shop, hunting for bugging devices. He stopped only when I pointed out that they didn't seem to be following him. They seemed to know where he would be even when he hadn't told anyone where he was going.

The last encounter was on January 30, 2014, with the smart-car long gone and him now driving something less obvious. Also, having put some distance between himself and the experiences, he had started to take some interest in the subject of UFOs. Having undergone such extraordinary events, and knowing first-hand how many experiencers felt, he wondered whether he could call on his professional experience to help people who underwent similar traumatic and inexplicable encounters to himself. I was all for it and encouraged him by loaning him a number of books I thought would be a useful introduction to the subject.

The day after I lent him some books, he went to the supermarket, purchased what he wanted and returned to his car. He was just starting to drive off, when that distinctive black 4x4 seemed to come out of nowhere., and on a collision course with him at high speed.

It was upon him so suddenly he was forced to swerve and hit a concrete post, Alan was unhurt but the car needed a new wing. This was enough for him to react in the same way that I had back in 1993 when I had isolated myself. He brought back the few books and abandoned the study of a subject into which he could have offered so much expertise.

I did suggest that he go to the supermarket and ask them to see if the incident was on CCTV, but he was too scared to do so in case it provoked an even more hostile response. I suggested I go instead, but he didn't want me to do that either. He wanted it left completely alone. Alan was in fear of his life.

I am not so self-deluded as to believe I am involved in anything so important that it would warrant such dramatic attempts at silencing, however,

I did as Alan requested and never discussed it again, nor did I approach the supermarket which may have filmed details of the vehicles license plate.

SHAMANIC SPACE-TIME

The Shamanic Path

What we refer to as *shamanism* is both an ancient healing tradition and a way of life, and as my training has shown, is a path to connect with all of creation. The word *shaman* isn't entirely accurate as it originates from a Siberia. When Russians colonised eastwards through Siberia in the 17th century, they encountered the Evenk, which in Russian was *Tungas*. The Evenk, along with their neighbours, the Buryats, use the term 'shaman' to identify their tribal spiritual leaders. Inevitably, the word spread from the Russians to the rest of Europe and the Americas via anthropologists who were studying Native Americans.

These anthropologists were in need of a word to describe what they *thought* the Native Americans were doing, and they were puzzled because they couldn't understand the very different world views that these people had. So with time, 'shaman' has changed in the West, and what formerly was a specific term used by specific Siberian tribes, has come to mean everything and yet nothing. We in the West had branded and merchandise anything earth-based as shamanism. Although clearly, the countless similarities between various ancient traditions across the globe have also encouraged the generalization of the word.

Over the past few decades 'shamanism' has been popularized throughout the western world via the internet from new-age groups. Today, it's often difficult to distinguish between traditional forms of shamanism and modern esoteric practices that use the label as convenience, and it looks 'traditional'. So with that history and explanation of the word, it just remains for me to say that my use of label is just for Western convenience, I have no specific word for what I and others like me do, it is not a marketable product that requires branding.

So moving on; one could view shamanism as the universal spiritual wisdom inherent to all indigenous tribes. As all ancient spiritual practices are rooted in nature, shamanism is the method by which we as human beings can strengthen that natural connection

Shamanism is as old as humanity itself, rock art depicting shamanic visions and shamanic journeying date back at least 30,000 years. This makes shamanism not only much older than any other spiritual practice and reaching across Europe, Africa, North and South America and Asia, but also from which every religion on Earth has it's deepest and most esoteric roots.

Shamanism is the original means of contact between humanity and the otherworlders – the gods, and angels, the demons and the djinn.

Harking back to its traditional form, the shaman – who would be selected for the vocation, perhaps because he or she was a loner, maybe marked as an outsider of the tribal community, possibly also prone to poetry or song – would ascend to the heavens and descend to the underworld. There the spirits transform the candidate through means of terrifying death-and-rebirth reformation. The result of this transmutative procedure endows the re-constructed shaman with the ability to heal the ills of the tribe, escort the dead to the afterlife and to hunt for - and bring back - the souls or soul fragments of victims that had been taken by an enemy. Last but not least, the shaman would mediate between the tribe and the spirits.

But this is at a price, as I well know. A shaman in the classic sense of the word is little more than a slave. You cannot leave the path, and you cannot defy the spirits. Did I use the word 'slave'? Yes, I did, that's because your existence is governed by a multitude of prohibitions, and to violate them, more often than not brings immediate retribution. This has been handed down to me on several occasions, not through being rebellious, but rather through not having a clue what was happening. But it seems that even ignorance is no defence.

The shaman would help ensure an ecological balance by guiding the tribe in their food-hunt. Through trance, animistic communication and sixth-sense, they would safeguard the herd which brought about conservation resulting in a balanced assurance of survival through the seasons for both the tribe and the animals that were so vital to the community. Unfortunately, this harmony is now all but lost due to the sweep of industrial civilisation. The plague-like and invasive proliferation of industrialised civilisation has pushed the imbalance to almost a point of no return: the bulldozed forests, the damming of the rivers, choking pollutants pouring into the atmosphere, chemicals and GM crops sown across the lands; the industrialists are terraforming the planet into something obscene and poisoned, causing a global soul-sickness.

What do I mean by 'soul-sickness'?

Humanity starves with a hunger for entertainment of an increasingly jaded nature, such as the proliferation of 'reality' TV, the craving for more and more possessions and wealth, as reflected in the seeming need for the very latest model of phone, or that elusive lottery win with its immense rollover figures that spiral into unimaginable millions. There is the grasping for ever more power by the very few, as demonstrated in the lies and betrayals of the politicians towards the people who naively continue to elect them. Those are symptoms of soul-sickness.

The acquisition of what we crave at a superficially material level will not lead to anything but transient satisfaction, fleeting at best. But like a junkie needing that next fix, it perpetuates an endless drive to acquire even more, and the inability to satisfy that hunger encourages increasingly corrupt methods to deal with it.

This has seen a resurgent interest in 'shamanism', entwined with the seven decades of UFOs and alien contact being popularised by the media, it results in people looking to the skies and considering what might be up there. Maybe it's an intentional nudge in the ribs, encouraging humanity to think beyond their own rapacious existence. The contactee messages channelled, and the abductee stories brought back, all hint at something more than the suicide that this industrialised, world-devouring monster of a civilisation is threatening us with.

Over the last sixty decades, the abductees have been returning with messages of doom. During the Cold War those warnings were focused on the proliferation of nuclear weapons and the imminent threat of global annihilation. After that, the emphasis was on the ecological damage humanity is doing to the planet, and many of the contactees bearing these warnings returned as 'reformed' people. For example, maybe they would give up a corporate way of life and devote themselves to a spiritual or nature-orientated vocation. Others have such mind-expanding experiences that they begin to study the Kabbala in order to try better understanding what they underwent. Or they might develop a deeper empathy with animals and plants and work in conservation.

This shows that many encounters leave the experiencer a very changed person, a more spiritually aware individual. But there are also great numbers who are left traumatised, frightened and confused by what they have been forced to undergo. Sometimes this resolves itself and at other times it does not. Most abductions can actually be seen as a form of death-and-rebirth ritual, because it changes their concept of reality and adds new dimensions to their existence. So do abductees undergo a form of shamanic experience? Is a global shamanic death-and-rebirth of humanity under way? I ask that because the life story you have just read is fundamentally shamanic in nature.

Raven Kaldera is a northern-tradition shaman and a pansexual FTM transgendered intersexual. That complicated string of titles translate as someone who was born with an intersex condition, raised female, transitioned to being socially and physically male, and became a transgender/intersex activist. This was at the time when he was claimed by the Norse death goddess, Hela, who visited him and informed him that he was required to undergo gender reassignment. 'I'm sending you where you're needed most,' she told him.

So he went through not only sex reassignment but also suffered a protracted illness that culminated in a near-death experience, then began to be plagued by gods and spirits. Afterwards, trying to make sense of what was happening to him, he began to read anthropological accounts of traditional tribal shamans and soon realised that he had suffered through experiences that were frighteningly similar to those of tribal shamans of western Eurasia.

Further research revealed that a good number of the things that the gods and spirits wanted him to do were things that northern tribal shamans were traditionally expected to do, and that was in spite of him being a white American. There was nothing left to do but either do the work and live the job, or go mad and die, so today Raven is a northern-tradition shaman in the modern world.

On his website, Raven says:

The word "shamanism" has been thrown around a great deal these days, and has been attached to all manner of things, sometimes with only a vague understanding of its meaning. Most people who go to a class on "shamanic this-or-that" have very little knowledge of what actual tribal shamans practised in any given culture, or what sorts of things were and are practised transculturally among them. A researcher or interested seeker, looking through all the widely varied literature, will notice both similarities and differences between anthropological descriptions of long-ago tribal shamans and modern-day shamanic practitioners. They may also run across specialised terms such as 'core shamanism', 'shamanistic practice', 'shamanistic behaviour', and so on. It can be rather confusing . I've chosen to use the term 'classic shamanism' to describe the cross-cultural set of experiences described by tribal shamans across the world. It shares with 'core shamanism' many of the same tools and techniques of consciousness - journeying, visualisation, drumming, ritual, working with animal and plant totems, nature spirits, or ancient gods; natural hallucinogens, cultural symbol systems, and so forth. It isn't the tools that differentiate the two, as core shamanism borrowed those tools from classic shamanism. Instead, it's the central spiritual experience that is strongly different.

So let's look at the key points in Raven Kaldera's classic shamanism:

- Is open only to those who are clearly chosen by the spirits. Although one can offer oneself to the spirits, they may or may not accept.

- Is generally entirely involuntary. The individual

is chosen by the spirits, often with no warning, and is not allowed to refuse the "gift", or else they will suffer illness, and/or insanity, and/or death. They can never stop being a shaman so long as they live, or it will recur.

• Is nearly always accompanied in the early stages by severe, life-threatening experiences, including but not limited to chronic serious illness, psychotic break, and/or near-death experience.

• Is nearly always accompanied by a traumatic death-and-rebirth experience, after which the personality is radically changed. A visionary experience of being dismembered and rebuilt differently by the spirits is evident cross-culturally in the accounts of many tribal shamans, and is almost a hallmark of the experience

• Causes radical, unusual, and permanent changes to the aura and astral body. This process is inflicted onto the shaman by the spirits, and is entirely out of their control.

• Shamanic practice occupies the main focus, time, and energy of the individual's life for the rest of their existence. All mundane careers, projects, loyalties, and relationships are secondary to the shaman's career of spiritual service.

• Primarily taught by divine and/or spirit teachers, although in the beginning stages the novice is usually taught the cultural context and symbolism by another shaman.

• Never taught in groups; always one-on-one as an oral tradition.

• Lives are bounded with dozens of increasing taboos, violation of which generally brings immediate illness, pain, or other physical and spiritual retribution.

- Cannot work entirely alone; must be attached to a tribe. If no tribe is in evidence at the time of their shamanic rebirth, one will be provided for them by the spirits. Ability to see clients outside their demographic group varies, usually depending on their tradition and their particular patron spirits.

- Is almost always seen primarily as a path of service to a particular tribe.

- Mental breakdown or temporary psychosis common to the early "death-and-rebirth" stage, after which shamans have been tested and found to be comparatively extremely sane and stable. Mental illness never returns as long as they continue to do their jobs.

- Generally requires one specific central cultural context, although they may borrow from neighbouring (and thus not radically different) cultures. The symbolic context seems to be a useful 'anchoring-point' for the training of beginning classic shamans, and aids in bonding them with the tribe that they are to serve.

- Relationship with the gods and/or spirits ranges from propitiating/coaxing to being their outright slave, for which the shaman gains access to their powers.
www.northernshamanism.org

When we consider the bullet-points that describe working with a tribe, in Raven's case he looks to the broad sweep of the transgendered community as his tribe. In my situation, and having interacted with a vast number of individuals across the globe, humanity itself is my tribe. But that statement isn't designed to feed my ego; it needs to be understood from the perspective of the Grey, an immersive illusion I adopt for the interaction required.

Raven describes the strict and unconditional terms forced upon a shaman: no negotiation, no compromise, and if you deviate, little mercy is shown. But for all its daunting implications, you are selected because you *can* bend to the regime. In the case of Raven Kaldera, during a critical life-and-death battle with physical illness he was confronted by a deity who revealed herself to be Hel, the Norse goddess of death, and it was she who set about his transformative process, just as happened to me following my path-working encounter with Cerridwen, following my accident. Hel also told Raven he was required to undergo gender reassignment, which isn't such an unusual request as Shamanism has always had a relationship with transgenderism, and you'll find pagan gods across many cultures are either hermaphroditic or at various times switched genders for one reason or another.

Says Raven:

> *Shamans have to work with their energy bodies a lot;*
> *they have to shape-shift and things like that. If you grew*
> *up with an energy body that was different to your*
> *physical body, you're used to that distance and you're*
> *used to being able to do things with your energy body*
> *that the ordinary person doesn't even think about. I*
> *found that many transfolk are able to see and know and*
> *move their energy body around much faster than others.*

In my case, one transition involved my so-called 'soul-fusion' with Shelagh, perhaps creating a hermaphrodite element to my energy body, which was then brought into perfect balance after my own gender-related switch. It's particularly interesting that it was only after this occurred that I went aboard the ships, and always as a - perhaps genderless - Grey. This then raises the question, why would such an otherworldly figure have been involved in a shamanic initiation scenario? It clearly linked with me some years before, perhaps whatever is behind the 'Red Eagle' image put a finger on me, by way of selection, and said *this one*. But why would it select me?

One far-flung idea could be that this intelligence is not only from the distant future but is in fact, *me* from that future! If the consciousness is a time traveller, it might not be just a random meshing with me, But a far-future incarnation which would put the consciousness into an eternal entanglement with its own former reincarnation!

However, we do know that these beings have a deep relationship with traditional and ancient shamanic processes, we also know they are often seen during DMT or other hallucinogenic-driven journeys. We know it through the cave art that prehistoric shaman have left behind. There are many legends of the Star-People coming down to earth. In Kimberley, Western Australia, there is a famous cave art depicting the Wandjina: Creators that came from the Milky Way to create the earth and people. So maybe far from being mystified as to why the Grey would be part of my own shamanic rites, perhaps we should understand it as a key element of all shamanic reality. So having now seen what a shaman is, let's have a look at what I underwent and see how it can be viewed in context.

Process Of initiation

If the entity we know as Red Eagle seems to have been brutal, even downright hostile in what he forced me to endure, it's because in shamanic initiation, he is what is known as the Threshold Guardian: a trans-personal being who offers the opportunity to directly experience every aspect of the Universe - not only the physical and sensual universe, but the Otherworld, which embraces parallel dimensions and alternate realities - it's a mind expansive experience beyond the illusory walls of four-dimensional space and time.

So, initially the would-be shaman is approached by way of a contact which often takes the form of a paranormal or psychic experience in which you meet the Threshold Guardian face to face and in which he or she questions you. It will be this Guardian's task to train you.

In my particular case, Red Eagle, through having taken on the image of the Maori Mystic and then The Man in the shop, questioned me about myself, my view of the world and my fears and hopes, before easing into a discussion about alien life and the paranormal. In fact, if it hadn't been for a gap of eighteen months, one conversation might could have almost been a continuation of the other.

To be honest, it's rather naive that I even continue referring to him as 'Red Eagle', as he's no more a Native American than he is a Maori mystic. Not only was he the Threshold Guardian, but he also became The Companion. One who accompanies me in my own role as The Journeyer. The

Companion is a friend and ally who works with and supports me as I enter the spirit world to heal, seek advice, communicate with humans during their sleep-time, or mediate between humans and the Greys. This Companion not only opened the various doors to the Otherworld for me, but also cements the links I have to it. So this entity I still refer to as 'Red Eagle' is so much more than that; much more than the Threshold Guardian; much more than a consciousness who assessed his pupil's potential.

From there, initiation moves on to that daunting stage in which you confront a critical personal crisis, and it's not an exaggeration to say this is an earthquake of soul shattering and life altering magnitude. This personal crisis usually takes one of two forms; either it's a serious and life-threatening physical illness, or it can be an overpowering mental condition. This deep psychological and emotional experience brings the shaman initiate into a transformative relationship with nothing less than the Angel of Death.

It sounds dramatic and I intend it that way because that's exactly what it is and it's what I endured following our late night visit to the cinema and my sanity was clawed to ribbons. So what's the purpose of such an ordeal? Well, it's a savage trial in confrontation with death and the ultimate goal of conquering the fear of it. Surviving this terrifying ordeal leads to nothing less than integrating Death into yourself; after all, how can you fear what is now a part of you? Successfully dealing with Death means the shaman has one foot firmly in the underworld, and has laid to rest his fear of death. This encounter is the well-documented 'death and resurrection experience' - dismemberment of the shaman's old personality and reformation into a new being.

So how did this ordeal work itself out within me. The footsteps that followed us home were representative of Death; an audible tool that started working on my senses to make me feel stalked and insecure. It is quite likely that Shelagh's involvement that night was purely as a witness, and to discourage me from being able to dismiss it as imagination; It was the same with the dinosaur apparition, part of a 'softening up' process before the enthusiastic attempt to unhinge my mind. That first night's horror was for my human consciousness to survive, and although it was delusion, it was so powerfully presented that my mind lost any way of distinguishing between real and illusory.

I was brainwashed into believing I was on a train bound for a death camp; but why was that particular imagery used? I can't say with any certainty, Maybe it was just because it was fresh in my mind from the film which made it easily accessible. On the second night, the Grey - my 'second consciousness' - was faced with its own critical moment of existence. But, unlike mine, it was a physical crisis.

The Grey, being seduced by the EVS, perceived it as not only an implacable evil, but also as something irresistibly alluring. Stepping through would have separated the Grey consciousness from myself, but as I was in a mental entanglement with that entity, it might well have permanently damaged my human consciousness.

So over those two nights of integrating Death, along with everything it could throw at me, it had me almost physically trying to claw my brain from my skull; It had the Grey survive some form of annihilation that only it seemed to recognise. This is why Red Eagle offered no help whatsoever when Shelagh questioned him, despite me passionately begging him for help. I suppose the problem was that I constantly lost sight of the fact that I was undergoing an initiatory process, not only because of our mundane urban environment, but because Shelagh was involved. This was all arranged to keep me in a state of confusion and driven to such despair that I often reached what I thought was a breaking point.

That absorption of Death was a triumph, but it came with a price attached. In later years, when Clive Potter arranged for me to meet individuals in order to compare experiences, many took an instant and inexplicable dislike to me.

An example was a trio from Coventry - one man and two women - whose claims, although at times rather vague, was a belief that they were being 'guided' towards recovering a buried sword. Its purpose was treated as a close secret and so was never revealed to me, but I understood from the cryptic remarks that it was very ancient and wielded 'great power'. Although we welcomed them into our home and did all we could to offer warmth and hospitality, it became immediately apparent that they didn't like me. In fact, although they arrived late Saturday afternoon with the intention of staying until late Sunday afternoon, all three rose very early on Sunday and made immediate and hasty preparations to leave as soon as they possibly could; by 8am they were gone.

I was baffled by their attitude and so sent the man an enquiring letter. Now a safe distance from me, he made his dislike very clear. In fact, as his letter continued, I found it bordered on pathological hatred. To these people - as well as others - I was a 'force of darkness', or there was 'something dark' about me.

This is a well attested reaction following the Death-and-Rebirth transformation. Some psychics are able to feel that you have fused with Death but are unable to interpret their feelings, so shy away - or as in the case of my Coventry trio, flee! - In other words, the horror that I've experienced and absorbed still exists as an internal energy and can be read by others, and will manifest within their consciousness as fear, apprehension or evil. This was to frustrate me in the years to come because whenever I attempted to get close to people to work with them in one way or another, they would, more often than not, back away.

What of the Men in Black? Were they a response to me attempting to circumvent the traditional shamanic process? Was I walking such a narrow path that to deviate even slightly would bring threats and intimidation to our door? It might be helpful if we take into account one of Raven Kandera's key points:

- Lives are bounded with dozens of increasing taboos, violation of which generally brings immediate illness, pain, or other physical and spiritual retribution.

So if that's the case, it means the MIB were a kind of regulator and intervening to maintain a set of parameters that I didn't understand. One thing about the MIB I do know is that many of these visitors are tulpa in nature. They turn up, usually out of nowhere, in vehicles and clothes that have clearly not experienced even a day of wear and tear. They seem cumbersome and clumsy in their attitude and movement. They seem unfamiliar with how they should behave.

Trauma

I knew for at least a month beforehand, that a particularly difficult encounter was going to take place. As is usual, I wasn't aware of any details, but I did know, somehow, that it would be emotionally distressing for me. Because of this I knew I needed to distance myself from Denise Lane.

My role with her had primarily been to help begin the healing of her mind from deep-rooted psychological issues - that and helping to expand her mind. I had accomplished all I possibly could, and there were clear improvements in her day to day attitude. But now I was being pressured by the 'other intelligence' to step back and detach myself emotionally in preparation for that next and apparently unavoidable encounter.

However, I faced two problems, one of them was that I had begun to form strong friendship connections with Denise and her family. It was my first experience of 'family', and whenever I visited them, I could feel the strong and loyal bond between them as a domestic group. All it really achieved was to strengthen the bond between us and is something which shouldn't have happened to begin with. I ought to have retained an almost doctor to patient relationship. The second problem was in trying to explain to Denise, that my work with her was finished and I needed to step back.

She wasn't able to understand what I was trying to explain; she told me that she'd become so accustomed to me being with her that she saw me as her 'comforter'. She also described me as her 'strength and confidence'. I wasn't really prepared for this, nor did I know how to deal with it. This was complicated even further when Denise told me that I would need to be around longer, and if I did step away from her and she needed me, all she'd need to do is 'sent out a call' and I would respond. Unfortunately, that isn't how it works, but our entanglement perhaps made it appear that way to her.

I couldn't explain why I felt the next person would be almost too much for me to handle, I just seemed to know it. Regardless of this sense of forewarning, the lack of any real understanding gave me reason to override the increasing urgency to remove myself from Denise's' environment - I knew I was going against my better judgement by not breaking the link, and in my mind, I was even being told that if I didn't break away from her the situation would be forced and it would have dire consequences for any future friendship with her. I continued to ignore the warnings and this was to lead to an almost catastrophic outcome.

In November 2013, I found myself on a ship. I was Grey-shifted and in a featureless rectangular room that appeared to be about five feet by eleven feet long. There was another Grey standing beside me and this creature had authority over whatever mission they were engaged in. Ahead of me was a large observation window that dominated most of the wall. Beyond that, I could see a large circular room in which five Greys were attempting to subdue a human female, a woman who appeared to be offering a remarkable level of defiance.

The Greys had managed to subdue her to an extent, but the ferocity of her resistance had taken them unprepared and she'd even been able to tear free of their pacification techniques that so often worked with others. I seemed to be there because they couldn't understand how her fight was defeating them, they needed me to absorb her emotions, and that would somehow make them available for analysis and help the Greys' understand how her fight or flight was being so successful.

You need to remember that during this experience, I was thinking as one of them, I was hooked into their hive-mind and because of that, I was finding this struggle just as intriguing as they were. I knew I would have to take her emotional content back with me so they might be able to define whatever it was that acted as a resistance, so I fixed my eyes on her and she responded by looking up towards the observational window and our eyes locked. I was suddenly consumed by a tsunami of raw and violent 'alien' human emotions. Nothing could have prepared me for the seething turmoil that stormed into my mind.

I crashed back to earth and into my human body.

I woke instantly, shaking and sick. I had no control over my body that felt as though it had undergone a deeply traumatic event; my heart was pounding and I was sweating. I could recall everything from that journey, and what eclipsed all else was the big dark eyes of the female, they had been filled with more terror and dread than I would have thought possible, and perhaps emphasised because of the alien mind I was using at the time. I have never seen anything like it in my life.

As soon as I recalled those eyes, I burst into tears and I felt as though I could have laid there forever, my body and mind felt demolished. My partner, stirred awake and asked what was wrong, I told him I'd had a disturbing dream and that I'd be OK. The fact is that I wasn't OK, I was haunted by those human eyes fixing on me and consuming my mind with the emotional turmoil I had invited into my head.

That next day I was a complete mess and sank even deeper. I can't go into any details because I seemed to be experiencing the emotional footprint of a single human lifetime, and within the space of a few hours I had sunk to the point of suicide. Although I know quite clearly it was the female's emotional trauma that I was experiencing, my human brain was trying frantically to process this information and was translating it as hatred towards myself.

I tried to discuss this problem with the few people I was able to confide in, Denise being one of them. It was only while talking to her that it suddenly dawned on me that this mental collapse was because I hadn't distanced myself from her, and I was realising that had I had done so, it would have put a 'buffer' of several months between her own emotional issues and those of this other female who also had emotional issues! But having ignored the prompting, I was now paying a dreadful price.

Now realising what was happening, and having no idea about how to proceed, I asked Denise for advice. I knew that she wouldn't have much of a clue but I had nowhere else to turn, and with my mind becoming unhinged, I was at the pinnacle of desperation.

Denise's advice was explicit and to the point. I needed to 'work through it'. Whatever that meant. I just couldn't get her to understand that the emotional effect originated with someone else, that I was collapsing under a kind of negative quantum entanglement.

Only a day later I located the female encountered on the ship. She was on the social media contact list of someone I had been talking to recently, for no particular reason I rolled through the profile pictures of some of her friends, Then stopped at one and stared at the face on the screen; I recognised those eyes and the face quickly resolved itself into the one I had seen on the ship.

I contacted this woman, Laura, who at that time was living in Bridport, in Dorset. I also found she'd posted something regarding her experience on an alien abduction website, so it was obvious she had some memory of it, which didn't surprise me in the least, not with the degree of trauma she had displayed. Her having some conscious memory gave me something of a doorway to her. I'd also had the 'inspired' solution to my problem. I could only cope with what she had passed to me by sharing it back, in a manner of speaking. To simply connect with her would be enough to lift the remorseless depression and thoughts of suicide.

I mentioned this idea to Denise, but she suggested I don't tell Laura anything about my involvement. I don't understand why she said that, but I knew it was the only way this could be dealt with. Besides, I couldn't see what I had to hide. Denise could only view this with a human state of mind, and assumed the depression was caused by the things I witnessed of a night. But that wasn't the case and that I'd reached a critical juncture; I had to do something because I didn't think I could survive many emotional clashes of this magnitude.

It wasn't until January 9, 2013, a month after the experience, that I made contact with Laura through the website. When I approached the subject with her I found she was extremely confused over what she could remember and felt it best to consign the entire memory as just a bad dream. At that stage it would have been very easy to encourage Laura further into that belief, and then to follow Denise's suggestion by not telling the woman anything.

But aside from a discussion being of help to me, I felt she needed to know. After all, it was her life it had impacted. Also, I was not prepared to live a 'secret life'. If I hid away on this occasion, it would probably happen again and again. I couldn't live while hiding this thing as a secret; making me feel like some kind of Jekyll and Hyde. However, once we were talking, I found her memory of the crazy dream to be quite lucid. She did say that she'd undergone other experiences, such as night paralysis.

Here is a portion of my opening conversation with her:

Laura: *I don't know what the hell went on but I am freaked out and going with the theory it was just a bad dream. I couldn't fall asleep for ages then all of a sudden I just got sleep paralysis. I could feel it happening so started fighting against it; but when I fought against it, I swear to God I was surrounded by aliens. One bent over and looked straight at me [as if to tell me] that I was awake then looked at the others. I couldn't see them properly - they were like translucent or something, but I got so freaked out I decided I'd rather not see and just gave in to my sleep paralysis and made myself close my eyes and go to sleep. This may sound so ridiculous; it's probably because I've been reading about UFOs and stuff. I've never had this happen before, but it was like they were trying to put me to sleep and I was fighting it like crazy then just thought 'to Hell with seeing this', and fell asleep. I was totally freaked out. It was really weird because Tom, [one of Laura's two dogs] wasn't in my room. When I woke up* *properly a bit later he came running in my room and jumped on my bed, tail wagging like I had been out. But I hadn't.*

Me: *Your encounter with aliens wasn't a dream. How do I know? I was there. I saw you and when I came back to earth I carried your fear and confusion. The following day I felt suicidal and was suffering severe depressions. I had connected with your life and experienced much of it within the space of a few hours. I was on the ship when you were taken.*

Laura: *So did you see what they did. Were you in the window?*

Me: *Yes, I was. You looked directly at me.*

Laura: *Did you see what they did to me? I know what they did to me so did you see it?*

Me: *I never come back with full memory. So if I did, it has been blocked*

Laura: *Why were you stood in the window?*

Me: *I was there as an observer, because they needed to have you monitored. I have done this before, but your emotions hit me so hard.*

There is more, but I just wanted to show how the subject was introduced. A short while later - just hours in fact - I began to feel much better. The suicidal depression dissipated, and by the following morning it had gone completely and I felt as though it had never been there at all. I have no idea how sharing the experience back with her could have helped, but I seemed to know that it would, and it did.

Because Laura had virtually nobody she could discuss all this with, I put her into contact with a couple of other experiencers I knew, and this is probably the best thing I could have done for her, and I was mindful that I needed to take a step back and not become as deeply bonded as I had with Denise.

Diane Tessman, in *The UFO Agenda* is quite clear about abduction experiencers who exhibit extreme and violent reaction:

When they take a human aboard, they have to assume she will react according to the collective human consciousness model they have constructed. She should be somewhat frightened, but also very curious. Instead, this woman might have had a traumatic abduction event during her childhood and that might explain why her abduction was absolutely horrifying. In other words, we humans have personal experiences which also determine our behaviour and reactions. So while we do act like humans (we do not act like swans, wolves, or whales), we also act according to what is personally psychological within us. According to the collective human consciousness, we are highly curious creatures; therefore we should be able to handle meeting new species. But, if we have had a traumatic childhood, and life has been difficult, we do not react with curiosity but with total fear. Of course, another individual who had a rough life might be more able to handle an alien experience, having been made strong and flexible by life itself. From the aliens' point of view, there is no way of predicting which human will react in what way. And yes, humans might be more emotional creatures than aliens. It is possible. The aliens may know we have our inner minds to contend with. They might also have individual experiences which cause them to vary from their collective consciousness. However, there is nothing they can do about reading individual human inner minds. Their instruments and abilities only "read" the outer field of collective human consciousness.

The last contact I had with Laura was in April 2014, at which point she moved to Basingstoke in Hampshire to live with her fiancée; she was still struggling to come to terms with what she had experienced the previous year.

So all this has led to me becoming some kind of interpreter of human emotion. The effects I felt from Denise Lane's turmoil and the horrific impact of those from Laura, are the two examples I've chosen for this book, They were also chosen because of how they are linked through me not stepping back from one before the other began. There have been others but of less spectacular impact.

All this activity happens at night when I am asleep, so the big question is how can all this have a real world impact if it's happening during sleep? How could Alan, for example, recall me walking through his dreamstate? Diane Tessman:

> *Australian Aboriginal people believe that every person exists eternally in Dream Time. This eternal aspect of the individual exists before the life of the physical individual begins, and continues to exist when the life of the individual ends. This sounds very similar to the concept of the morphic field which stretches into infinity. When we leave our physical shell, we return to the vast consciousness of the universal quantum field. Aboriginal teachings are about each individual being a quantum-child. He or she is the Infinite Dreamer and is only initiated into physical life by being born through a mother. The spirit of the child is understood to enter the developing foetus during the fifth month; when the mother feels the child move in the womb for the first time. It is believed that this was the work of the spirit of the land in which the mother then stood. Upon birth, the child is considered to be a special custodian of that part of his or her land and is taught the stories and songs about that place. What a dynamic connection between human and planet!*

> *The Aboriginal teachings are that before humans, animals, and plants came into being, their souls existed; they knew they would become physical, but not at what "time." When that time came, all but one of the souls became plants or animals, with the last one becoming*

human and acting as guardian to the natural world. Here is ancient wisdom for the human species today as our Planet Earth now struggles to sustain its life-forms, due to our own recklessness and uncaring ways! The hypnagogic state is a strange phenomenon which happens at the onset of sleep. Also known as hypnagogia, it induces visions, voices, insights and peculiar sensations as you go bouncing through this borderland terrain. Hypnagogia varies; sometimes it is the reality you know flashing in and out in crazy ways, but other times, you briefly see, hear and even touch realities which are completely alien to you.

Extraterrestrials and time-aliens can and do show up in this level of reality. It is only that old Day Reality which tries to filter out these beings, telling you they do not exist in any way because it (your day-mind), refuses to conceive of them. Your Day Mind is easily frightened and is a rigid censor - a heartless filter - of anything it does not comprehend. The old Day Mind deals with the boss, the headache, the money problems, the wayward son, the computer, and so much more, so we need to give it a break, too. It is not "bad," but it is not ALL either! It only thinks it is ALL. Hypnagogic imagery as you fall asleep contains faces, landscapes and geometric shapes, perhaps like the Aborigines crop circle-like art, which emanated from their Dream Time over thousands of years. Complex patterns flow across your field of vision, becoming almost hypnotic in nature. You can manipulate the hypnagogic state with intense focus, but you must not let your Day Mind awaken fully to delete the whole thing. It is very skilled at doing that! What many people don't realise is this imagery can be used to induce lucid dreams. Is there a connection to our Dream Reality and ancient myths, legends, and Jungian archetypes? Do our dreams link to the consciousness of our living planet? Our Dream Reality to her Dream Reality – a pathway to our Mother Goddess? I believe so! Fairies and other nature spirits are quite at home in our Dream Reality! In dreams, we are all shape-shifters, starting out as ourselves and then becoming another 'actor' in the dream. We can shift our perception, looking out of female eyes or male eyes, perceiving as human or alien. Quantum dream portals open to extraterrestrials and other-dimensional beings so that they can interact with their human cousins safely; the Dream Reality is safe for both human and other- world beings. (UFO Agenda Pp 54-55).

Everybody exists in the dream reality. It's where we go - and is the only place - you are truly yourself. You can't hide behind a mask to deceive yourself or others. What people have communicated to me while an energy form is quite often different from what their physical form will say. I have experienced this so many times with people when I have dream-walked with them. It's a shame that most people cannot recall their journeying, or if they do, they can't recognise it for what it actually is: 'It was just a dream.' They say.

Not so, what happens here is an echo of what has been set in motion there. It's where I made my initial contact with Clive, and prepared him for a meeting in the physical world. It's where I prepared Denise for that first crucial meeting. It's where I prepared Terry for the shape-shift in the street; The dream reality is where you make those short term plans to meet those who will have a significant effect on your life; It's where we deal with our problems and plan how to take our life several steps in the right direction.

The dream reality is where we wrestle the demons brought into existence by our emotional states; The dream reality is where we write the script that we try to follow in the physical world. But the dream-reality is ignored and has no place in a materialistic culture. Given a different spiritual evolution, humanity would be stepping from one world to another. 'Aliens' wouldn't be seen as something threatening, invasive and to be feared. We wouldn't be proscribing natural substances such as Ayahuasca, Peyote, Wachuma, and psychedelic mushrooms such as Fly Agaric; just a few of the consciousness modifying drugs which are a gateway to a multidimensional existence.

By forbidding controlled use of mind-expanding drugs, and by trying to ridicule the notion of contact with non-human intelligence, those who hold the material world in their hands will continue to retain control the population.

But change is in the air and it's happening around you now; People reporting contact with non-human intelligences are not always held up to immediate ridicule or considered crazy, with the exception of the mainstream media, which as both an entertainment industry and mouthpiece to the establishment, will portray the experiencer as an 'oddity' sitting outside of normal society and easy prey to ridicule.

But, there *are* increasing numbers of experiencers revealing their alien contact, and the tide is slowly turning. When humanity has turned away from its current path, which can only lead to a reckless self-destruction of itself and the obliteration of the planet, and when it has begun to free itself of its fears and xenophobias, and removed itself from its imagined pinnacle of creation, there is a future for humanity as a trans-dimensional race. Even now, the framework for this future is being put into place as the children of the next evolution are born.

A RESEARCHER'S VIEW

Holographic

The holographic view of consciousness is the nearest approach that physics will get to mysticism as it posits the idea that there is a network of interconnected and interpenetrating things and events. What this means is that conventional ideas of memory and information storage have been displaced in favour of information being stored and accessed similar to how a computer memory works.

Information is accessed through association, in the same way that a search-engine will bring up a whole number of word associations, simultaneously. On a mystical level the holographic view of consciousness is simply a metaphor that shows that all thoughts are one, with every thought inside every other thought.

It's suggested that consciousness is a field and if this is indeed the case, then it offers an explanation as to how consciousness may interact with matter, and how the reality-structure of consciousness allows reality to be manifested, even at times overcoming the laws of physics. Mind and matter are, in essence, a continuum, and both become a multidimensional projection in space, both affecting one another like ripples on a huge pond. However, at the fundamental level, matter and consciousness are one since at the deeper level (*implicate order*), everything is indeed one and co-exists together. What is of fundamental significance is not only the chameleon-like nature of subatomic particles, which can be either wave or particle in nature, but how such quanta can manifest in either form merely by the act of observation.

It was proposed by theoretical physicist, David Bohm, (1917-1992,) that there is a deeper reality beneath the quantum level which he termed the quantum potential. At this level specific locations lose their validity, nothing is separate, and hence space becomes non-localised. If the universe possesses a holographic nature, then matter is contained within the very essence of that hologram (or the *implicate order*), hidden until it is manifested (*explicate order*). Using this model to understand reality, we can view the brain as an instrument that converts frequencies emanating from the holographic universe in which it is enfolded within, interpreting a reality that is consistent with its manifesting beliefs.

The material universe is really only a second-generation reality, brought into existence from within the implicate order. The universe is one huge web, but everyone and everything are at the centre because of non-locality. The world that we create is infinite, reality being composed of a multitude of reality fields that shift with time and thought'. The only permanence is consciousness; in effect, we live within a 'Living Universe'.

Using this model we can determine that Jungian archetypes are implicit within all of mankind and are equally accessible to all, dependent upon how the brain interprets certain frequencies. Mankind has no borders, since we are all one at the implicate level. Our sense of separation is due solely to the ego and its myriad set of identities which lead to the situation of 'them' and 'us'. The threat to mankind is the fragmentation of the world. There is a conflict going one between man's ego, the urge to be separate - dividing the world up into races, ideologies, religions - and nature which seeks to bridge that gap to maintain species-connectedness.

The holographic model may be able to explain the concept of parallel universes in that such universes may be smaller holograms within the greater hologram. I find this the most logical way of perceiving the nature of such parallel worlds. When Lucy travels across dimensions she is perhaps travelling across bubbles of other holograms that are contained within the Super hologram? Since time and space are not fixed within the *Super hologram* this may allow for precognition and prophecy to take place. Hence an individual can determine the future by tuning into a particular hologram encoded within the implicate order. If there are many separate holographic futures, then we can choose which one to manifest. In that sense can transcendent beings help us to shift the future from one unrealised hologram to another?

The holographic model can also allow us to understand the subtle worlds, the afterlife and other hidden non-physical worlds where imagination is the creative force. These realms may be the generators that give rise to this physical universe, which again is a feature of the holographic model in that the whole is contained within each component as well as the location, thus embodying both the holographic and the non-local natures of the model. The saying of Jesus that, "the kingdom of heaven is within' is perhaps the clearest expression of the holographic model, so the idea is not exactly new.

In a sense the Indian Yacqui shaman Don Juan, written about by Carlos Castanda, was very close to describing the holographic model when he spoke of the *tonal* and the *nagual*. For within the holographic universe all appearances are illusions, created by the consciousness, but perceived from something that is there, frequencies which exist within the implicate order (*the nagual*), and which are given birth to realities through the midwife of perception (*the tonal*).

Metamorph

I see the shape-shifting ability of Lucy as primarily an aspect of her mental and spiritual consciousness, possessing a coherent perception of itself and of the universe, so that she is able to move in between worlds and bodies (through the holographic nature of reality) at will. Her consciousness is free from the shackles of our reality and as she possesses shamanic abilities and perception, this is - in my opinion - the source of the shape-shifting.

Her Grey form - as far as I can understand - is less of a genetic entity and more of a spiritual vessel that is overlaid by other non-physical bodies. Her alien body is an avatar-like vessel, and I tend to view it as an AI (Artificial Intermediary) construct, a solidified tulpa hidden beneath layers of non-physical bodies which contains the 'operating vessel' for her nocturnal activity as a Grey, encasing her consciousness within another, perhaps artificial and machine-like, consciousness.

There are two approaches to this issue. We are dealing with either:

1) A futuristic technology, or

2) A sophisticated development of traditional anthropocentric shamanism, but one which originates from a post-human or parallel dimension.

The key to this may lie in the fact that when she begins to shape-shift as a whole entity into the Grey, in daylight on a city street - and once we had begun to publicise it - she attracted the attention of a negative and dark power. The question is, why? Why would such activity have threatened this dark power and why did it want to stop her from continuing? I am beginning to consider seriously, that we live in just one of many realities - possibly even a simulated one.

Once humanity realises that fact it may threaten, or even end, the control that this dark power has over humanity. shape-shifting shows the mind that concentrated imagination can surpass what we believe to be reality. By revealing who she is and her nature and origin, and the fact that reality is indeed plastic and transient, Lucy may have begun to undermine the very fabric of this *system of control*, deception and reality manipulation that the dark power has over this planet and of mankind. Whether this dark force is an alien and extra-terrestrial or extra-dimensional intelligence I do not know.

The 'alien' shape-shifting could begin the meltdown of the consensual reality that binds together this control system (this intelligence may involve such beings as Archons, Djinn and so forth). Once that meme, or 'cultural virus' that carries ideas or behaviours from one mind to another, takes root within man's consciousness, there would be a loosening of those mental and hence spiritual shackles that currently chain humanity to a perpetual prison. As humanity begins to evolve man no longer remains a bystander, but rather he realises that he is both a participant as well as an observer in the creation of reality. In the realm of quantum possibilities, we appear to be made to participate in our creation. Since we are universally joined at the quantum level, our connectedness ensures that *even* small changes can have huge influences on the world as well as within the universe, maybe even beyond.

Butterfly Effect

Look at that remarkable incident in Sarajevo on 28 June 1914, after the first failed assassination attempt. Archduke Franz Ferdinand of Austria chose to continue with his motorcade tour, and in order to avoid the city centre, General Oskar Potiorek decided that the Archduke should travel along the Appel Quay to the Sarajevo Hospital.

However, the driver took a right turn onto Franz Josef Street. The reason being that Potiorek's aide Erich von Merrizzi was hospitalised, and unable to give Lojka the information about the change in plans and the driving route The Sarajevo Chief of Police Edmund Gerde, should have told the drivers of the new route but neglected to do so, due to the confusion and tensions of the moment.

Consequently, as he drove away from the hospital, Lojka took a wrong turn down a backstreet. Then, realising his mistake, Lojka began to reverse out. However, it so happened that the young Bosnian assassin Gavrilo Princip was sitting in a café on the street just as the Archduke's car began to pull into it. Princip grabbed the opportunity and ran out of the café with his Model 1910 7.65 mm FN Browning. Lojka attempted to reverse faster, but his foot missed the accelerator pedal, which allowed Princip to shoot and kill the Archduke with a bullet to his jugular vein, and to his wife, in her stomach.

Just a foot slipping from the accelerator led to the death of Ferdinand, igniting first Europe, then the globe in what turned out to be the First World War. This ultimately led to Russian communism, which helped to precipitate the Second World War, and ran into a 46-year Cold War, whose effects the world is only just beginning to emerge from. Such 'butterfly effects', can begin with a seemingly minor event; but can evolve into a major outcome.

The effects of the mind-body connection are the key to this, and Lucy's shamanic training has provided her with the key to synthesise the relationship between her inner and outer experiences, so that she can achieve this 'miracle' almost at will, as if it was a natural part of herself (which, of course, it is). I believe also that a being such as Jesus may well have been a Master who could transcend realities in a similar way as do shamans in their dream-walking. What individuals such as Lucy do is to remind us that the universally connected holographic nature of the universe ensures that our consciousness can create new realities, and lead us to a freer future of unlimited potential. Everything is interconnected and a change anywhere means a change everywhere (compare this to the parable of Jesus when he spoke of the mustard seed).   .

Holographic World

Film concepts such as *The Matrix* and *The Thirteenth Floor* are interesting in that they explore the possibilities of simulated universes. I am beginning to wonder whether an intelligence that exists outside of this consensual reality is able to project consciousness into physical beings as humans.

In that scenario, it's possible that Lucy's body is merely a vessel containing a human personality and soul, but her 'true' and primary essence exists outside of our consensual time and space. If that is so, her dream-walking and shape-shifting is less of an expression of an inner embodiment than another reality projecting her essence, or program, into a physical container - her body.

I prefer to think of Lucy's true essence and shape-shifting abilities as being dependent upon her *coherence*. If we assume the Divine, the Ultimate Mind, is *total* coherence, then her essence can be considered perhaps to be coherent, certainly if compared to the mass of humanity. That is to say, her energies are systematically organised in a synchronised way. It denotes the fact that her energies come together as one. shape-shifting is therefore a natural way of her patterning her energies to transform, and for her consciousness to travel across the boundaries that separate the multitude of realities and dimensions. Whether this is because that is the natural state of beings from where she originates, or whether it is because she has been initiated and trained over many earthly incarnations, remains unknown to me. Possibly both suggestions have some validity.

Since physical reality can be expressed as, essentially, the interaction of frequencies, then her dream-walking and shape-shifting could best be described in terms of the interaction of these frequencies at certain scales of existence. Her consciousness would mean that it is totally coherent and synchronised and is in unity with her source. Like enlightened spiritual human individuals her being can produce a full spectrum of frequencies, from alpha, beta, gamma and delta, all at the same time and, in so doing so, this systematic brain functioning must be the basis for the shape-shifting, the invisibility and healing, amongst other external phenomena that has been reported.

All of our minds operate at an entangled level. Consciousness is operating as quantum events with mind and matter interacting. As far as the psychic phenomena that Lucy experiences, such as the powerful healing, as well as her experiences on-board 'craft', these are examples of quantum entanglement within the holographic universe. As far as I am aware I do not consider these 'craft' to be physical, but merely 'constructs' created by the interaction of 'alien' minds and matter through entanglement. In a way, perhaps similar to the science fiction programme 'Star Trek', these constructs may be more akin to holographic programmes created by a 'holographic environmental generator' which is able to produce realistic and three-dimensional creations; in this case what we call 'UFOs', 'ships' or 'crafts'.

Someone who touches a shape-shifter whilst transmogrifying, may incur burns. This is an expression of kundalini energy, and it's interesting to note that Julian could not get near to Lucy when she began to shape shift, it was as if her body was surrounded by an energy field. This may have been for Julian's protection, as it was to maintain the energy equilibrium during her morphing.

I believe that Kundalini may be the source of the shape-shifting, which is related to the chakras of the body and Qi energy (or *mana* energy).It is through the long and intensive training that Lucy has undergone that she has been able to achieve this process of shape-shifting. I think she has rediscovered something essential about herself when she suggests that maybe Red Eagle 'simply' re-educated her during her shamanic initiatory work. From what I understand such adepts as Lucy require sustained and intensive training, probably over many human lifetimes, to attain that level of reality shifting. Those few years spent with Red Eagle as her instructor really could not have led to such feats of shape-shifting, dimensional travel and similar phenomena. The fact that her brain has been able to maintain such coherence and hence to act in a synchronised manner has meant that such achievements have been possible, but it would have required lifetimes of spiritual training and no doubt much wisdom and painstaking work on herself.

The list of common signs that signify an awakened Kundalini, include such physical and mental symptoms as involuntary jerks, tremors, or shaking, itching and tingling sensations; headache, and possibly migraine; increased blood pressure and irregular heartbeat; emotional numbness and antisocial tendencies; mood swings with periods of depression or mania; pains in different areas of the body, especially back and neck; sensitivity to light, sound, and touch; trance-like and altered states of consciousness; disrupted sleep pattern; loss of appetite or overeating; a feeling of bliss, feelings of infinite love and universal connectivity and 'transcendent awareness'.

It is conceivable that Lucy may have had several lifetimes spent as a Tibetan and Japanese Budddhist, learning those energies and how to manipulate them in preparation for later incarnations. Intuitively there has always been a sense of an oriental energy around her that is also perceived as an oriental which seems to be reflected in the discipline and austerity that she takes towards life.

When she leaves her physical body, or has her human consciousness and identity moved 'out of the way' for shape-shifting, it's likely that she is being 'plugged' into a much larger reality - or super-human intelligence - whose connection is far more consistent with the divine matrix than humanity and this physical world is. Instantly she has access to greater knowledge and more dimensions, as well as possessing abilities that are not easily demonstrated on earth as a human. I guess that it's probably akin to switching channels on a radio or TV set. The human physical body is merely the receptor of the signals which come from her source/reality, but in order for those signals and programming to be received and displayed, an appropriate mechanism is required.

An *avatar*, within computing terminology, is the graphic representation of either the user or the user's alter-ego in any computer programme game. The 2009 science fiction film *Avatar* encapsulates perfectly the concept of the 'Grey', a device that is able to contain the injected intelligence of a consciousness into a remotely located body. The 'Grey avatar' is a tulpoid, essentially a materialised thought form. Hence the 'Grey avatar' construct acts as such a device, a bio-computer of spiritual energies sustained as a tulpoid and held together by unified thought patterns. Since only the hidden, subconscious, part of Lucy is utilised within the device, it is like dreaming and, like a dream, time and space are different to the waking state as is our own identities. The human ego is relinquished and pure consciousness that drives the avatar, the holographic construct, the bio-computer programme taking the place of the thinking and rational ego state of mind. When she is connected to the Grey avatar, she experiences a totally different state of being; one that is coupled to a contrasting reality.

Is this free from the ego consciousness of a human? Perhaps it is akin to a state of consciousness that Buddhist meditators aspire to. When Lucy exists as a human on the physical plane, she feels separation, a duality. But in other experiences she exists as a totality, an absolute, where she is able to engage in the oneness of matter and energy.

Professor William Tiller, a physicist (formerly of Stanford University), has described in his book, *Conscious Acts of Creation*, how there are two levels of reality. One is our physical reality that is all around us. The second is a non-physical reality that used to be termed the 'etheric level' but which Tiller refers to as the magnetic information wave level. This second reality is outside of space-time, but can be influenced by consciousness. This reality forms the template, the blueprint if you like, of physical reality.

Whilst these two levels remain normally 'uncoupled', Tiller has shown how through human intention these two levels can 'couple', resulting in physical events and manifestations. This is how I believe the Grey avatar can manifest and how the holo-programmes, or 'ships', can manifest.

When Lucy shape shifts or engages in nocturnal experiences as a Grey, she switches thought systems and exists as wholeness outside of common space and time. Like the film 'Sliding Doors' or 'Source Code' she is switching between alternative realities, and hence can modify human daytime responses, such as transpired with Denise Allen and me. Her Grey avatar serves as a template, a blueprint, from where, I would suggest, her etheric, or magnetic informational, energies are moulded around and into. I would suspect that her physical body is made invisible through altering its holographic nature rather than physically changing, and in this state these energies become rather like ectoplasm which is described in some forms of physical mediumship phenomena.

The avatar which describes her 'Grey' consciousness acts as a 'conditioned space' (some might say a 'sacred place') in which this coupling of realities occurs. The energy field of the avatar is a matrix that contains the template of the non-human body as well as the mental and spiritual information of the 'Grey', a bio-computer in essence. Possibly the reason why Red Eagle trained Lucy as a shaman was because these devices are in fact 'magical technologies' and their programming and operational drives require an understanding of technology that we call 'shamanism'. The coherence that she is able to maintain within her consciousness is attributable to the lack of ego manifesting and, like enlightened masters and similar individuals, she has unchained herself from the fetters of the physical universe and hence able to shape-shift and travel in OBE states across dimensions.

What her Grey consciousness represents is open to speculation. It is the sixty-four million dollar question. To determine that, will be to understand her true nature and source. But since working with her in the 1990s my earlier thoughts have radically shifted from considering that her 'Grey' consciousness is a non-human alien source, to one that encompasses ideas that include a post-human source utilising time-travelling technology, to that of an inter-dimensional source, and even to notions involving a superior and enlightened spiritual human source existing on this planet.

The Grey does seem to represent a universal being, an archetype, and maybe this is how humans will evolve through hundreds or indeed thousands of years, becoming a universal and cosmic being, perhaps best symbolised by the birth of the childlike human at the end of the science fiction film, '2001: A Space Odyssey'. Are beings such as Lucy here to witness and assist as midwives to the birth of a new human - overseeing the death of homo sapiens and the emergence of a post-human species ready to begin exploring both outer space and inner dimensions? Does the Grey consciousness represent Lucy's future self which has become entangled with her present self? If so, her Grey consciousness is the embodiment of a future, post-human, species that has become adapted to inter-dimensional travelling and altering realities.

Is the Grey consciousness an artificial mind that is able to perform like any sentient, conscious mind? When she is 'plugged' into the bio-morph, or 'Grey avatar', is this what acts as 'Lucy's' mind and hence shifts her consciousness from an anthropocentric perspective, to a more non-human, alien state of mind?

I see that her shape-shifting has many similarities with her nocturnal experiences as a Grey entity. The only difference is that when the daylight shape-shifting occurs, her waking mind is in dominance, and it is perhaps this that has to be controlled through the intervention of an external intelligence. The other difference is, of course, that the shape-shifting occurs within a physical realm that requires a great expenditure of energy and witness preparation, as well as the processes necessary to contain the energy whilst it moulds itself to the template of the avatar. At night whilst her mind is asleep, her spiritual bodies do not require this process.

The outstanding question for me, though, is why she has been enabled to travel as a Grey on-board 'ships' *now*. I can only think that the answer is because previously there was no need. I would be hesitant to suggest that she would have been able to travel on board ships had her guiding superiors not wanted her to. Possibly something occurred during the hospital operation and the 'soul fusion' which made this possible, but somehow I don't think that is correct. I simply think that that one mission had ended and that *particular* identity was rendered unsuitable, for any number of possible reasons, for the work required later. A being with compassion, empathy and a feminine nature was required to act as the emotional processor for dealing with the human abductees. That being was Lucy combined with Shelagh, and from that moment her role as an on-board 'emotional translator' was initiated.

The shamanic initiations, or perhaps more accurately, her shamanic re-education at the hands of Red Eagle, a superior consciousness of unknown origin and nature, essentially opened Lucy up to realising and working with the holographic nature of reality, enabling her to journey across dimensions, to perform paranormal phenomenon, or 'miracles', and later to travel within an OBE state as a ' Grey consciousness'. This ensured that she could interact on board what we refer to as 'ships' or, more accurately perhaps, as holographic programmes from holographic generators.

This 'oneness' that she has been opened up to was essential to allow her to have personal interaction with the 'spirit world', or non-local realities. Allowing her to experience the dissolution of the boundaries between life and death and between physical and non-physical universes has meant that she can perform her mission not just within this physical world but also within other realities. She has become, in effect, an intermediary between the 'gods' and 'spirits' and mankind. She has also become the embodiment of a new relationship between humanity and nature, a relationship that is particularly important today as humanity unconsciously practises ecocide upon this planet and its life forms.

Lucy's experiences have also crossed and dissolved the boundaries between male and female, the soul fusion on a mythical level embodying the Hindu god and goddess Shiva and Parvati, in a synthesis depicted as Ardhanari, similar to the Greek myth of Hermes and Aphrodite. This spiritual androgyny has enabled her to span the divisions of not only gender boundaries but of other boundaries also. Within traditional shamanism such individuals are more identified with non-ordinary realities and able to mediate far more effectively with 'spirits', the process of reconciling opposites and hence such dualities having been achieved.

The Grey consciousness experienced, to all intents and purposes, a Near-Death Experience (NDE). Within the NDE, there are several stages and within her own, Lucy experienced a separation from the physical body, as the Grey emerged from within her, experiencing a separate existence. It then experienced darkness as it confronted the Void (the EVS). This Void could easily be perceived as the beginning, or end, of the archetypal tunnel that many of those who experience an NDE see. This tunnel is a passage between one state of being to another and therefore perhaps may not actually represent a portal to another, alien, universe.

What the Grey experienced has many of the features ascribed to a negative NDE, as opposed to the commoner positive NDE. The experience is accompanied by fear or panic, emotional and mental anguish (sense of evil?); feeling of being lost or helpless; feelings of being tricked into death. The NDE results in the ego-death of the individual undergoing the experience as all sense of reality is lost from the reduction in sensory-based input to the brain. The individual becomes aware of a higher transcendent power and the realisation that consciousness is independent of the physical body.

Was it a necessary requirement for the Grey consciousness to undergo a NDE to fully experience this realisation? I view the Grey consciousness as a consciousness in its own right, having perhaps been created artificially. In a sense it is an AI that has attained a highly developed sense of awareness and consciousness on its own accord. As that non-human, perhaps machinelike, consciousness evolves, it also requires a knowledge and experience of spiritual realities for it to evolve in accordance with its own independent sense of self.

The Grey also needed a spiritual and psychic rebirth for it to evolve. The transformative processes involved would have led to a tremendous alteration of the Grey's consciousness, enabling it to fuse more closely with Lucy's human consciousness. The evolutionary imperative is to allow the Grey collective consciousness to evolve, to ensure growth instead of stunted development. This heralds the creation of a new species as humanity enters a collective near-death crisis. It is a call to a cosmic, universal brotherhood. That process may be what is manifesting within her as an archetypal manifestation of this process.

When the Grey within Lucy separated from her human form and

confronted the black hole that appeared on her bedroom wall that night, was this a portal to another, alien world? Or was this perhaps, and more likely, a shamanic initiation for the Grey consciousness? Within shamanic tradition the spiritual Lower World is accessed through a hole in the ground perhaps like Alice in Wonderland? The Lower World is the place of healing, of power and of our own human ancestry.

Was the Grey being shown a glimpse of its own ancestry? If so, it may have also glimpsed elements that could be construed as evil. Elements often associated with evil include "unbalanced behaviour, involving expediency, selfishness, ignorance or neglect". We could even postulate Jung's ideas as to the nature of evil here, it being expressed as the shadow unconsciousness; a projection of ourselves. Was the Grey consciousness being confronted with its own dark, unconsciousness shadow self? Was this what the confrontation with the Void was really all about?

Within Buddhist beliefs good and evil is sometimes seen as opposing dualities that must be overcome through a process known as ' Sunyata', which is about achieving emptiness and so recognising that good and evil are fundamentally opposite principles through achieving oneness.

All things and events, whether 'material', mental or even abstract concepts like time, are devoid of objective, independent existence. Things and events are 'empty' in that they can never possess any immutable essence, intrinsic reality or absolute 'being' that affords independence."

All shamans deal with the Death World, as Lucy experienced it during that period of time. These experiences, typified by the dinosaur, were a process that perhaps freed her of the concept of time barriers and limitations, hence enabling her to perform her tasks.

This process, perhaps sees the shaman acting as the midwife at the birth of a new soul from the death of the old soul. From that point, Lucy was no longer afraid of death; it had become an ally to her as she had overseen the delivery of a new soul. Perhaps on a collective, holographic level, she had also overseen the death of the old collective soul of humanity and the emergence of a new.

The Death World appears to be vital to the work of the shaman who uses it to allow a new perception within the physical world. This allows the mind to engage with other non-physical realities for the simple fact that the consensual reality is no longer leading to the survival of the physical body. In a sense it is a necessary process to the kind of training that Neo had to undergo in the sci-fi film *The Matrix* as Morpheus tried to get Neo to rid his mind of its mental and emotional attachment to the confines and limitations that he once experienced within the reality of the Matrix. Through this process the mind, freed from such restrictions, will engage with other realities. Beliefs have to be confronted and destroyed; fixed ideas about consensual perceptions have to be purged from the mind.

Don Juan Matus, an Indian Yacqui shaman who taught a student called Carlos Castaneda (who later wrote about his experiences) described perception as the 'tonal'. The tonal was everything that we can perceive, what the consciousness creates from the information that it receives to give the illusion of a single universe. In the terms of physics, it could be described as 'constructive interference'. The 'nagual', on the other hand, is the actual frequency of the information, or 'destructive interference'. It is the paradigm of reality. It could be construed as Schrödinger's Cat which can exist in several states until it is observed. It is the potential of reality since it represents the reality that exists beyond perception. Through the shamanic training of Castaneda by don Juan, he was able to see the transparency and illusion of the tonal, and understand the nature of the nagual. Within Buddhist training a Buddhist must also learn to see beyond the tonal and to become at one with the nagual.

Lucy has been trained to use the powers available to her within the super-hologram of reality to not only to travel across realities but furthermore, to also create realities. Within the physical world these powers can produce healing, to enable the perception of information from remote locations, and even to create matter; all can be considered as 'miracles'. She has learned to accept that the consciousness is superior to the world of matter and to the physical universe, and hence she has become a free spiritual being whose consciousness is not defined or limited to a physical body.

Could the 'Grey consciousness' be more akin to a tulpa? Could an advanced spiritual consciousness create a tulpa that can exist independently of its creator(s), that although can exist, act and think on its own volition, can perhaps remain attached to Lucy's human consciousness? In a sense, a magical being that is fully under the control of her consciousness? Alexander David-Néel, in *Magic and Mystery in Tibet* describes a Tibetan shaman as saying, "Visualising mental formations, either voluntarily or not, is a most mysterious process. What becomes of these creations? May it not be that like children born of flesh, the children of our mind separate their lives from us, escape our control, and ply a path of their own?" I am making the suggestion that perhaps the Grey consciousness is a tulpa that is so advanced and controlled that it is both a part of her and can also exist outside of her, taking with it a fragment of her own consciousness to perform roles assigned to it. That may perhaps be why her own consciousness loses its human perception and emotional capabilities as it is purely animating the tulpa.

The shaman is a reality-structurer and within the holographic universe, Lucy is capable of changing reality. She is able to use symbols, archetypes and metaphors to communicate with what we call meta-programmes which are, in a sense, the tonal of reality. Humans are capable of doing this, but, trapped as we are within this 'Matrix' of illusion, with our consciousness tied to a physical reality, we are powerless. A predatory intelligence that knows how potentially powerful humans are would want to ensure that we remain trapped within this illusion and ignorant of our own potential. Such an intelligence could use the meta-programmes to guide and direct our thought processes and behaviour and hence to manipulate humanity. Such meta-programming can be through religious or occult symbols and metaphors designed to reinforce human conditioning involving perhaps aggression, greed, hate and subservience.

The symbiotic relationship between human consciousness and that of the Grey consciousness may be the beginnings of the birth of a new species, a new consciousness and perhaps a new order. From death through the delivery of a new being, will humanity, perhaps shed its old self and destroy the cancerous destructive components of itself, to emerge as a new child, born into the cosmos, giving rise to a new brotherhood?

Abductions, A Shamanic Process?

I have also been wondering whether all UFO abductions, or some of them, are perhaps in some sense 'shamanic abductions' or 'shamanic initiations' on a collective scale. Missing time episodes and some of the mental, emotional, spiritual and indeed, physical symptoms, or side-effects of abduction seem to relate to certain shamanic illness or 'shamanic sickness'.

I am beginning to wonder whether an intelligence is staging collective events, not to perform some sort of medical experimentation or genetic hybridization, but to perform a spiritual crisis within those whom they abduct. Through experiences that seem to be remarkable to both NDEs and to some shamanic initiations.

Is it possible that the abductors are engaging in a mass shamanic initiation of humanity to begin the birth of a new humanity, on a spiritual level? In that essence, perhaps the abductors are some sort of cosmic midwife, preparing mankind for its own death and rebirth of a new self. The sickness within mankind may not just be a reason for this, but also a sign that it is happening. Perhaps the aggression and hatred, lack of identity and depersonalisation that we see amongst humanity are signs that deep down within the collective psyche, mankind knows that he is dying, and that before he can be reborn, he, as a species, must also die.

Thinking about how Lucy suffered acute bouts of illness: chronic fatigue, which she had suffere4d for several years when I met her, and other signs, such as an aversion to alcohol and tobacco, she did seem to lose parts of herself. I recall her telling me that over time, the human part of herself was dying, and that her 'alien' self was becoming stronger. It was as though she was losing more and more of herself, and becoming more - well - 'alien'.

At the time, we both took it that the 'alien' consciousness within Lucy was growing, and her humanity was being discarded. Now I'm not so sure. I am starting to see it more of a sign that she was indeed dying, or rather, parts of her were dying in accordance with suffering the onset of 'shamanic sickness'. The blockages and unhealthy parts of her were being removed, cleansed and purified during this period. It was a form of death. Pieces of herself were dying, to be replaced by new growth and consequently, the birth of a new being. She was being broken down under Red Eagle, experiencing trauma after trauma and being re-moulded into a new being that the 'gods' or 'spirits' could use. Through a process of spiritual sacrifice, death and rebirth she has undergone remarkable transformations, enabling her to perform her missions within a conscious and living spiritual universe.

Clive Potter 2014

Further Reading

Jacques Vallée, *Dimensions (*Souvenir Press,1988)

Jacques Vallée, *Passport to Magonia* (Neville Spearman 1970)

Budd Hopkins, *Missing Time* (Ballantine Books 1988)

Budd Hopkins, *Intruders* (Ballantine Books 1987)

John. E. Mack *Passport to the Cosmos: Human Transformation and alien Encounters* (Crown Publishers 1999)

Dr David Jacobs Ph.D. *The UFO Controversy in America* (Indiana University press1975)

Dr Karla Turner Ph.D. *Into The Fringe* Kelt Works(1992)

Dr Karla Turner. Ph.D. *Taken -Inside the Alien-Human Abduction Agenda* Kelt Works(1999)

Dr Karla Turner Ph.D.*Masquerade of Angels* Kelt Works 1994

Diane Tessman. *The UFO Agenda* (Eye Scry Publications 2013)

Whitley Strieber, *Communion: A True Story*. (Avon Books, 1995)

John. G. Fuller. *The Interrupted Journey: 2 Lost Hours "Aboard a Flying Saucer"*, (Dial Press 1966)

Ruth Montgomery. *Strangers Among Us: Enlightened Beings from a World to Come* (Coward, McCann & Geoghegan, 1978)

Dr. William Tiller Ph.D. *Conscious Acts of Creation – The emergence of a New Physics.* (Pavior Publishers, 2001)

Alexander David-Neel. *Mystery and magic in Tibet.* Dover Publications 1971)

About The Author

Lucy has spent most of her career in a variety of security roles, from that of store detective for major department store chains to guarding the property of a Middle East king.

In April 2011, four years after moving to Manchester from Reading, she decided to start her own small business. Turning to her experience and knowledge of paganism and a diversity of spiritual paths she opened a shop in Afflecks Palace in Manchester's famous Northern Quarter.

Pagan Planet was a very successful small business and became popular with pagans across the North-West of England. In June 2012 Lucy decided it was time to put her astonishing story into print. So using the office in her shop, she spent the next two years working on this project.

Lucy's shopped ceased trading in 2014 when her partner was suddenly taken ill.

www.ingramcontent.com/pod-product-compliance
Lightning Source LLC
Chambersburg PA
CBHW051950090426
42741CB00008B/1333